RURAL LABOUR MARKET

RURAL LABOUR MARKET

Editor

DR. M. SOUNDARAPANDIAN
Reader in Rural Industries & Management,
Gandhigram Rural Institute,
Deemed University,
Gandhigram-624 302.
INDIA

SERIALS PUBLICATIONS
New Delhi

First Published-2005

ISBN : 81-86771-67-0

Published by

Head Office : SERIALS PUBLICATIONS
4, B.S.S. Hall, Khyber Pass Market,
Civil Lines, Delhi-110054 (India)
Phone : 23245225
Fax : 91-11-23272135
e-mial : Serials @Satyam.net.in

Branch Office : *4830/24, Prahlad Street, Ansari Road,*
Daryaganj, New Delhi-11002 (India

Printed at : R. K. Offset Process, Delhi-110032,

PRINTED IN INDIA

PREFACE

It is widely recognised today that India's organised sector accumulated over the years, a sizable stock of surplus labour. There are three basic reasons for this, firstly the problem of industrial sickeness (i.e. non-viability of enterprises); secondly the Government kept many non-viable enterprises going in order to protect employment; and thirdly, job creation was viewed as a social obligation of the State and public enterprises. There has been a considerable debate in the country regarding the impact of economic reforms on rural labour market adjustment.

In wake of the reforms, immediate task has been the redeployment of persons found surplus on the one hand, and training and retraining them for their absorption in certain emerging specialised skills on the other.

The self employment generation programmes need to be expanded, and the necessary environment and support system need to be created for the promotion of self-employment, particularly in the urban informal sector. So far as the rural areas are concerned, appropriate integration of various on - going employment generation programme among themselves and with the programmes for rural infrastructure building and other development programmes is necessary. It is against this background that a national level seminar conducted in our institution, to examine the impact of economic reforms on rural labour market. A few selected papers presented in the seminar are edited as a book on "Rural Labour Market.

The book consists of 24 papers of eminent contributors. The first ten papers examine the Employment level in rural areas after liberalisation, next four papers deal with the industrial employment and other four papers analyse the women entrepreneurship. A few other papers discuss the Rural-urban migration, child labour and employment generation through Self Help Groups.

Undoubtedly, the book will be immensely beneficial to the administrators, policy makers, planners and researchers. I am thankful to Dr. N. Thillainayagam, Professor and Head, Department of Rural Industries and Management, Gandhigram Rural Institute, Gandhigram for his encouragement for publishing the book. It gives me great pleasure to thank my wife Mrs. S. Indhumathy and my children S. Diwakaran and S. Vidhya for their support in completion of this work. Finally, my sincere thanks to Serials publications for their acceptance in publishing the book.

M. SOUNDARAPANDIAN

CONTENTS

LIST OF CONTRIBUTORS

1. Dr. G. Valentina, Asst. Professor (CSED), National Institute of Rural Development, Hyderabad.
2. Dr. R. Naagarajan, Faculty, Department of Economics, Nallamuthu Goundar Mahalingam College, Pollachi.
3. Dr. S. Benjamin Christopher, Reader, Department of Commerce, Nallamuthu Goundar Mahalingam college, Pollachi.
4. R. Ravindrapirabu, Research Scholar, Department of Economics, Bharathidasan University, Trichy
5. Dr. C. Thangamuthu, Professor of Economics, Department of Economics, Bharathidasan University, Trichy
6. R. Albert Christopher Dhas, The American College, Madurai.
7. M. Helen Mary Jacqueline, Lady Doak College, Madurai
8. Dr. S. Kannan, Reader in Commerce, Kamaraj College, Tuticorin.
9. A Padrakali, S. G. Lecturer in Commerce, A.P.C. Mahalakshmi College for Women, Tuticorin.
10. Dr. A. Balakrishnan, Senior Lecturer, Department of Applied Research, Gandhigram Rural Institute (Deemed University), Gandhigram - 624302.
11. T. Raj Pravin, Research Scholar, Department of Agricultural Extension & Rural Sociology, Tamilnadu Agricultural University, Coimbatore-641 003.
12. Dr. V. Ambumani, Faculty, Department of Economics, Bharathiar University, Coimbatore 46.
13. T. Lingamurugeshwri, M. Phil Research Scholar, Department of Economics, Bharathiar University, Coimbatore 46.

14. N. Rajeshwari, Ph.D., Research Scholar, Department of Economics, PSG Arts College, Coimbatore 14.

15. S. Gandhimathi, Lecturer in economics, Avinashilingam Deemed University, Coimbatore 641 043.

16. Dr. L. Radhakrishnan, Reader in Rural Industries and Management, Gandhigram Rural Institute, Gandhigram 624 302.

17. Dr. A. Annadurai, Guest Faculty, Department of Economics, Gandhigram Rural Institute (Deemed University), Gandhigram 624 302.

18. Dr. B. Shyamala, Prof & Head, PG Department of Economics, Fatima College, Madurai 18.

19. Dr. Aroma G Sam, Dean, Professor & Head, Department of Social Sciences, Tamil University, Thanjavur.

20. Dr. N. Manimekalai, Reader, Department of Economics, Bharathidasan University, Trichy.

21. Dr. P. Ambiga Devi, Prof of Economics, Avinashilingam University, Coimbatore - 641 043.

22. Dr. Samwel Kakuku Lopyetum, Senior Post - Doctoral Research Fellow, Department of Cooperation, Gandhigram Rural University, Gandhigram - 624 023.

23. R. Velu Raj, Lecturer, Department of Cooperation, Dr. R. K. Shanmugam College, Kallakurichi - 606 202.

24. Dr. K. Ravichandran, Senior Lecturer, Department of Cooperation, Gandhigram.

25. M. Revathibala, Ph.D., Scholar, Department of Cooperation, Gandhigram - 624 302.

26. Dr. T. R. Jeyaraaj, Reader in Development Studies, Department of Economics, Annamalai University, Annamalai Nagar - 608 002.

27. Dr. N. Malathi, Professor of Economics, Annamalai University, Annamalai Nagar-608 002
28. Dr. Soukath Ali, Reader in Economics, M.S.S. Wakf Board College, Madurai.
29. V. Saravanan,. Ph.D. Research Scholar in Economics, Centre for Research, Arul Anandar College, Madurai.
30. N. Mukundan, Lecturer in Economics, A.V.C. College, Mannampandal –5, Mayuram.
31. Dr. A. Selva Kumar, Reader in Commerce, Pope's College, Sawtyerpuram, Tuticorin - 628 251.
32. Dr. G. Karunanithi, Prof & Head, Department of Sociology, Manonmaniam Sundaranar University, Tirunelveli - 627 012.
33. Dr. S. Padmavathy, Reader in Economics, K. N. Government Arts College for Women, Thanjavur.
34. M. Malarvizhi, Lecturer in Economics, K. N. Government Arts College for women, Thanjavur.
35. Dr. D. Solomon Raj, Reader in Economics, Pope's College, Sawyerpuram-51, Thoothukudi Distirct.

ECONOMIC REFORMS AND RURAL LABOUR MARKET BEHAVIOUR IN HYDERABAD

Dr. G. Valentina,*

1.1 INTRODUCTION

The context of migration, urbanization and the creation of labour markets received much attention in the developing worlds. In the recent past agriculture is viewed to effect significant changes in the labour markets, yet certain sections of the population continue to remain poor. India's economy has under gone tremendous changes, in the 90's with the inititation of economic reforms which has set the Indian economy to accelerate. In the 80's the Indian economy accelerated to 3.5per cent per annum, the decade of 80's witnessed a growth of 5.8 per cent per annum, further to 7 percent in 90's. Now the target is set to achieve 8 per cent annual growth rate in the present decade. However, the growth of economy has not been commensurate with the growth of employment. Instead there has been an overall deceleration in employment growth, emerging problems of open employment, growth of casual labour, growth of unemployment in unorganised sector and swelling labour markets with the rural-urban migration.

1.2 OBJECTIVES

In the existing context, the objective of the study is to study the economic reforms and rural labour market behavior in the city of Hyderabad.

1.3 METHODOLOGY

In order to study the behavior of the rural labour market in view of the economic reforms a detailed study as made by

* Asst. Professor (CSED) National Institute of Rural Development, Hyderabad

drawing a questionnaire for the migrant labourers in the city of hyderabad. Primary data was collected through the interviews and questionnaires by gaining responses from the migrant labourers., while the secondary information was collected through the census data and the labour commissionarate. The sample respondents were interviewed at the market squares and their dwellings were also visited.

1.4 STUDY AREA

To study the labour market behavior in the context of the economic reforms four areas from the east, west, north and the southern directions of the city of hyderabad were choosen.

The four locales taken up for study are the following.

- Addagutta- Secunderabad
- NTR huts - karmanghat
- Bapu nagar - Langer house
- Ashok nagar - near Indira Park

1.5 SAMPLE SIZE

A sample of one hundred house holds were taken up for the study, covering twenty five house holds from each region.

2.0 A PROFILE OF HYDERABAD CITY

Andhra Pradesh is the biggest state of South India. It is the fifth largest state inhabiting the fifth biggest population in the country. It is spread out on 2750685 sq. kms of area. with a population of 76111243 persons. Being endowed with an extensive irrigation system it is one of the food grains surplus states of India.

Hyderabad constitutes the state capital and also smallest districts in the state of Andhra Pradesh. The district of Hyderabad is divided into the Hyderabad-urban and rural districts. The rural part is called Ranga Reddy district. Hyderabad urban ranks the first in possessing the highest urban population in the state. The following table provides the demographic features of Hyderabad-urban.

Table 1: Demographic Features of Hyderabad District (1991-2001)

Item	Unit	Number	Census
Area	Sq. km.	217.00	2001
Population	'000	3686.46	2001
Male	'000	1894.99	2001
Female	'000	1791.47	2001
Urban	'000	3686.46	2001
Population Growth (pa)	%	3.92 + 17.18	2001
Population Density (Person/Sq. Km.)	Nos.	16988.00	2001
Urbanisation	%	100.00	2001
Literacy	%	79.04	2001
Male	%	84.11	2001
Female	%	73.67	2001

Source : Hyderabad.com

The population of Hyderabad is 3686.46 lakhs, with the male population out numbering the female population. 71.52 per cent of the population are educated. Hyderabad is 100 per cent urban with a population density of 16988 persons per sq. km. The population figures in the city of Hyderabad increased from 3145.94 in 1991 to 3686.46 persons in 2001. The population growth per annum (1991 census) stands it 3.92 per cent with a decadal growth for the yearl(1991-2001) at + 17.18. While increase in the ratio of population density from 14497.00 to 16988 persons per sq. km. indicates the concentration of the population in the urban areas.

2.1 ECONOMIC REFORMS AND RURAL LABOUR MARKET BEHAVIOUR IN ANDHRA PRADESH

Employment in Andhra Pradesh is mostly un-organised, rural and non-industrial, with a rich work participation of women in the rural areas.

The labour market in Andhra Pradesh is categorized by the following:

- High work Participation rates for male and females.
- Rise in the share of agricultural labourers from 37 per cent in 1981 to 41 per cent in 1991.
- Movement of the population towards unorganised sectors for employment.
- high rates of female participation in the rural areas.
- Highest incidents of child labour (25.1 per cent) with children in the age group of 10 to 14 years.

With the introduction of economic reforms the economy has picked up and the growth rate reached an average of 7 percent during the period 1994-95 to 1998-99. This is a legitimate achievement of economic reforms. The emphasis was to sustain a high growth rate to take care of poverty and unemployment. But the results of economic reforms have turned out to be different, which will be high lighted as the discussion goes on.

In Andhra Pradesh from 1993-1994 to 1999- 2000 the growth of employment declined. Andhra Pradesh has 6 per cent of the total work force in the organised sector. Here also there has been decline in the growth of work force. While the post-reform period registered a growth in the private sector and decline in the public sector and the status of unemployment in the state registered a significant increase in 1990's. With the rising casualisation in the labour, the state has occupied a second highest percentage of casual labour in the country with 48.3 per cent being the casual labourers.

In lieu of the economic reforms it does not seems to have contributed favourably towards the labour market. Employment growths in rural Andhra Pradesh declined in 1983 from 2.40 per cent per annum to 0.29 per cent during 1999-2000. While in urban areas form 4.28 per cent to 0.01 per cent. As a result the employment growth (rural + urban) from 1993-94 to 1999-2000 was 0.3. per cent per annum. The reasons for the decline in the work participation could be non-participation by the lower age groups, movement of people into sectors other than the labour force for employment and demographic pressures.

2.2 ORGANISED SECTOR EMPLOYMENT

In 1988, 20.5 lakh workers were engaged in the organised sector in Andhra pradesh, which is around 5.5. per cent. While the un-organised work force constitute about 94.5 per cent. In 1990 and 1999 (economic census) employment in un-organised sector increased form 67.34 lakh to 72.46 lakh with a growth rate of 0.80 per cent per annum. The employment in organised sector increased from 12.35 lakh in 1975-76 to 20.72 lakh in 1999-2000. However, the GSDP grew from 57868 crores in 1993-94 to 125236 crores in 1999-2000 yet employment since 1996-97 in Andhra Pradesh has been marginal. These have largely being the impacts of the economic reforms at a larger level in Andhra Pradesh.

Hyderabad too experienced movement of a vast majority of the population into the un-organised sector. By the year 1999, the main workers in Hyderabad were engaged in various categories of works such as; agriculture and allied activities, mining and dnarrying, manufacturing in industries, household industries, industries, construction and services. The following table provides the details of distribution of the population in various activities.

Table 2 : Total Workers in Hyderabad (2001 Census)

Workers % of main workers	percen-tage	Number	Census 1991
Agriculture & Allied activities	%	0.79	"
Mining & Quarrying	%	0.08	"
Mfg. (Non-household) industries	%	18.55	"
Household industries	%	0.50	"
Construction	%	7.59	"
Services	%	72.49	"

Source : ibid

The Number for works employed in agriculture and mining has been comparatively low (0.79 per cent and 0.08 per cent respectively). However, the higher concentration of population are figured in the manufacturing industries (18.55 per cent), household industries (0.05 per cent), construction (7.9 per cent) and services (72.49 per cent) Literally 98 per cent of the workers population is engaged in un-organised sector by 1991.

2.3 LABOUR MARKET BEHAVIOUR

With Agriculture contributing only 30 per cent towards the GDP, Agriculture has to absorb 65 per cent of the work force for employment. As a result of low absorption capacity in agriculture, rural-urban migration became the escape route for the agricultural labourers. Large masses of the labour force started being employed in in-organised sectors in the urban areas of the city of Hyderabad.

The rural population seems to migrate to the urban centers in search of a livelihood to better their future employment prospects. The modern manufacturing industry, public sectors and the private enterprises, constitute the modern formal/ organised sector, which are lucrative. With the inability of the formal sector in providing jobs, the informal sector turns out to be the ultimate agent to absorb the labour force. This provides a source of livelihood to the urban poor.

2.3 [A] MIGRATION

The total migrant workers population into the city of Hyderabad is 1,98,113 lakh population according to the 1991 census. The male migrants (167332) out numbering the female migrants (30781). The following table analyses the various categories of employment in the un-organised sectors by the migrant labourers in the city of Hyderabad.(Migration 1991 census Andhra Pradesh, Hyderabad).

In a study taken up in the four locales of the Hyderabad city, a large percentage of the agriculture labourers and agricultural cultivators have migrated into the city. The migrants are from the neighbouring rural areas of the districts of Ranga Reddy, Medak, Warangal, Mahboobnagar and the Bidar district of the State of Karnataka. The migrants have migrated in search of a livelihood. Due to severe drought conditions and lack of employment opportunities, the city of Hyderabad experienced mass migration

A majority of the population migrated from the adjoining villages of Medak warangal, Mancherial, Karim Nagar and Karnool etc. The migrants seem to have migrated in search of a livelihood. All these migrants are from the land owning families, on an average each migrant holds 2-3 acres of land in the village. But there are also migrants coming from the non-land owning families who have migrated for a livelihood support in the context of crisis created by the persistent drought situations and limited employment opportunities available in the agriculture sector. However, the economic reason dominates the reason for migration.

Due to lack of water the migrants subsisted by producing maiz, pulses and jowar with which they could earn an amount of Rs. 5-600 only per year otherwise if through good rains persisted the households produced rice which gave an income of Rs. 6-7000 per year. Conceptually the push and pull factors have been responsible for migration. Nearly 70 percent of the migrants have migrated 5-10 years back. With rural -urban migration, the households in the study have migrated with their immediately families leaving behind their parents.

Evidence through the study indicates that 98% of the migrants are young, educated (upto primary schools), newly married persons have shown a high propensity to migrate. The migrant workers were in nuclear families with not more than 2-3 children.

2.3[B] EMPLOYMENT IN THE UNORGANISED SECTOR

The un-organised sector is characterized by a work force including agriculture labour, construction labour, leather and tanning, handloom, fishing, forestry, household industry, village and urban artisans, these migrants are seen distributed in the various categories.

Table 3: Migrant Workers other than Cultivators and Agricultural Labourers in the City of Hyderabad in 1991

S.No.	Item	Number
1.	Total Migrant Workers Population	198113 (5.37)
2.	Total Migrant Workers Male	167332 (4.5)
3.	Total Migrant Workers Female	30781 (0.83)
4.	Livestock, Forest Fishery ... Industrial Category III Male	564 (0.28)
5.	Industrial Category III Female	46 (0.23)

6.	Mining and quarrying... Industrial Category IV Male	220 (0.11)
7.	Industrial Category IV Female	20 (0.010)
8.	Manufacturing, process, service... Industrial Category Va Male	555 (0.28)
9.	Industrial Category Va Female	291 (0.14)
10.	Other than households... Industrial Vb Male	30333 (15.3)
11.	Industrial Category Vb Female	2900 (0.14)
12.	Construction ....Industrial Category VI Male	12956 (16.5)
13.	Industrial Category VI Female	2659 (1.3)
14.	Transport, storage, communication... Industrial Category VII Male	47941 (24.1)
15.	Industrial Category VII Female	4816 (2.4)
16.	Industrial Category VIII Male	19195 (9.6)
17.	Industrial Category VIII Female	1293 (9.5)
18.	Other services... Industrial Category IX Male	55568 (28)
19.	Industrial Category IX Female	18746 (9.4)

Source : Census of India 1991
The numbers in parenthesis are percentages

Industrial Categories

III- Livestock, Forestry, Fishing, Hunting and Plantations, Orchads and allied activities; IV Mining and quarrying; V(a) – Manufacturing, Processing, Servicing and Repairs in Household Industry; V(b) - Manufacturing, Processing, Servicing and Repairs in other than Household Industry; VI– Construction; VII– Transport, Storage and Communications; IX – Other Services.

The total migrant population amounts 5.3 per cent (1991). in the city of Hyderabad. About 98.23 per cent of the population is engaged in the unorganised sector excluding agricultural labourers. The largest population have taken to other than households category of work (30333), construction (12956) and transport, storage and communication (47941).

The study analysis reveals that the bulk of the agricultural labourers constituted the labour adopting to non-agricultural occupations with a majority of them being employed in earth works\ construction works [97%], painting [1%], road laying [2%] etc.. Majority of the women too adopted the same occupation [97%], a very small number are also employed as house maids [3 percent]. Girls in the age group of 10-12 years are also seen taking up these works [2%] and earn an income of Rs.700-800 per month.

On an average they received work for only 15-20 days in a month and were free for the rest of the time. Both the man and woman in a family went to work and the children had the privilege of being educated [20%]. The wage structure available in the urban un-organised sectors too is high (Rs. 80-120 for men and Rs. 60-70 for women) in comparison to the agriculture wage rates (Rs.20 for men, less than Rs.20 for women) back in the villages.. On an average each working family (male + women) earned an income of Rs.1,400.00 and 1,225.00 respectively per month. Their expenditure per month is as follows:

Table 3 : Table Showing the Expenditure of the Migrant Labourers in the study made in City of Hyderabad

S.No.	Item	Amount (Rs.)
1.	Food	Rs.1,500-00@ Rs.50 per day
2.	Meat	Rs.240-00 @ Rs. 60 once in a week
3.	Rent	Rs. 700-00 per month
4.	Water	Rs.100-00 per month (Tanker Water)
5.	Bore Well Water	Rs.50-00 per month
6.	Drink	Rs.40.00 per month @ Rs.10-00 once in a week
7.	Clothes twice in a year	Rs.500-00
8.	Medicines	Rs.100-00 to Rs.200-00 (occasional)
	Total	**Rs. 3230.00**

Source : Computed data

As such the lives of these labourers have not improved beyond recognition as their expenditure is un-doing their income but they are able to subsist through their income. But due to high cost of living in Hyderabad the house holds could not save any money. Back in the village this merger subsistence was also quite questionable.

2.3 [C] LABOUR SETTLEMENTS

With rapid urbanisation, industrial growth, rural -urban migration and changes in the land use, increased the pressure on the civic infrastructure which resulted in the over crowding, congestion and in sanitation, this has manifested in the development of the slums from 1982-83 to 1991. The slums have grown from 470 to 964 slum settlements there by accommodating 0.6 percent of the population. These slums lack safe drinking water, toilet and electricity facilities. The following table gives the details of slum population of Hyderabad in 2001.

Table 6: Table Showing the Slum Population in Hyderabad

S.No.	District/ Town	Total Population	Slum Population	% of Slum Population
1.	Hyderabad District	3686460	621295	16.85
	Municipal Corporation	3471071	592414	17.07
2.	Secunderabad contonment	204182	28881	14.14
3.	Ranga Reddy District	3506670	549129	15.66
	Portion of Hyderabad	24899	8922	35.83
4.	Serilingampally	150525	73866	49.07
5.	Kukatpalli	290591	19585	6.74
6.	Quthubullapur	225816	138360	61.27
7.	Aiwal	106424	62585	58.81
8.	Malkajgiri	175000	47396	29.08
9.	Kapra	159176	47064	29.57
10.	Uppal Kalan	1182519	43586	36.86
11.	L. B. Nagar	261987	23478	8.96
12.	Rajendra Nagar	143184	84287	58.87

Source : Census of Andhra Pradesh, 2001

Higher concentrations of these slums are seen in the periphery of the city of Hyderabad, as the peripheries are marked by industrial activities. These increases in urbanisation and increasing concentration of urban population has led to severe problems of accessing basic amenities. As a consequence there is a decline in the living standards of the slum dwellers. They suffer from lack of safe drinking water, sanitation and lack all basic facilities which makes the environment hazardous. In Andhra Pradesh the estimate of percentage households with safe drinking water in 1991 is 73.82, with toilet facility was 54.60 per cent, having electricity facility was 73.31 per cent (census of India, 1991, Housing and Amenities, a brief analysis, 1993, SETTLEMENTS

The migrants lived in the slums which are available on rent at Rs.700.00 per month. Each dwelling possessed a plinth area of 9×6 foot. The dwellings are provided with electricity but lacked water, toilet and ventilation facilities. They are all single room dwellings and the whole family stays in that room only

3.0 URBANISATION AND THE STATUS OF LABOUR

In the face of continuous increase in migration of the rural people to the urban areas, it manifest itself in urbanisation as a consequence of the push and pull factors. The economic pressures of push factors in the country side have compelled the people to migrate, and take up secondary and tertiary sector occupations. As a result the urban population in India has quadrupled from 50 millions in 1947 to 217 millions in 1991. The urban growth rate in Andhra Pradesh in 1951 is 17.42 and it ranks the eight in terms of urbanised states in the country. The rate of urbanisation gradually increased to 26.84 per cent in 1991 maintaining the existing rank. However, the decadal growth rate of urban population rose from 15.76 in 1951-61 to 42.64 in 1981-91. According to 1991 census Andhra Pradesh has 213 urban agglomerations and towns. With the level of urbanisation at

26.89 per cent. The percentage share of Andhra Pradesh in urban population in India is 8.20 with a urban population of 17.88 millions in India (1991 census). The following table provides the details of level of urbanisation and decadal growth rate in Andhra Pradesh.

Table 4 : Urbanisation Trends In A.P. (1961-91)

Year	No.of Towns	Population	Levels of Urbanisation	Annual Growth Rate %
1961	212	6.27	17.43	1.47
1971	207	8.40	19.31	2.97
1981	234	12.46	23.39	4.05
1991	213	17.88	26.89	4.50

Source : Urban Poverty and Urbanisation

The Telangana region (including Hyderabad urban agglomeration is the most urbanised with 44% percent urbanisation.. The state as a whole, witnessed a decline in the decadal growth rate from 3.96 to 3.55. The Telangana region, more or less, maintained its growth rate. The Hyderabad urban agglomerating, however, witnessed a substantial decline from 5.03 to 3.47 percent. Of the 23 districts in the state, the Hyderabad district encompassing the MCH, has hundred percent urban population. Hyderabad being the fastest growing city has witnessed rapid urbanisation and industrial growth in the last two decades. From 1971 to 1991 the urban agglomeration area has expanded from 245 sq. km to 522 sq. km. It's population doubled from 1.8 million in just two decades with a growth rate of 9.5 percent per annum.

Andhra Pradesh experienced a higher growth rate of the urban population through a natural increase and also by the net in migration. A classification from 1961-71 reveals the following:

Table 5 : Table Showing Components of Urban Growth in Andhra Pradesh

S.No.	Year	Natural Increase	Net in Migration	Level of Urbani-sation
1.	1961-71	52.86	27.92	19.22
2.	1971-81	43.05	49.30	7.25
3.	1981-91	48.00	33.50	18.50

Source : Urban Poverty and Urbanisation.

The net increase in urban growth in Andhra Pradesh is more than half of the growth through it's natural increase. However the net in migration in the year 1971-81 has been more than the natural increase.

(RGI, New Delhi; quoted in urban poverty and urbanisation).

4. REHABILITATION

In view of these developments the Hyderabad slum improvement project was initiated by the Government of Andhra pradesh through a community development approach. It tried to provide infrastructure like housing, roads, electricity, drainage, drinking water, etc., in addition to the health, education and welfare measures. The following has been the expenditure [in US $] of the state government to uplift the slums in a phased manner.

Table 7 : Expenditure for Slum Development

Phase	Year	No. of Slums Involved	Funds Allocated
I.	1980-1983	1,228	US $ 3.5 Million
II.	1983-1989	210	US $ 110 Million
III.	1989-1993	300	US $ 250 Million

Source : Hyderabad.com

5. POLICY IMPLICATIONS

Policy implications even after more than 55 years of independence and literally a century spent on industrialisation there is a dearth in the comprehensive legislation for the un-organised labour in the state of Andhra Pradesh and India at large. It was only in the year 2003 the law was proposed, constituting of two components, following the recommendation of the commission.

- Social Security
- Setting up of a board in lieu of the Andhra Pradesh Welfare Board.

The social security aspects would take care of the medical and educational aids, and assistance on the event of accidental deaths. While the board would study the schemes for different categories of population by setting up Corpus Fund and raising contributions from employers and employees. It would also be responsible to probe into the working conditions of various unorganised labour, undertake compulsory registration of workers which would held them in accessing ESI and Provident Fund.

6. RURBANISATION

To counter balance this rural- urban migration there is an urgent need to transform the rural areas. The new agenda for rural prosperity as enunciated by professor Indiresan is by Rurbanisation which involves providing the basic amenities to the villages through the formation of a ring road around the village. By provision of the basic amenities in the village on par with the cities the potential for rural -urban migration can be reduced. Building a basic infrastructure in the rural areas, as found in the cities, there is also a possibility to sustain markets by enhancing income and generating job opportunities. These markets in the future can perform as service centres. Adopting this strategy, it is envisioned that rural-urban migration can be arrested to a larger extent and simultaneously it paves the way for the establishment of schools, hospitals and other service centres around the villages itself. This way a decongestion of the agriculture sector can also be made possible by deviating the excess about in to the various sectors created by induced employment. As employment opportunities are strengthened in a house hold, there is a possibility to create income in other sectors too. There improvements are hoped to have a potential in curtailing rural-urban migration.

Another facet of transforming the rural areas is counter-urbanisation, which has happened in the developed nations wherein the rich preferred to settle in the rural areas, which is happening in New Delhi.

7. CONCLUSION

- In view of the various transformations sparked off by economic reforms and the associated changes that have been brought about in the behaviour of the labour market in the city hyderabad there is an urgent need to transform the rural areas.
- Improving the economic growth in the rural areas with the emphasis on generation of employment to the poor by shifting the workers from agricultural to the non agriculture sectors should be the focus.
- The prevailing rural-urban migration needs to the reversed to urban-rural migration.
- Paradoxically the state must intervened in the affairs of the workers employed in the informal sector who are not assured of a regular income.
- The role of institution credit and the non-governmental organisation is vital in pursuing the objective.

To sum up it can be stated that economic growth in Hyderabad has brought about a growth in the GDP, which was not commensurate with the employment situation. The economic development brought about by the economic reforms in the state has been accompanied by rapid migration leading to urbanisation and urban growth. This has resulted in a labour market characterized by unorganised sector, urban poverty, urban poor lacking all skills and the proliferation of slums, which threaten the environment, thus reverting to rurbanisation constitutes an effective solution in handling the existing status of the labour market in the city of Hyderabad.

8. BIBLIOGRAPHY

1. Economic Reforms in India An Appraisal and Policy Directions for Second Generation Reforms, Ruddar Datt, 2001, Book Well Publications.
2. Urban Poverty and Urbanisation, Reena Bhasin, Deep and Deep Publications, 2001.
3. Job Creation in Urban Informal Sector in India: Issues and Policy Options, Edited by A.S. Oberai, G. K. Chadah, June, 2001.
4. Challenges of Economic Reforms Impact on Labour and Industrial Relations, 1997, DR Publishers.
5. Andhra Pradesh Economic Reforms and Challenges Ahead, Economic and political Weakly, 38 (1213), 2003 March.
6. Law on Un-organised Sector, The Hindu, April 24, 2003.
7. Making Rural India Magnetic, P. V. Indiresan, Hindu, April, 2003.
8. Business Line, 12th November, 2002, C. P. Chandrasekhar and Jayati Ghosh.
9. Rural to urban migration and the urban labour market; Biswajith
10. Banerjee; Himalaya Publishing ; 1986.

EARNINGS, OCCUPATIONAL MOBILITY AND LABOUR MARKET SEGMENTATION — AN ECONOMETRIC ANALYSIS

Dr. R. Naagarajan*

Dr. S. Benjamin Christopher**

INTRODUCTION

India adopted the policy of economic liberalisation/ reforms in 1991. As is well known, such a policy has been designed following the guidelines provided by the "Washington consensus". The main ingredients of the policy have been : (a) to attain macroeconomic stability by controlling inflation and reducing fiscal deficits; (b) opening of the economy to the rest of the world through trade and financial sector liberalisation; and (c) liberalisation of domestic policy believed that its adoption would bring about an increase in economic efficiency that would lead to attainment of higher economic growth in India, which is so crucial to address, inter alia, the twin problems of unemployment and poverty that have afflicted the country over the years.

In recent years, a large number of empirical studies have been initiated to examine the effect of economic liberalisation policies on the Indian economy. In this context, once again, there has been a clear dearth of unanimity of opinion among the researchers on issues relating to the effect of economic liberalisation policies on growth performance of the economy, poverty, inequality and so on (Ahluwalia, 2000; Nagraj, 2000;

* Faculty, Department of Economics, Nallamuthu Gounder Mahalingam College, Pollachi.

** Reader, Departmetn of Commerce, Nallamuthu Gounder Mahalingam College, Pollachi

Sen, 1996, 2002; Datt, 1999; Gupta, 2000; Dasgupta *et al* 2000; Dev, 2000). In any case, the recent debate on the impact of economic liberalisation policies in India has remained by far inconclusive.

In a service oriented era, the quality, quantity and utilisation of human resources are of central importance. Capital and natural resources are vital factors in an economy, but it is the quality of labour- the human resource-which contributes most to the contemporary 'Wealth of Nations'. In this context, policy makers and planners interested in the development of Human Resources and in Social Welfare have a fundamental concern with trends in employment, wages and labour incomes. They will consider the measures which are required to improve both the Productivity and the Welfare of Labour. It will help to understand who obtains them, how they are remunerated and the response of this system of relationship to social policy (Harriss, Kannan Rodgers, 1992). For this, we must understand the way in which the labour market operates and performs the functions in an economy.

FUNCTIONS OF LABOUR MARKET

Evolution and operation of labour markets has been a subject of considerable research and controversy in the economic analytic literature. (Praveen Jha, 1994). The emergence of the concept of labour market reflects growing need of human resource allocation for the mechanism of economic welfare which is consistent with optimum production structure. Labour market may be defined as a system of allocating and rewarding labour. Its main function is to match workers and jobs and to fix remunerations in a manner that ensures required quantity as well as quality of labour supply; its performance is judged by the efficiency with which labour market process performs this function (Prohit, 1985).

Labour markets play a central role in determining the macro economic success of stabilisation and adjustment policies and in mediating the impact of policies on living standards of the people in general and the poor in particular. As different types of labour exist, differentiated by skill, allocation, gender and so on, different types of labour market also exist. But these markets are linked with each other since the conditions in one can influence the working of other. The labour market has been variously categorised as primary and secondary, formal and informal, organised and unorganized sectors. It is widely accepted that among these classifications not much variation is identified. In India many researchers preferred to consider organised and unorganised classification of Indian labour market. Based on the classification of industrial sectors as organised and unorganised, employment and labour market also have been classified and analysed in related terms.

LABOUR MARKET IN INDIA

In India about 25 per cent of population live in urban areas where 40 per cent live below poverty level (World Bank, 1989). Evidence indicates that many Indian urban workers are trapped into the unprotected segment of the labour market, where the incidence of poverty is high (Harriss, 1989). The evidence also suggests that the disparity between the earnings of protected and unprotected worker is widening, and the earnings of unprotected workers are stagnating (Khandker, 1992) in India. However, of late, the problem that the Indian economy facing is, the employment creating capacity of the organised sector which appears to be on the decline (Papola, 1992; Sanjay Kumar and N. K. Sharma, 2003) while open unemployment of the rise. And the unorganised sector, far from readily absorbing all who seek jobs, is increasingly perceived as riddle with barriers to access, making it almost as difficult to penetrate as in to the organised sector.

Employment in the unorganised/informal sector has always been an important part of the urban economic structure in India. The issue of poverty and inequality of the disadvantaged groups needs to be specially looked after. The workers of the urban unorganised sector constitute on esuch disadvantaged group. For this proposition, a plea is often made for a policy to favour unorganised sector in matter of government policy of providing public utility services, financial help and other assistance (Banerjee, 1983).

Empirical research on urban labour in developing countries has tended to concentrate on configuring labour markets, studying mobility, migration, occupational choice and earnings among the workers. The extent of occupational mobility is one facet of labour market segmentation literature. A second is the process of wage determination (earnings) within each labour market segment. Third is the occupational choice of the labourers. An understanding of how the urban labour markets operate and interact with the occupational choice, earnings and mobility among workers may help to understand better the role of labour market segmentation.

Objectives of the Study

1. To study the nature and structure of the Coimbatore urban labour market,
2. To analyse the determinants of earnings in urban labour market,
3. To study the occupational mobility and their determinants among the organised and unorganised industrial workers and
4. To know whether the Coimbatore urban labour market is segmented and how far earnings, mobility are supported the segmentation of the market.

Data Sources and Methodology

The available research works, both theoretical and empirical, on the supply and demand side of the labour market has been inadequate. In this context, it is hoped that the present research work at the micro level, in a modest way, would cover, consider, explain and reveal the process of labour market. Segmentation, determinants of earnings of the worker's in a labour market. Though the emphasis is more on economic aspects, adequate importance has also been given to the non-economic aspects like the so-called institutional factors. And this would help to understand the whole gamut of Indian Labour Market from analytical perspective at the micro level.

Having selected Coimbatore city, the next task was to identify the industrial units to conduct the study. From the information and data obtained from the office of the Registrar of Companies, Coimbatore (Tamil Nadu is unique in one sense that it has a second office of the Registrar of Companies at Coimbatore, Other one at Chennai), it was found that textile units stand first in terms of number of units and size of the employment and second was engineering units. Hence, it was decided to have sample from these two types of industries, which brought prominence to Coimbatore, both at national and international level.

The names and addresses of the textile units were obtained from the office of the South India Mill Owners Association (SIMA) and South India Small Spining Mills Association both at Coimbatore. Similarly the names and addresses of the engineering units were obtained from the Coimbatore District Small Scale Industries Association (CODISSIA). From both the lists only those units which fell under Coimbatore City Corporation limit and also functioning for the preceding five years without interruption due to strike or lockout were considered. The final list contained 12 textile mills, 18 small textile units, 14 large scale engineering units and 51 small scale engineering units were identified.

Having selected the units, the next stage was to select the workers from the industrial units. The name list of workers from the selected units were obtained. Workers in the selected textile units were 2060 and in the engineering units 1400. From the respective industrial category to have a meaningful-study it was decided to have 10 per cent as sample. So we have identified a total of 346 workers by taking 210 organised and 136 unorganised industrial workers. Our study did not cover the women workers as they constituted less than one per cent in the industrial units of our sample and the numbers we have collected might not be helpful for meaningful analysis.

As we aim to examine the earnings structure, mobility and existence of segmentation, the primary data was collected from a sample of 346 industrial workers of Coimbatore urban labour market, covering organised and the unorganised sectors. To get the relevant data in fulfilling the objectives facts were collected from the sample workers through personal interview by the researcher with a pre-tested questionnaire. The questionnaire called information's from the respondents on personal and house hold characteristics, earnings and choice of occupations, the pattern of mobility. The data were processed by using the simple statistical tools like mean and standard deviation. Multiple regression technique was used to estimate the earnings differentials of workers in the labour market. The Tobit model was fitted to analyse the determinants of mobility.

REVIEW OF EMPIRICAL STUDIES

Labour Market Studies in Developed Countries

A number of empirical attempts have been made in advanced industrial countries to test the theoretical hypotheses of the labour market segmentation. In this section an attempt is made to briefly review some of the important studies on labour market segmentation [viz. Andrisani, 1973; Bosenquet and Doeringer 1973; Wulf 1974; Osterman, 1975; Rosenberg, 1975; Carnoy and Rumberger, 1976; Carnoy, Girling and Rumberger, 1976; McNabb and Psacharopoulos 1977; Oster, 1979; Mayhew and Rosewell, 1979; Rumbereger and Carnoy, 1980; McNabb, 1981; Kumar and Lou Coates, 1982; Bertil Homelund, 1983; Dickens and Lang, 1985; Meng, 1985; Miller and Volker, 1985; McNabb, 1987; Shackett and Trapani, 1987; Kruggers and Summers, 1988] in developed countries, especially in USA and U K.

Labour Market Studies in Developing Countries

In the last decade several econometric studies have been carried out on labour markets in the developing countries. Interestingly enough, econometric studies in the industrialising countries [Zehra Kansnakoglu, 1968; Andorsan, 1973; Alexandor, 1974 velloso, 1975 Liu, 1975; Clignet, 1976; Lobo, 1977; Barbosa and De Souza, 1978; Majumdar and Massoori, 1978; Corbo and Stlcner, 1978; Toledo, 1979; Fields, 1980; Neuman and Ziderman, 1986; Heckman and Hotz, 1986; Uthoff, 1986; Susanne Schmitz, 1989; Sakamota and Dechien 1991.] provides quite different empirical evidence on labour market compared to that in the industrialised countries.

Labour Market Studies in India

In India, labour market studies, particularly studies on segmented labour markets are few in number. Exclusive theoretical and empirical studies on segmented labour markets have not been done in India. It may be because of the peculiar characteristics of the labour market or because of the lack of availability of suitable cross-section and time-series data on the existing labour force. Moreover, factors like caste, religion and culture may have greater influence on the functioning of the Indian labour market. Perhaps for this reason, we do not find an integrated labour market in India which makes it difficult for empirical analysis [Kannappan 1985 Papola 1985]. However in the present section, we will review the few available (Papola and Subramaniam, 1973; Mazumdar, 1974; Tilak 1978; Deshpande, 1979; Mazumdar, 1979; Harriss, 1982, 1986 Despande 1983; Mazundar 1983; Dota, 1985; Papola , 1986; Saila bala Debi, 1988; Harriss, Kannan and Gary Rodgers, 1989; Acharya and Jose, 1991; Khandher, 1992) empirical studies on segmented labour markets have been carried out in India.

Determinants of Earnings in Organised and Unorganised Labour Markets

To estimate the determinants of our sample workers of

Coimbatore labour market a semi-logarithmic earnings function was fitted. It related logarithmic earnings to workers' education, experience, (time spent on labour market) training (Human Capital Variables) religion, caste, location of the job, (Workers Background Variables) and some industry specific, job characteristics such as whether or not labour laws apply and sector of employment.

Empirical Model

To test and verify the answers to the above questions, equations were estimated using ordinary least squares. The semi-log form was chosen after a review of the recent literature on earnings functions.

$$\text{Ln EAR} = \propto + ß1\ A + ß2\ M + ß3\ K + e.$$

Where, `log Ear'is the natural logarithmic earnings function of the industrial workers. In our case we can write the specification as

`A' is a vector of human capital variable such as age, [proxy for experience] age square, education and training experience (time spent of labour market)

`M' is vector of background variables of individual workers such as caste, religion, migration and area dummy where the worker was born;

`K' is a vector of industry specific, job-related characteristics such as the location of the job, whether any labour law applies to job and sector of employment And ∝ and ß 's are the parameter estimates.

Equation No.1. Determinants of Earnings for Organised and Unorganised Workers

(All Workers)

Ln EAR =

∝+B1 AGE+B2 AGESQ+B3 EDUI+B4 EDU2+B5 EDU3

+B6DUTECH+B7SCL1+B8SCL2+B9RELI+B10REGION

+B11 ARYMIG + B12FAILL + B13 FOCCI + B14 FOCC2

+B15MTUPRJ + B16 CI+B17 NAW+B18 NWI + B19 LAPRJ

Equation No.2. Determinants of Earnings for Organised sector Workers

Ln EAR =

∝+B1 AGE+B2 AGESQ+B3 EDUI+B4 EDU2+B5 EDU3

+ B6 DUTECH + B7SCL1 + B8 SCL2+B9 RELI + B10 REGION

+B11 ARYMIG+B12FAILL+B13 FOCCI+B14 FOCC2

+B15MTUPRJ + B16 CI+B17 NAW+B18 NWI + B19 LAPRJ

Equation No.3. Determinants of Earnings for Unorganised Sector Workers

Ln EAR =

∝+B1 AGE+B2 AGESQ+B3 EDUI+B4 EDU2+B5 EDU3

+ B6 DUTECH + B7 SCL1 + B8 SCL2+B9 RELI + B10 REGION

+B11 ARYMIG+B12FAILL+B13 FOCCI+B14 FOCC2

+B15MTUPRJ + B16 CI+B17 NAW+B18 NWI + B19 LAPRJ

Table 1.
Mean And Standard Deviation of Selected Variables

Variable	Label	Mean	Standard Deviation
Lear	Log Earning	9.72	0.60
Human Capital Variables			
AGE	Age	29.88	9.23
AGESQ	Age Square	977.81	630.49
EDU0	Illiterate	0.04	0.20

EDU1	Primary	0.09	0.28
EDU2	Secondary/HSC	0.67	0.47
EDU3	Diploma/ITI/ Degree	0.20	0.40
DUTECH	Training Duration	3.83	9.75
Workers Background Variables			
SCL1	Forward caste	0.12	0.33
SCL2	BC/MBC	0.82	0.38
SCL0	SC/ST	0.05	0.22
REL 1	Religion	0.94	0.23
REGION	Rural	0.24	0.43
ARYMIG	Migration	0.34	0.48
FAILL	Fathers Education	0.64	0.48
FOCC1	Agriculturalists	0.39	0.49
FOCC2	Workers in (manufac)	0.27	0.44
FOCC0	Other Jobs	0.34	0.48
MTUPRJ	Trade Union Member	0.41	0.49
Industry, Job Specific variables			
CL	Industry	0.60	0.49
WORUN	Sector	0.61	0.49
NAW	Nature of Work	0.46	0.50
NWI	No. of Workers	272.85	259.46
LAPRJ	Labour Law	0.63	0.48

Number of Valid Observations (Listwise) = 346.00

Excluded categories in dummy independent variables

1. Edu0 = Illiterate workers
2. SCL3 = SC/ST category
3. Religion = Other than Hindus
4. Region = Urban
5. Fathers Education = Illiterates
6. FOCC3 = Fathers employed in other occupations
7. CI = Classification of Industry - Textile/Engineering
8. WORUN = Sector of employment -Organised /unorganised
9. NAW = Nature of Job - Permanent/ Temporary

Table 2.

Determinants of Earnings For Organised And Unorgnaised Sector Workers

Variable	Equation 1 All Workers		Equation 2 Organised Workers		Equation 3 Unorganised Workers	
	ß	t	ß	t	ß	t
Human Capital Variables						
AGE	.091050	5.434*	.061032	3.542*	.128209	3.452*
AGESQ	-.001000	-4.194*	-0.0007	-2.811*	-0.01703	-2.9.2*
EDU1	.110998	.872	-.093950	-.675	.051516	.204
EDU2	.077900	.708	-.042350	-.343	.019700	.098

EDU3	.123368	1.021	.008634	.066	.098504	.437
DUTECH	.000500	.204	.000838	-.266	.001431	.391
Workers Background Variables						
SCL1	-.210837	-1.882*	.020595	.143	-.218003	-1.269
SCL2	-.072765	-.742	.101869	.748	-.084771	-.623
REL1	-.057689	-.626	.063324	-.603	.028482	-196
REGION	.074102	1.376**	-.103274	-1.758*	.186276	1.926*
ARYMIG	-.024356	-.531	.012346	.272	-.090432	-1.030
FAILL	.055671	1.214	.000130	.003	-0.32177	-.350
FOCC1	-.112333	-2.177*	-.051614	-.936	-.103439	-1.184
FOCC2	-.098388	-.1.726*	-.034542	-.609	-.155400	-1.378**
MTUPRJ	.367293	5.436*	.281119	3.728*	.065371	.537
Industry, Job Specific variables						
CI	-.143356	-2.569*	0.11926	.178	-.280937	-3.121*
NAW	.283047	4.552*	.496735	6.827*	.068142	.712
NWI	.000283	2.421*	.000213	1.923*	.000267	.686
LAPRJ	-.054442	-.932	.202997	2.934*	-.167785	-1.820*
Constant	7.822786	26.549*	8.012839	23.885*	7.586446	14.925*
R Square	.61088		.77463		.36265	
Adjusted R Square	.58820		.75210		.25825	
Standard Error	.38543		.30594		.40368	
F	26.93636		34.37241		3.47384	
Sample Size	346		210		136	

*Significant at 5% level** Significant at 10% level

RESULTS AND DISCUSSION

The results partially support the human capital model of Neo classical labour market (NLM) view that earnings variations were partly explained by variations in workers' human capital such as experience (age as proxy, i.e. time spent on labour market) and education [Becker 1964; Mincer, 1974]. Our findings are similar to that of the findings of Andrisani (1973), Velloso (1975, Clignet (1976). Meyhew and Rosewell (1979) and Mc Nabb (1981). Among the workers background variables, castes (FC, BC/MBC) had a negative impact on earnings. Forward caste was significant (for Forward caste) as compared to SC/ ST on earnings. The location (rural) of a job was significant on earnings as compared to the urban sector. When father's occupation was agriculture, or worker in manufacturing unit had negative influences on earnings compared to fathers employed in other jobs. In general Trade union membership improved the earnings of industrial workers. Increased earnings may result from the positive feedback of a union, as suggested by Segmented Labour Market (SLM) model. Religion did not influence worker's earnings in the industrial sector.

Based on the results of the industry specific characteristics, the variable textile category of industry has negative relation with earnings. The other variables such as nature of work and scale of enterprises also found having significant. An industry's scale of operation increase worker's earnings in the industrial sector and the earnings may suggest that benefits were more in large scale enterprises. Our findings are similar to that of the findings of Dipak Mazumdar and Misoori, (1978). So among the industry specific variables category of industry, nature of work and size of units had significantly influenced the variables.

The results indicated that contrary to our expectation education variable failed to emerge significantly. They had a negative influence in organised but positive in unorganised sector. The findings of Liu's (1975) study was consistent with the results of this study Similarly the study conducted by McNabb (1981) suggest that lower segment (secondary) educational attainment have positive impact on earnings. So it revealed that in organised sector other factors might have dominated in influencing earnings and many workers would have entered the service with less education and on the job training would have played its role. Whereas in unorgainsed sector education had the positive association but not significant in both the sector.

The workers background variables, such as forward Caste, Backward Caste/Most Backward Caste in organised sector had a positive role (as evidenced by Harriss, Kannan and Rodgers, (1989) on workers job and earnings than the unorganised sector workers. However they were not significant. Religion was found to have contrary sign in organised sector. It had positive impact on earnings of the unorganised sector but no significant in both the sectors with reference to in-Hindus. Trade union membership was found to have significant influence on the earnings, in the organised sector but not in unorganised sector. Alternatively, higher wages would have followed with union pressure and fight as contemplated by NLM model. So our findings support the NLM model.

An industy's scale increase workers earnings in the organised sector (this is in conformity with the results of Dipak Mazumdar and Masoori, 1978) but not in the unorganised sector. Labour law had positive influence on earnings and significant in the organised secotor and negative influence on earnings and significant in the unorganised sector. The results indicated that the wage-setting process differed among the segments. In the unorganised labour market, earnings seemed to depend more on the amount of time worked, as expressed by the unemployed and weekly hours variables. An interesting aspect we obsere in the equations was the differences in magnitude between the two sectors. There was a substantial difference in the explanatory power of the two equations, a fact which emphasized that the industry-job-specific variables better explain wage-setting practices in the organised than in the unorganised.

Tobit Estimation of Occupational Mobility

This section deals with the following questions that may have important policy implications.

1. Has better human capital enabled a worker to change jobs more?

2. Do characteristics such as caste, religion, and other background variable influence workers' occupational mobility?

In our empirical model, we estimate the determinants of occupational mobility rate by using Tobit method.

The functional Forms of Tobin Model.

The Tobit model is specified as

Yi = B'Xi+Mi if B'Xi+Mi 0

= 0 if B'Xi+M1 0

i=1,2,3......N. Where N denoted the number of observations, Yi the dependent variable, Xi a vector of independent variables, `B' a vector of unknown parameter, and -- i an independently distributed error term assumed to be normal with zero mean and constant variance--2.

Specification of the Empirical Model

Using the above functional form of the model to estimate empirically the determinants of the occupational mobility among our sample workers at Coimbatore labour market we have framed the empirical model by incorporating the workers human capital, workers background and job specific variables. By modifying the specifications of the empirical equations we have tried to obtain a best explanation of the situation using the Tobit model.

Occupational Mobility

Let us consider first the occupational mobility which is defined as the number of time a worker changes job divided by the length of time he works in the labour market. It was expected that the human capital variables, workers background variables and job specific variables would influenced the dependent variable. Before we provide the results of the multivariate analysis in a table let us have the mean and standard deviationof the variables we have considered in the Tobit model. Now the empirical estimation of the model may be presented.

(Determinants of Occupational Mobility of Organised and Unorgainsed sector workers)

All the Education, training and experience (time spent on labour market) variables have important positive influence on occupational mobility by our sample workers and it was significant. Similar results evidenced by Andrisani, (1973); Mayhew and Rosewell, (1979) and Khandker, (1992). Within the background variables compared to SC/ST workers, variables such as workers belonging to Forward Caste, BC Caste, father's occupation had negatively influenced the mobility.

Table 3.
Tobit Estimates Of Determinants Of Occupational Mobility Of Organised And Unorganised Sector Workers

Dependent Variable : Occupational Mobility

Variable	All Workers		Organised Sector Workers		Unorganised Sector Workers	
	Nomalized Co-efficient	T-Ratio	Nomlized Co-efficient	T-Ratio	Nomalized Co-efficient	T-Ratio
Human Capital Variables						
Age square	-0.08336	-1.8074*	-0.10888	-1.8730*	0.36546	3.1777*
Primary	0.00217	3.2891*	0.00254	3.1910*	-0.00524	-2.8410*
Secondary	0.88094	2.1860*	0.62001	1.1697	0.07135	0.08935
Post -Secondary	1.2763	3.4916*	1.1682	2.4073*	0.26239	0.40005
ITI/Diploma	1.3981	3.2939*	1.4513	2.6069*	-0.08525	-0.10929
Training	1.0069	2.4432*	0.67598	1.2506	0.19296	0.26173
Experience	0.00887	1.2187	0.01807	1.5529**	-0.05573	-0.05321
Workers Background Variables						
Forward caste	-0.63238	-2.0742*	-0.75052	-1.5228**	-0.79234	-1.6933**

BC/MBC	-0.61644	-2.3521*	-0.82699	-1.7586*	-0.67887	-1.9270*
Religion	-0.09333	-0.89766	0.18823	0.51225	-1.1275	-2.9089*
Region	0.25387	-0.61451	-0.09220	-0.46089	-0.25851	-0.91508
Migrants	0.00635	1.9964*	0.19319	1.2408	0.30799	1.2830
Father educate-	-0.10997	0.04980	0.11420	0.70455	-0.58284	-2.2917*
Fat. Occu. (agr)-	0.17564	-0.75010	-0.18131	-0.95798	-0.11664	-0.45041
Fat. Occu. (Man)	0.12701	1.1073	0.10215	0.52200	0.40230	1.3249**
Trade Union. Me		0.67586	0.15631	0.60097	0.11079	0.33186
Industry, Job Specific Variables						
Organised	0.16547	1.0473	0.17582	0.76233	-0.30712	-1.1727
Permanent	-0.22810	-1.3069	-0.33863	-1.3490**	-0.11060	-0.42368
Scale of enter	0.00063	2.0921*	0.00031	0.82720	0.00109	1.7075**
Labour law	-0.07177	-0.44358	-0.23016	-0.96904	-0.40649	-1.6073**
Constant	0.01197	0.01452	0.59743	0.52499	-3.6061	-2.3369
Sample Size		346		210		136
Log-Likelihood Function	-1265.8849		-859.96805		-363.72584	

*Statistically significant at 5%level ** Statistically significant at10% level

The migrant character had positive influence on bob mobility and significant. Trade union also had positive impact on worker's job mobility but no significant. It may be treated that trade union did not influence on worker's job mobility in our study. In the industry job specific variables namely type of industry, Sector of employment, and scale of operation had positive influence on workers job mobility among industiral workers.

Education and experience (time spent on labour market) of workers had an influence on worker's occupational mobility among organised sector workers, But not in unorganised sector.

In contrast, training did not help job mobility for unorganised workers. This result supports the findings of the study made by Rosenberg (1975). The workers background variables such as Caste, religion, father's education and father's occupation didnot have much influence on job mobility as evidenced by the study made by Hariss *et al* (1989). Workers who were born in Coimbatore were more mobile than men who were born in areas outside of Coimbatore. The Trade union had positive impact on worker' job mobility but not significant on both the organised and unorganised workers. With respect to job specific variables such as type of job had negative influecne on workers job mobility in both textile and engineering industry. Scale of operation had positive influence on workers job mobility in both organised and unorganised workers. The protected job had a negative impact on the mobility of the industrial workers.

Labour Market Segmentation

Over the years several labour market models have been developed to provide alternative explanations to the operational mechanisms of urban labour markets. Most of these models, which draw their basic propositions from the classical model of labour market analysis, have limited applicability in explaining the structure, functioning and consequences of urban labour markets in developing countires in general, and India in particular. Howerver, in late 1960.'s a non-neo classical 'theory of labour market segmentatioin was evolved to help understand the labour market mechanisms and outcomes in both developed and developing countires.

Many economists working in the field of Labour market, want to know why the distribution of earnings is more unequal in some counties than in others. They are motivated by a desire to understnd the determinants on inequality in income. The pertinent question is what causes inequality in the distribution of labour market rewards? One answer that is increasingly being offered by analysts at the World Bank and elsewhere is 'Labour Market Segmentation' [LMS] [Fields, 1980 b]. It implies the process of compartmentalisation of the labour market into separate segments having distinct reward structure and circumstances of employment.

Existence of Labour Market Segmentation

A number of empirical studies on labour Market segmentation in India (viz., Deshpande, 1979, Mazumdar 1979, 1983; Hariss, 1986; Papola, 1986; Hariss, Kannan and Rodgers, 1989; Khndkar, 1992) have been carried out. Most of the labour economists agree that the Indian labour market is segmented. An attempt has been made to assess whether Coimbatore labour market was segmented or otherwise by taking the characteristics considered by the three major approaches to urban labour market which preferred to call the labour market as segmented when there exists primary/ secondary and organised/unorganised and formal/informal labour market conditions.

Various researchers have described the labour market dualism, as formal and informal, protected and unprotected and organised and unorganised. In all these classifications characteristics attributed to primary, organised, formal and protected labour market are more or less same. Similarly the features attributed to secondary, unorganised, informal and unprotected market are common. Hence, we have applied organised and unorganised labour market classificaiton of the labour market and attempted to test the nature of Coimbatore labour market. Most of the Indian researhers have used such classification and more particularly the other important study on Coimbatore labour market done by Harriss, Rodgers and Kannan also followed the same classificaitons. The widely accepted caharacteristics of organised sector are: high wages, job stability (permanence), good working conditions, seniority rights (scope for promotion) and benefits, and high degree of unionisation. And the characteristics for unorganised sector are: low wages, job instability (impermanence), poor working condition, no seniority rights and benefits, low or non unionised, scale of enterprises. Hence, to assess the labour market segmentation a discussion of characteristics of earnings and mobility were necessary. We have considered the features of organised and unorganised segments in our earlier analysis on earnigns and mobility, using those explanations or results of analysis and additional informations were collected from the respondents, verified the nature of Coimbatore urban labour market from the organised and unorganised point of view in the following lines.

Table 4.

Tallying Coimbatore Labour Market Condition With Segmented Labour Markets Characteristics

Characteristics Labour Market Segmentation		Coimbatore Urban Labour Market Characteristics	
Organised Sector	Unorganised Sector	Organised Sector	Unorganised Sector
1. **WAGES** High Wages	Low Wages	High Wages (57% earned more than Rs.50 in average per day	Low Wages (only18% earned more than Rs.50 in average per day)
2. **JOB STABILITY** Stability (permanence)	Instability (impermanence)	High proportion of permanent workers (80% workers)	Low proportion of permanent workers (56% workers)
3. **WORKING CONDITIONS** Good working conditions	Poor working conditions	Working conditions Fair	Working conditions Poor
4. **SCOPE FOR PROMOTION**	No seniority rights and benefits	Relatively more scope for	Less scope for promotion

Seniority rights and benefits		promotion than in unorganised sector	
5. **UNION MEMBERS** Unionised	Non-unionised	More number of workers in union (59% workers)	Less number of workers in union (14% workers)
6. **EMPLOYMENT** Low unemploy-ment	High unemployment	More waiting period	Less waiting period
7. **SCALE OF ENTERPRISE** Monopoly sector industries (large firms)	Competitive sector industry (small firms)	More large firms (46% large units)	Less Large Forms (62 % small units)
8. **ADVANTAGED GROUPS** Prime age males	Disadvantaged groups (minorities youth, older workers)	More experienced workers (44% of workers in 20 to 30 years of age) Less minorities and weaker sections	Less experienced workers (84% of workers in 20 to 30 years of age) More minorities and weaker sections

SUMMARY AND CONCLUSIONS

An attempt has been made to verify the nature of Coimbatore labour market by considering the characteristics attributed to segmented labour market by approaching the market on the baiss of organised and unorganised. In additon we made an attempt assess the natue of Coimbatore labour market on the basis of the role of variables asuch as set of human capital, workers background and job specific variables on earnings, mobility and occupational choice. The first approach revealed that all the widely accepted features of segmented labour market prevailed at Coimbatore during the period of our study. The second approach also proved that in the determinants of earnigns of workers human capital variables were not significant, but other two set of variables were significant. While for mobility and occupational choice all the three sets of variables played their role. As the role of institutional variables like, caste, religion, trade union, region, occupation of father as well as job specific variables were significant in all the aspects of labour market, it is reasonable to conclude that Coimbatore labour market was segmented.

References

Ahluwaia, Montek S. (2000). "Economic Performance of States in Post-Reforms Period", *Economic and Polictical Weekly*, Vol. 35, No. 19,May 6.

Banerjee, B. (1983), "The Role of Informal Sector in Migration Process ; A Test of Probabilitic Migration Models and Labour Market Segmentation in India".

Biswal K. (1995), "Theory of Labour market Segmentation: Implications for Analysis of Urban Labour Market in India", Common Wealth Publishers, New Delhi.

Cain G. C. (1975), "The Challenges of Dual and Radical Theories of the Labour Market to Orthodox", discussion Paper, Institute for Research on Poverty, University of Wisconsin, Madison.

Carnoy, M. (1978), "Segmented Labour Markets : A Review", Working Paper, International Institute for Economic Planning, UNESCO, Pairs.

Datt, gaurav (1999), "Has Poverty Declined Since Economic Reforms? Statistical Data Analysis", *Economic and Political Weekly*, Vol. 34, No. 50, December 11.

Deshpande, L. K. (1983), "Labour Market Segmentation – A Study of Bombay", Kunda Datar Lectures, Gokhale Institute of Politics and Econmics, Pune.

Deshpande, L. K. (1991), "Human Capital Theory and Labour Market Analysis", Edited by V. N. Kothari "Issues in Human

Capital Theory and Human Resources Development Policy.

Dev, S. Mahendra (2000), "Economic Reforms, Poverty Income Distribution and Employment", *Economic and political Weekly*, Vol. 35 No. 10, March 4.

Gupta, S. P. (2000), : "Trickle Down Theory Revisited: The Role of Employment and Poverty", *The Indian Journal of Labour Economics*, Vol. 43, No.1.

Harriss, J., K. P. Kannan and Gerry Rodgers (1990), "Urban Labour market Structure and job Access in India. A study of Coimbatore." Research series. ILO Geneva. (Khandker R Shahidur (1992). "Earnings, Occupational Choice, and Mobility in Segmented Labour Market in India'. The World Bank) Khandker. The World Bank Staff Working Paper No. 154,

Mazumdar Dipak (1983), "Segmented Labour market in LDC's", *The American Economic Review,* Vol. 73 No. 2 May.

McNabb, R. (1979), "Further Evidence of the Relevance of the Dual Labour Market Hypothesis of the UK", *Journal of Human Resources,* Vol. XVI, No. 3 Spring.

Nagraj, R. (2000), "Indian Economy Since 1980: Virtuous Growth or Polarisation", *Economic and Political Weekly,* Vol. 35, No. 32 August 5.

Papola, T. S. (1984), "Urban Informal Sector in a Developing Economy", Vikas Publishing House Pvt Ltd., New Delhi.

Pascharopoulos G. (1987), "Economics of Educatioin : Research and Studies". Pergmon Press, Oxford.

Rosenberg Sam (1989), "From Segmentation to Flexibility", *Labour and Society,* Vol. 14.

Sailabala Debi (1988), "Labour market Segmentatioin: A Case Study", *The Indian Journal of Labour Economics,* Vol. XXX, NO. 4, Jan.

Sanjay Kumar and N. K. sharma (2003), "Informal Sector ; An

Indian Perspective", *The Indian Journal of Labour Economics*, Vol. 46, No. 1, January– March 2003.

Sen. Abhijit (1996), "Economic Reforms, Employment and Poverty', *Economic and Political Weekly*, Vol. 31, Nos. 35-37, Special Number.

Sen, Abhijit (2000)., "Agriculture, Employment and Poverty: Recent Trends in Rural india", in Ramachandran, V. K. Adn Swaminathan, Madhura (eds.), *Agrarian Studies: Essays on Agrarian Relations in Less-Developed Countires*, Tulika Books, New Delhi.

ECONOMIC REFORMS AND RURAL LABOUR MARKET BEHAVIOUR —A STUDY ON OCCUPATIONAL DIVERSIFICATION IN RURAL AREAS

R. Ravindrapirabu*

Dr. C. Thangamuthu**

INTRODUCTION:

The economic reforms have been largely perceived that they would result in casualisation of organised labours, if labour market reforms are vigorously pursued (Joshi, 1995). But in rural sector, where agricultural labour is already unorganized and mostly depend on casual employment, the reforms as such may not have directly adverse consequences. The marketisation reforms in farm sector may force the farm labour to seek non-farm employment. Whatever little institutional bonds left in villages may be slackened, freeing the agricultural labour to seek contractual employment either in the farm operations or in the non-farm operations within or without the villages.

The post liberalization period has witnessed a rapid increase in the migratory character of the rural population into urban areas. This migratory character has taken different shapes. Numberless people from the rural areas migrate to cities daily for work and return home in the evening. There is another segment of the rural population that migrates to the cities on a periodic basis because it has arrangements for stay here. These people make weekly (or) fortnightly visits to their villages.

* Research Scholar, Dept. of Economics, Bharathidasan University,

** Professor of Economics, Dept. of Economics, Bharathidasan University

Then, there are people who have almost permanently migrated to urban areas despite their links with the rural areas. This segment of population is more interested in calling itself urban than rural . Thus it will be seen that the post liberalization period has been witnessing an employment oriented rehabilitation and realignment of population in the country with a pasture tilt towards urbanization. (M. P. Goswami and B. B. Lal, 1999).

But the shift of employment for rural labour into non-farm employment would be conditioned by the degree and patterns of rural industrialisation and the skills/capabilities of the labour who migrate to non-farm jobs. Though our results indicate that increasing opportunities for employment in agriculture would help improve rural income distribution, the opportunities for wage employment in agriculture seem to be limited due to decreasing size of land holding and increasing landlessness. The alternative is to develop agro-industries in rural areas based on locally available raw materials, which would strengthen the linkage effects of agricultural growth on rural employment. This is likely to promote many other activities like, repairs and maintenance, small seale business and other tertiary activities. However, to reap the benefits of rural industrialization and the externalities associated with it for equitable socio-economic development it is imperative to upgrade or impart the technical skills and education to the rural population at the lower end of income distribution. (Pratap Singh Birthal, 1997).

The non-farm employment has a tendency to expand if the farm itself gets diversified giving scope for processing industires with linkage effects. The strategy of agricultural growth must contain the elements of not-only growth and efficiency but also equity and sustainability. For proper output growth, diversification of agricultural activities must be stepped up into areas such as dairy production and other animal products, horticulture and floriculture, where demand is more elastic than that for food grains. Increased trade will help modernize production and processing and marketing should emerge as major rural activities providing agro with industry and trade and enhancing opportunities for rural employment. Since rainfed (or) dry land areas in the country have a coprative advantage in animal husbandry, horticulture and floriculture agricultural diversification in the context of trade can benefit backward areas where poverty is widespread. [Bishwa Nath Singh and H. N. Sing, 1995].

The experience in rural non-farm employment in India in the post reform period has not been quite encouraging. G. K. Chadha (2002), while highlighting the relevance and significance of the rural non farm sector (RNFS), holds that the employment scenario during 1990s was marked by a serious setback in rural non-farm employment. In an attempt to assess future employment potential in RNFS, identified a wide range of manufacturing activities, Construction, Hotels, Tourism, Transport, Storage, Communications and some activities in the social sector. With regard to employment diversification in the rural area however suggested a selective approach to rural employment expansion keeping in view the ground realities and future potential in each State.

The structural changes in the economy have led to selective withdrawl of labour force from agriculture and shitting of the same to non-agricultural activities either within the rural sector or to the urban and semi urban areas through short-term migration. Further, the development of infrastructure especially the transport and communication network, albeit not substantial in magnitude, has subserved the process of short-term migration of work force from rural to urban as well as semi-urban areas. Alongside the employment elasticity's not only in the agricultural sector but also in the economy as a whole has been found to decline (Bhalla, 1993, 1997). The user of new land augmenting technology in agriculture seems also to have produced worse impact on the employment through the replacement of labour by machineries particularly in the technologically developed regions along with the increase in productivity per unit of land. Surprisingly there has been significant acceleration in the growth rate of GDP and per-capita income during the post liberalization period albeit it is accompanied by a fall in the growth rate of agriculture. However the impact of growth rate on employment has been found to be declining. (Bhalla, Shiela., 1993)

The trends in rural employment have been similar to those for the whole economy. Growth in rural employment has decelerated sharply from 1.87 percent Per annum during 1973-74 to 1993 -94 to only 0.66 percent per annum during 1993-94 to 1999-200. Agricultural employment also decelerated the most, from 1.44 percent per annum during 1973-74 to 1993-94 to 0.19 percent per annum during 1993-94 to 1999 -2000. In both the rural and urban sectors, the non-agricultural sector has recorded a higher growth rate in employment than agriculture in almost all period. In rural areas during the over all period and during all the sub periods the growth rate of employment in non-agricultural sectors was appreciably higher than that in agriculture. As a result the manufacturing, trade, and transport and service sectors are emerging as an important source of rural employment. This is indicative of a gradual diversification of the economy away from the primary sector, albeit at a low rate. This shift from agriculture to non-agricultural sector is not a distress phenomenon. Some studies also show that there was less poverty among non-agricultural works than agricultural works. The relationship between agricultural growth and growth of non agriculture through input, output and consumption linkages has been well documented. In India the emergence of numerous, growth poles, including corridors of development along highways and above all, public expenditure on anti-poverty and other rural development programmes and on rural infrastructure have all been instrumental in increasing out put and employment in the non-agricultural sectors. The need therefore, is to develop a strategy to eliminate poverty in rural areas within a generation through accelaraning the growth of agriculture for providing productive employment in agriculture and no agriculture through diversification of non agriculture and accelerated growth of non agricultural activities. [G. S. Bhalla, Peter Hazell, 2003].

The sex distribution of rural non-farm employment has been found to be adverse to the fain sex. The contribution of female labour force participation in explaining inter-state variations in NFE has so for been negative indicating thereby that the States with higher female participation have lower non-farm employment. Although the non-farm employment turned out to be non significant in this extremes in explaining inter-State variations in rural poverty, it has shown strong potential to raise the real agricultural wages, which have shown significantly positive impact on rural poverty. Therefore, it's required to develop female labour market for non farm activities in the States having higher female labour force participation for reducing rural poverty (V. N. Misra 2000).

The level and growth of RNFS differ from region to region. The analysis of RNFS with reference specific region may throw more insight than taking in terms or rural areas of a state as a whole. While it is difficult to estimate the exact number of workers in RNFS due to multi-occupational status, it's observed that the income from RNFS as a percentage of total household income has increased rapidly in industrially developed region. While analysing the factors affecting the growth of RNFS, one should recognize dualism in RNFS, such as formal and informal RNFS. It is wrong to assume that non-agro-based formal RNFS industry (or) public services are determined by agricultural development (or) distress. It is more likely that agricultural development may influence informal RNFS positively or negatively. (Kishore C. Samal, 1997).

The recent years provide a disappointmenting employment scenario for the rural workers in general and rural female workers in particular whatever additional employment came, that was largely confined to agricultural sector; perhaps the locale of such jobs is shifting from rural to urban areas or the slackening pace of public (and private) investment in rural areas is squeezing the total size of this sector, or whatever new job or coming up in this sector are quantitatively superior for which the big mass of 'unskilled' or 'un-educated' female workers are not qualified. For all that one can anticipate for the further, job markets, the Non-Agricultural sectors are sure to pose more severe difficulties for the rural, especially female workers. Even a number of agricultural jobs are going to be more and more education and skill incentive if Indian agriculture gets truly globalized. In India, the imagination of the illiterate rural labour force in general, and rural female workers in particular, would not stir beyond there village life and economy. As production agents, they remain dormant, and as formal job seekers in the imagine labour market scenario, they are unwanted. (G. K. Chadha, 1999).

The Indian, scene in terms of sex-distribution of Non-Farm Employment (NFE) across the State reveal that:

a) There has been greater and increasing share of Non-Farm Employment among the relatively more developed States;

b) Between male and female, the latter leg behind the former in Non-Farm Employment and

c) During the period 1971-91 there have been some sharp decline in female NFE particularly in those States with agricultural advancements (implying the growing dependence of female workers on agriculture, a sort of "feminization of agriculture").

From the Table - 1 that the non-farm work force residing in rural areas, it is evident that the total non-farm expansion has been quite uneven among the States. The non-farm employment expanded fast especially during the 1970s and

1980s in Punjab, Haryana, Gujarat, Himachal Pradesh Rajasthan, and Tamilnadu Similarly the States such as Karnataka, Maharashtra, Orissa, orissa and West Bengal have witnessed a modest expansion. Slow expansion is noticed in the case of Bihar, Kerala and Madhya Pradesh. The States where the non-farm employment is very high especially during 1990s are Assam, Himachal Pradesh and Kerala - while there was no substantial change in other States (Koteswara Rao, 2000).

The NFE has been largely the bastion the male labour force. During 1971-91 the proportion female non-farm workers in the total rural work force increased substantially only in Kerala and marginally in HP , Up and West Bengal. There sharp decline (around 50 Percent fall) in the States of Punjab, Haryana, and Orissa. In other States, there were negligible changes (mostly on the decline).

In this regard, it is relevant to study the role of non-farm activities as a vital segment of rural economic structure. It is very relevant to study the dimension involved in the contribution of this sector to the farm households, their growth, employment pattern, income level, resource generation.

But the scope of NFE within the village area may not be adequate enough to sustain the growing work force. Hence, almost on a daily basis, the village people may commute to the neighbouring towns for non-farm employment as a source of livelihood.

Such growing nonfarm employment contributes to the rural economy and addresses the basic problems of unemployment and poverty to a considerable extent. The question as to how such non-farm employment benefit the scheduled caste households (the weakest and landless who are prone to migrant jobs) vis-a-vis the non-Sc households belonging to backward and most backward communities becomes the focus of the present study.

Table-1

State-Wise Percentage Distribution of Male Non-Farm Employment To Total Employment

States	1961	1972 - 1973	1977 - 1978	1981 - 1988	1993 - 1994	1999 - 2000
Andhra Pradesh	20.0	21.4	19.7	25.9	24.4	25.6
Assam	---	18.5	14.5	23.5	21.8	35.3
Bihar	14.7	17.8	17.0	20.0	18.0	21.0
Gujarat	15.9	16.1	15.5	31.4	28.9	28.6
Haryana	19.4	19.9	22.0	29.1	39.1	40.4
Himachal Pradesh	15.4	18.9	22.6	31.3	34.2	46.2
J & K	---	--	25.0	36.9	38.7	32.1
Karnataka	13.9	14.8	16.9	20.4	212	21.5
Kerala	40.4	44.3	41.0	45.8	46.8	57.2
Madhya Pradesh	11.7	3.6	10.8	14.7	21.8	15.8
Maharashtra	14.8	17.6	19.6	24.2	24.7	26.2
Orissa	12.1	18.4	15.5	25.1	21.3	33.0
Punjab	23.2	20.2	22.1	31.2	31.8	36.3
Rajasthan	11.9	15.6	18.0	34.7	30.4	32.7
Tamil Nadu	20.7	24.6	26.0	34.8	36.0	31.8
Uttar Pradesh	13.9	18.1	19.7	21.1	23.7	28.2
West Bengal	20.0	22.1	22.2	27.8	35.3	33.6
All India	16.3	16.7	19.5	25.5	26.0	28.6

Source:- Census Reports

Table-2

Non-Farm Female Workers as Percentage to Rural Workforce 1971 to 1999-2000

States	1971	1981	1991	1993 - 1994	1999 - 2000
Andhra Pradesh	12.96	12.27	12.20	16.3	15.7
Assam	6.10	7.66	6.80	8.1	14.3
Bihar	6.10	7.66	6.80	8.1	14.3
Gujarat	7.24	11.42	14.60	9.4	8.0
Haryana	23.06	14.89	13.70	6.8	7.9
Himachal Pradesh	5.12	5.91	7.60	4.5	4.9
Karnataka	19.17	16.60	14.80	15.4	12.2
Kerala	41.17	46.09	51.50	37.0	40.2
Madhya Pradesh	6.05	7.32	6.00	6.1	8.4
Maharashtra	5.94	6.70	6.50	8.8	6.1
Orissa	23.02	16.53	14.70	15.0	19.6
Punjab	67.15	17.69	37.90	7.3	9.4
Rajasthan	9.95	11.27	6.40	7.3	8.1
TamilNadu	15.47	13.43	15.50	21.5	24.1
Uttar Pradesh	7.86	9.55	10.40	10.0	12.5
West Bengal	30.56	33.46	34.30	41.0	45.9
J & K	--	--	--	4.6	6.5
All India	**12.96**	**12.73**	**13.10**	**13.8**	**14.6**

Source:- Census Reports

OBJECTIVES

1. To find out the magnitude and characteristic features of non-farm employment in the study village

Vadakkumadevi, Perambalur District, Tamil Nadu;

2. To study the impact of non-farm employment on the household income and living standards of SC and non-Sc households, from comparative perspective.

METHODOLOGY:

The present study is based on primary survey of all the 78 SC households and BC sample of 50 households in Vadakkumadevi Village located near Perambalur town. All the 128 households are engaged in non-farm employment on full time or part-time basis. The study Village was chosen because of the predominant role played by non-farm employment and the location of the Village near the town of Perambalur enabling the people to have easy access to employment opportunities in the non-farm sector.

A pretested structured questionnaire was used to collect the date through personal interview methods. The data were compiled, analysed and interpreted using simple statistical methods.

FAMILY SIZE AND SEX DISTRIBUTION:

The data on family size and non-farm employment reveal that (a) higher income group tend to have larger family size (large family induced by greater income or perhaps incentive to go in for large family because of the possibilities of getting more wage income through increased number of working hands in the family) and (b) irrespective of the income groups, the incidence of female in non-farm employment is relatively lesser as the non-farm employment is in the urban location. Female labour urban areas; they are inclined to settle down in low-wage farm work within the village.

When compared with the SC group, the non-SC group shows that relatively more number of persons are in the higher income brackets. Average family size is higher in the higher income groups as in the case of SC group. But more number of women in non-SC group are found in the higher income group, indicating a better family status of the non-SC groups.

Table-3

Family Size Sex Distribution and NFE

Income groups	N.O. H.H.		Average Family Members		Male		Females	
	BC	SC	BC	SC	BC	SC	BC	SC
less than 10000	1	1	2	2	-	-	-	-
10000 to 15000	1	14	2	4.1	1	9	-	1
15000 to 20000	4	31	4.5	4.36	4	31	-	3
20000 to 25000	4	12	4	4.75	4	17	-	3
25000 to 30000	4	7	5.5	5.42	7	12	2	3
30000 to 35000	6	9	4.3	5.6	5	22	4	2
35000 to 40000	13	5	5	5.4	15	7	13	2
40000 Above	17	---	4.05	---	31	---	9	---
Toal	50	78	---	---	67	90	28	15

Source : Primary Data

Sex Distribution and Non-Farm Employment:

Sex distribution and non-farm employment indicates that still the non-farm employment is dominated by male workers because the women find it difficult to search for some casual hobs in the town. Further women tend to concentrate on farm work though less paid while men tend to commute to urban area in search of high paid jobs in the non-farm employment.

Thus the study village also corroborates the prevalence of "feminization of agriculture" i.e. women workers tend to occupy the employment space in agriculture vacated by the men labourers moving to non-farm employment in greater number.

When it comes to non-Sc group, the incidence of non-farm employment among the female members is almost double that of the SC group.

Table-4

Male And Female Distribution of NFE

Income groups	N.o H.H.		Non-Farm Employment			
	BC	SC	Male		Female	
			BC	SC	BC	SC
less than 10000	1	1	-	-	-	-
10000 to 15000	1	14	1	9	-	1
15000 to 20000	4	31	4	31	-	3
20000 to 25000	4	12	4	17	-	3
25000 to 30000	4	7	7	12	2	3
30000 to 35000	6	9	5	22	4	2
35000 to 40000	13	5	15	7	13	2
40000 Above	17	---	31	---	9	---
Toal	**50**	**78**	**67**	**90**	**28**	**15**

Source : Primary Data

Table 5

Occuptional Profile Of Non-Farm BC Household

Type of active	NO. H.H.		Cons		Qua.		Ser.		Hotel Work		Driver		Load Men		Elec		Busi.	
	BC	SC	BC	SC	BC	SC	BC	SC	BC	SC	BC	SC	BC	SC	BC	SC	BC	SC
Less than 10000	1	1	—	—	—	—	—	—	—	—	—	—	-	—	—	—	—	—
10000 to 150000	1	14	—	8	—	—	—	—	-	—	—	—	1	1	—	1	—	1
15000 to 200000	4	31	—	17	—	1	—	3	1	3	1	2	2	5	1	—	—	—
20000 to 250000	4	12	1	10	—	—	—	—	—	—	—	3	-	5	3	—	—	1
25000 to 300000	4	7	—	9	2	—	1	—	—	2	3	—	3	4	—	—	—	—
30000 to 350000	6	9	1	12	5	—	1	—	—	1	1	—	—	7	—	—	1	—
35000 to 400000	13	5	6	2	18	—	1	—	—	1	2	4	—	2	1	—	—	—
40000 to above	17	---	6	---	15	---	4	---	1	---	9	---	5	---	---	---	---	---
Total	50	78	14	58	40	1	7	3	2	7	16	9	11	24	5	1	1	2

Source : Primary Data

OCCUPATION PROFILE:

Among the 78 households a high as 105 members are occupied in various non-farm jobs. The major non-farm employment in which maximum members are found in clued construction followed by loadman work. It is quite impressive to find that out of 105 members, 9 are drivers followed by 7 in hotel work. There is only one skilled worker, namely, electrician. By and large there is heavy incidence of unskilled hobs among scheduled caste in NFE.

The occupational profiles of the two groups show some differences. The quarrying (dominated by odders), Service sector (Teachers, LIC agent, etc), driving occupations are dominated by the non-Sc groups while SC dominates in construction and load carrying which involve more manual work.

WAGE RATE, TRAVEL COST AND INCIDENTAL EXPENDITURE:

The data an average wage rates of male labour and the travel cost and other incidental expenses show that (a) the travel cost and other incidental expenses including the lunch (many do not lunch from their homes) and other items of consumption take away about 20 to 30 percent average wage income and (b) among the items of incidental expenditure, one concealed item is the regular expenditure incurred on liquor consumption by almost all the workers engaged in NFE activities. They become addicted to liquor in due course, but for which, the living standard of those households might rise substantially more than what it is at present.

The average wage rates for the non-SC groups are marginally higher. That is, more number of persons are in the higher wage rate classes. SC households spend higher travel costs. The incidental expenses are almost the same.

Table-6

Average Wage Rates, Travel cost and Incidental Expenditure

Income groups	NO. H.H.		Average Wage Rate Per Day		Average Travel cost		Average Other Incidental Expenditure	
	BC	SC	BC	SC	BC	SC	BC	SC
less than 10000	1	1	---	---	---	---	---	---
10000 to 15000	1	14	80	80	5	6.81	20	15.15
15000 to 20000	4	31	90	74.16	5	6	15	11.37
20000 to 25000	4	12	95	92.5	8.5	6.8	18.5	18.75
25000 to 30000	4	7	95	81.42	5	9.7	19.28	19.28
30000 to 35000	6	9	100	88.12	5	6.87	22.5	18.12
35000 to 40000	13	5	100	95	5	5	25	18.75
40000 Above	17	---	100	---	5	---	25	---
Toal	50	78	---	---	---	---	---	---

Source : Primary Data

Income from Farm Employment

The composition of income sources indicates that (a) at the lower income groups, there is a lesser dominance of NFE'S share (and the farm income still remains a sizeable share (b) at the higher income groups (more than Rs.20,000 level) there is a very sharp decline of the relative share of farm income while the non-farm employment income share is strikingly significant (roughly more than 70 percent) : implication is that higher the relative share of income from non-farm employment, higher the average household income.

The income from non farm employment is higher for non-SC whereas income from farm employment is marginally higher for SC group.

Table-7

Income From Farm And Nonfarm Employment

Income Groups	No H.H.		Income from Non-Farm Employment		Income From Farm Employment	
	BC	SC	BC	SC	BC	SC
less than 10000	1	1	---	---	100	100
10000 to 15000	1	14	75	65.70	25	34.29
15000 to 20000	4	31	73.71	73.71	26.29	26.26
20000 to 25000	4	12	85.82	86.72	14.18	14
25000 to 30000	4	7	87.78	85.83	12.22	14.16
30000 to 35000	6	9	94.8	87.87	5.2	12.16
35000 to 40000	13	5	97.5	96.67	2.5	3.31
40000 Above	17	---	98.9	---	1.1	---

Source : Primary Data

Conclusion:

The proximity of the village to the town and the improved transport facility by greater frequency of mini buses have increased magnitude of NFE in the study village. Particularly after the town, Perambalur (which was till recently only a town panchayat) becoming the headquarters of the newly formed district, the pace of NFE among the village around has improved markedly. When such opportunities emerge more literate and better skilled labour get higher income from NFE.

Even among the SCs, the lowest in the SC ladder namely chakkiliyar households do not get as much benefit from NFE as the parayar households. Not that chakkiliyars are discriminated against. But they are perhapsless motivated than the parayars. Though almost all SC households have some small (but uneconomic, dry) landholdings, they are prudent in seeking NFE because of the relatively higher wage rates in the NFE. As evident from the study, the female members of the SC households do not get equal job opportunities in NFE as their male counterparts do. Many female members contend with locally available farm jobs or their low-skilled NFE with low wage rates in the neighbouring town.

Thus the study brings out a revealing trend: the SC households have the prospect of improving their economic standards by migrating to (or daily commuting to) the urban areas and getting better paid jobs in NFE. Some types of better paid jobs in NFE which the SC labour can access to in the urban areas, may not be available, or accessible to the SCs in their villages, given the social hierarchy and labour market imperfections arising out of the caste system. The study further signifies the need for an in depth empirical evaluation of the SCs in the urban-based non-farm employment.

The non-SCs have also been attracted towards non-farm employment partly out of push factors (poverty, lack of jobs in the rural sector) and party out of pull factors remunerative jobs in the non-farm sector).

REFERENCE

1. G. K. Chadha (1999)," Economic reforms and Emerging Demand Supply Hiatus in India's Rural Labour Market," IEA (The Indian Economic Association) 82nd Conference (Conference volume) Amritsar, pp722-742
2. Bhalla, Shiela, (1993 a), "The Dynamics of Wage Determination and Employment generation in Indian Agriculture", Ind. Joun. Of Agri. Eco., Vol. XIVIII, No.3
3. Bhalla, Shiela, (1993 b), "The test of some Propositions about the Dynamics of Changes in Rural work force Structure", The Ind. Joun. Of Labour Eco., Vol. 36, No.3.

4. M. P. Goswami and B. B. Lal (1999), "Economic Reforms and Employment Rural-Urban Scenario IEA (The Indian Economic Association) 82nd Conference (Conference volume) Amritsar, pp 757-762.

5. Pratap Singh Birthal (1997), "Occupational Diversity income distribution: some implication for Rural Development", Jou. of Rural Development, Vol. 16, No. 3, pp 465-475

6. Bishwa Nath Singh and N. H. Singh (1995), "Structural Adjustment, Rural Labour and Poverty in India," Indi. Jou. of Labour Economics Vol. 38, No. 4 July-Sept, PP-633.

7. Naches V. Joshi (1995), "Structural Adjustment, Labour Market and Poverty", Ind. Jou. Of Labour Economic, Vol. 38 No. 4 July-Sept, PP634.

8. G. K. Chadha (2003), "Rural Non-Employment 44th Annual Conference of the Indian Society of Labour Economics : A Report, " Ind. Jn. Of Labour Economics, vol. 46, no. 1, Jan -March

9. V. N. Misra (2000), "Role of Female Labour force Participation in Rural Poverty and NFE: Indian Experience," Indi. Jou. of Labour Economics, Vol. 43 No. 2 APRIL-JUNE, PP-221.

10. Kishore C. Samal, (1997), "Rural Non-Farm Activities In Specific Regions or Orissa", Jon of rural Development, Vol. 16, No. 3, July -Sept, pp-457-464.

11. G S Bhalla, Peter Hazell (2003), "Rural Employment and Poverty: Strategies to Eliminate rural Poverty within a Generation", E.P.W., Vol. XXXVIII, No. 33, August 16-22, Pp 3473 to 3484.

REFORMS AND DISEQUILIBRIUM IN LABOUR MARKET IN INDIA

R. Albert Christopher Dhas
The American College, Madurai
&
M. Helen Mary Jacqueline
Lady Doak College, Madurai

INTRODUCTION

The Economic Reforms with its central focus on "globalisation" gained importance and created significant influence on the various facets of the Indian economy. In a general sense, 'Globalisation" refers to cross -national flows of goods, investment, production and technology (James Petras and Henry Velmeyer : 2001). It involves liberalisation, privatization, minimizing economic regulations, reducing expenditures on public goods, tightening fiscal discipline, favouring free flows of capital, strict controls on organised labour, tax reductions and unrestricted currency repatriation.

India's experience in globalisation could be divided in to two phases. The first phase of economic liberalisation began in 1981, under pressure from the International Monetary Fund and the World Bank. The second phase of globalisation began in 1991 where the economic measures initiated were based on the World Bank's Structural Adjustment Programme (SAP) designed to restructure the economy (Dalip S. Swamy: 1997).

The overall objective of this paper is to examine the impact of the economic reforms on the labour market in India. However, the specific objectives are (a) to highlight the major trends in labour force in India and (b) to examine the impact of reforms on the labour market in India.

The discussion on this paper is organised in the following manner. In section 1, a review of studies on globalisation and labour employment in India is attempted. In section 2, the trends in labour supply and demand in India are discussed. In section 3, the impact of reforms on the labour market is discussed. The last section summarises the main findings.

REVIEW OF STUDIES

The issues related to globalisation and its impact have drawn the attention of researchers and policy makers in the recent past. Though their coverage is wide and vast, we shall review the major studies that are relevant for our theoretical understanding and clarity.

Dalip S. Swamy (1997) highlighted the possible effects of globalisation on employment and worker's standard of living in India. According to him, employment is the second major causality of globalisation, next to infrastructural output. He estimated that restructuring the economy through privitisation, import liberalisation, exit policy, and the deflationary fiscal policy would lead to an increase in unemployment at least by 2.8 million per year. He argued that growing unemployment in the organised sector, owing to increasing capital intensity, is likely to push workers into the informal and agricultural sectors. More over, as prices rise and recessionary impact on the economy spreads the worker's standard of living will decline.

Ngaire Woods (2000) argued that workers who rely upon government-set minimum wages or working conditions would lose out since such government policies become anachronistic in a new era of global competition. Further, many workers do suffer-at least in the short term-from the effects of globalisation. According to him, even the most otimistic accounts of economic integration and transformation accept that workers who are not mobile, or whose skills are not transferable, may suffer in a globalising world economy. He has cited that in industrialised countries the low-skilled workers are already paying the price.

Neeraj (2001) argued that globalisation is threatening to destroy the very livelihood of the hundreds of millions of working people of the unorganised sector in India. He analysed the impact of globalisation on the unorganised sector, particularly in fishereies, dairying and handlooms, and agriculture. He concluded that the costs of globalisation includes large-scale unemployment in the organised sector and small scale industries, and destruction of livelihood of the hundreds of millions working in the country's unorganised sector.

Shridhar Pandy and J. S. Tiwari (2001) argued that with the start of the process of liberalisation and globalisation, the employment opportunities in the organised sector have been continuously shrinking. They observed that the annual growth rate of employment in the organised sector in 1991 was 1.44 per cent, which fell to only 1.09 per cent in 1997. With the policy of disinvestments of public sector undertakings, employment opportunities in this sector have practically vanished. In the meantime, this process has resulted in sickness in increasing number of small and large-scale units. They concluded that the economy is suffering from recession resulting in more and more unemployment due to globalisation.

Dutt Ruddar (2001) observed that the unemployment rates, which showed a declining trend during the period 1977-78 to 1993-94, got, reversed during 1993-94 to 1999-2000. He argued that it would be futile to pursue the failed strategy of liberalisation which has a focus on 7 per cent of the labour force. The need of the hour is take care of the 93 per cent of the labour force engaged in the organised sector. He concluded that liberalisation has driven more and more people from the organised to unorganised sector.

Chakraborty, Debashis and Prabal Kr. De (2001) observed that the employment growth rate in the organised sector, particularly in the public and government sector is not very promising. Among these, reduction in employment is particularly strong in central public sector undertakings engaged in manufacturing. The recent stress on voluntary retirements scheme to retrench excess labour also contributed to this declining trend. They also argued that though the private sector is expanding in the post liberalisation period, the corresponding employment growth rate is still insufficient to absorb the ever-increasing labour force. Owing to the rigidities in the existing labour regulations, firms are generally reluctant to employ more labourers even if the demand is high. They concluded that the economic reform has manifested in the increasing trend of casualisation among the labour force.

Irani Dutta Medhi (2001) observed that the rate of growth of private employment is 0.4 per higher during reform period, but self employment and regular wage employment are higher during the pre-reform period.

Kunhaman M (2002) viewed globalisation in a subaltern perspective. He argued that the process of globalisation would lead to progressive pauperisation and extermination on the marginalised sections in India. He also argued that there would be loss of employment for the agricultural labourers.

The impact of liberalisation on employment and unemployment levels in various countries were extensively discussed in Borkakoti and Milner (1997). In countries like Chile, Spain and Yugoslavia, the net effect of liberalisation on employment was positive; in Mexico and Morocco, it did not affect employment levels; in Argentina, Israel, Indonesia, Korea, Philipines and Turkey, the increase in unemployment was rather small and was attributed to the factors other than reforms; and, in Uruguay the trade reform had affected employment and wages (Edwards and Edwards: 1997). These evidences suggested that the effect of globalisation on employment depend on the institutional characteristics of the labour market.

In this background, an examination of Indian case is attempted.

Trends in Demand and Supply of Labour in India

As per the 2001 census, the total work force in our country is 402 million, of which 313 million are main workers and 89 million are marginal workers. Out of the 313 million main workers, only about 28 million (9 per cent) are employed in the organised sector[1] and the remaining about 285 million (91 per cent) are in the unorganised sector[2] (Government of India, Economic Survey : 2002-03).

The extent of workforce in the organised and unorganised sectors, and their changes over time could be under stood by the information provided by the Alternative Survey Group. Accordingly, the share of organised workforce was about 8.33 per cent by 1983 which declined to 7.65 per cent by 1999-2000. The corresponding share of unorganised workforce was about 91.67 per cent by 1983 which increased to 92.65 per cent by 1999-2000 (Table 1).

Table 1

Trends in Employment in Organised and Unorganised Sectors in India (in lakhs)

Year	Organised	Unorganised	Total Workforce
1983	240.10(8.33)	2640.00 (91.67)	2880.00
1987-88	257.00(8.75)	2680.00 (91.25)	2937.00
1991-92	267.33(8.27)	2966.22 (91.73)	3233.55
1992-93	270.56(8.20)	3027.42 (91.80)	3297.98
1993-94	271.77(8.09)	3089.14 (91.91)	3360.91
1994-95	273.75(7.98)	3157.21 (92.02)	3430.96
1995-96	275.25(7.97)	3224.26 (92.03)	3499.51
1996-00	277.89(7.65)	3355.41 (92.35)	3633.30

Source : Alternative Economic Survey : 1991-1998.

Note : Figures in brackets are percentages to the respective totals.

If we assume the total workforce as the supply of labour, the total employment could be considered as the total demand for labour. But, in a real sense, all those employed under the organised and unorganised sectors could not be treated as the demand for labour. This is because of the fact that high level of disguised employment is found in the unorganised sectors and those who are not demanded or absorbed by the organised sectors are invariably pushed into the unorganised one. If one accepts the above argument, the study of labour market becomes more complex. Hence, in our analysis, though we analysed the employment trends in general, for the model building exercise, the organised labour alone considered.

IMPACT OF REFORMS AND LABOUR MARKET DISEQUILIBRIUM

The impact of reforms on employment in general is said to be divergent. In fact, unemployment and disguised unemployment are the normal features to Indian economy. There is heavy dependency on unorganised sector by the labourforce for their employment, income and livelihood. In such a situation, the policies towards de-linking budgetary support to the public sector enterprises and reducing labour absorption on public sector as part of the globalisation strategy leads to adverse effect on employment situation in India and create 'disequilibrium' in the labour market. The growth of employment (overall and organised sector) from the Seventies is given in Table 2.

---

1. The organised sector included both under public and private sector employment.
2. Ministry of Labour has categorised this unorganised labour force under four groups in terms of occupation, nature of employment, specially distressed categories and service categories

Table 2

Growth of Employment in India

Period	Growth rate of overall employment	Growth rate of employment in the organised sector (%)		
		Public	Private	Total
1972-73 to 77-78	2.75	---	---	2.45
1977-78 to 1983	2.36	2.99	1.41	2.48
1983 to 1987-88	1.77	2.17	0.43	1.38
1987-88 to1993-94	2.37	1.00	1.18	1.05
1993-94 to 1999-2000	1.07	(-)0.03	1.87	0.53

Source : Economic Survey 1998-99 and Planning Commission, 10th Five Year Plan, Vol. 1.

DISEQUILIBRIUM IN THE ORGANISED LABOUR MARKET:

It can be seen that the growth rate of organised sector employment maintained its declining trend from the period 1977-88 to 1983-84. The growth rate of public sector employment declined sharply and this trend continues up to the present. From 1997, the public sector employment grew negatively (Economic Survey: 2002-2003).

As the labour absorption in the organised sector declines during the period of reforms, it would lead to disequilibrium in the organised labour market . The situation gets worsen if pruning or retrenchment activities by the public sector as initiated under reforms are taken into consideration. Taking into account the backlog of unemployment and overall magnitude of additional employment to be generated, there lies a major gap between demand and supply of labour in India. The immediate effect of the observed disequilibrium in the labour market would get reflected in the wage levels (Table 3).

Table 3

Real Wages for Organised Workers in Selected States in India

Sate	1987	1988	1989	1990	1991	1992	1993	1994	1995	1996
Gujarat	4.68	4.86	4.97	4.88	4.83	4.91	4.70	4.34	4.45	4.38
Maharashtra	4.50	4.51	4.44	5.28	4.31	4.31	4.31	4.30	4.28	4.25
Karnataka	5.14	5.16	5.20	5.33	5.32	5.33	5.34	5.31	5.34	5.32
Tamilnadu	6.24	6.37	6.31	6.27	6.27	6.30	6.29	6.31	6.32	6.32
Madhya Pradesh	4.51	4.49	4.41	4.35	4.32	4.32	4.30	4.27	4.27	4.25
Uttar Pradesh	5.28	5.35	5.33	5.21	5.72	5.76	5.51	5.68	5.21	5.20
West Bengal	5.59	5.64	5.73	5.67	5.59	5.60	5.62	5.64	5.60	5.78

Note : Rupees at 1980-81 prices
OL = Organised Labour (cotton textile industry labour)
Source : Unni (2001)

The trends in the real wages revealed that while the real earnings of organised labour is maintained in Karanataka, Tamilnadu and West Bengal, it declined marginally in all the other states during the period 1987 and 1996. The observed trends in West Bengal could be due to the contribution of Trade Union Movements and that of Tamilnadu could be attributed to the liberal wage policy, salary/wage revision as per Central Government Policies etc., during the early nineties. How ever, these trends would have got reversed in recent years as the unions bargaining strength were nullified, deliberate controls on wage revision, fulfillment of vacancies and appointments and the voluntary retirement schemes followed. Thus, the above analysis clearly indicated the disadvantageous position realised by the organised workers in terms of their earnings in the recent years; In fact, this trend could be attributed to the negative impact of globalisation on the organised sector.

DISEQUILIBRIUM IN THE UNORGANISED LABOUR MARKET

In the context of declining growth rate in employment generation in organised sector and no scope for creating additional jobs, the additional labour force have to find work on self-employed activities or remain casual workers. In other words, when the labour absorption in the organised sector declines during the period of reforms, it would naturally push the additional labour force to the unorganised sector leading to further swelling of unorganised workers. As a large number of labour force is pushed into the unorganised category of workers, the excess labour supply creates disequilibrium or imbalance in the labour market that leads to several adjustments in the unorganised labour economy. The surplus or excess labour supply into the unorganised category leads to partial or casual employment at low wages and without job or social security of any kind (Rao and Rao; 1994). Unni (2001), based on the study conducted in Ahemdabad highlighted the differential benefit between a regular and casual employee. It revealed that the casual labourers are highly exploited in terms of assurance of employment, contract procedures, paid leave, PF/pension, medical and other benefit and notice for termination. If the argument that the disturbance in the labour market would be disadvantages to the unorganised workers it will get reflected in the movement of the real wages (Table 4)

Table 4

Real Wages for Unorganised Workers in Selected States in India

State	Type of Worker	1987	1988	1989	1990	1991	1992	1993	1994	1995	1996
Gujarat	UNAL	6.70	6.50	6.03	5.39	4.34	5.03	4.35	3.66	3.29	3.76
	UAL	1.84	-	1.66	1.75	1.63	2.84	2.25	1.69	1.71	-
Maharashtra	UNAL	-	-	5.34	4.27	4.08	-	-	4.39	4.45	3.82
	UAL	-	-	2.23	2.08	1.87	-	2.57	2.82	2.46	-
Karnataka	UNAL	2.16	-	3.07	3.10	2.47	-	4.08	3.64	3.16	-
	UAL	-	-	1.71	1.73	1.19	1.05	2.14	2.34	2.20	-
Tamilnadu	UNAL	3.39	3.34	3.22	2.97	2.83	2.92	2.97	2.83	3.62	3.35
	UAL	1.65	-	2.07	1.91	2.66	-	2.38	2.43	2.17	-
Madhya Pradesh	UNAL	3.87	3.67	3.35	3.33	2.18	3.22	3.16	3.17	2.80	3.25
	UAL	1.79	-	1.68	1.97	1.95	2.06	1.78	1.86	9.73	-
Uttar Pradesh	UNAL	4.26	3.74	4.02	3.91	-	4.48	3.57	4.84	-	-
	UAL	2.10	-	2.10	2.08	-	2.24	1.79	1.94	2.59	-
West Bengal	UNAL	3.20	3.87	3.74	3.76	4.09	4.36	3.99	3.64	4.33	3.90
	UAL	1.69	-	2.38	2.08	2.56	2.26	2.26	2.26	2.10	2.07

Note : Rupees at 1980-81 prices

UNAL = Unorganised Non-Agricultural Labour; and UAL= Unorganised Agricultural Labour.

Source : Unni (2001)

It could be seen that the real wage rates were low for the unorganised agricultural labourers compared to that of the unorganised non-agricultural labourers in all the states observed The trends in the real wages indicated almost the similar pattern as observed among the organised sector. The relatively better movements in the real wages in the unorganised sector could be due to the forward and backward linkages of the organised sector. Thus, the above analysis clearly indicated the disadvantageous position realised by the unorganised workers in terms of their earnings in the recent years. This argument could be also attributed to the negative impact of reforms on the unorganised workers.

The disturbances in the labour market causing disequilibrium between the demand and supply of labourers is further aggrevated by the jobless growth promoted by the new technological changes and structural shifts in the global economy in favour of the so-called new economy. Though a country like India needs a labour intensive technology to accommodate the job-seeking labour force, the process of globalisation and liberalisation sets on a shift towards capital-intensive technology. Needless to say that in order to meet competition and to increase productive efficiency, firms are forced to modernise their operations involving machineries, capital and high technologies, setting aside the labour intensive technologies. The choice of labour intensive technology becomes obsolete.

The immediate and direct consequence of the shift in the industrial technology is the replacement of unskilled personnel with skilled people (Rao and Rao:1994, Wood 1997). Under the new production environment, the nature of work changes and that warrants skilled workers. Taking into account the basic qualifications and nature of an Indian worker, it is difficult to visualise the effort and time needed to shift an unskilled person into a skilled worker. Till then , the inefficiency would continue even in the new production environment and the labour market would be in the state of disequilibrium.

Based on the above discussion, the observed changes in the labour market, in the present context of globalisation, could be explained based on the following three models (see chart-1). Model-1 indicates the equilibrium state of labour market. Model-II and III are of disequilibrium situations.

Model I

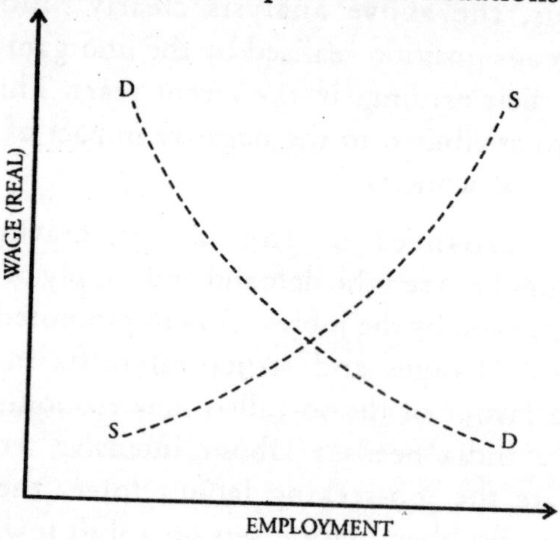

Model II

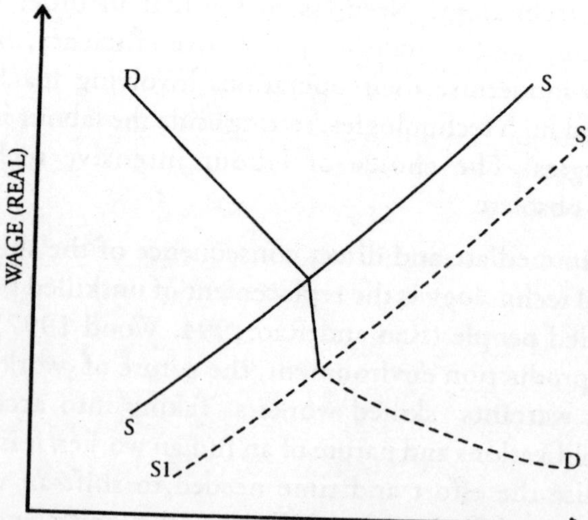

Model III

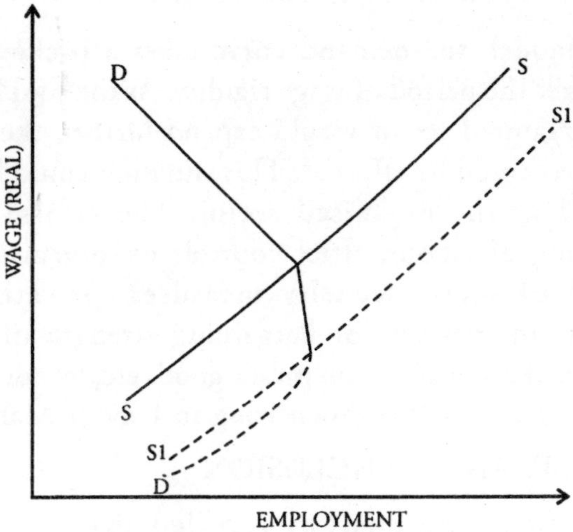

Model I (Normalcy in Labour Market)

In this model, the demand and supply of labour are in equilibrium. With employment and real wages on the X and Y axis respectively, labour demand and supply curves assumes the usual patterns. The labour supply curve is upward sloping, with each point depicting the trade off between real wages and employment. The demand curve sloping downwards from left to right. The wage rate is arrived at the point where both demand and supply of labour curves intersect.

Model II (Stagnancy in Labour Market)

In this mode, the demand curve takes a kinked position due to rigidity in wages. The rigidity of wages continues, till there is increase in demand for labour. However, during this phase the supply of labour may increase leading to outward shift in supply curve. This phenomenon is empirically observed in our analysis. Theoretically, one can argue that after a point of time, the demand for labour would increase due to higher labour absorption, and subsequently wage rigidity would get altered.

Model III (Downsizing in Labour Market)

In this model, the demand curve takes a backward sloping trend after the period of wage rigidity. As the supply of labour to the organised sector would expand further, the reversal of real wages could be effected. This situation could be stikingly observed in the organised sector. The reform efforts of downsizing of labour, strict controls on organised workers, removal of social security measures, privatisation, de unionisation, removal of bargaining strength of labourers, reduction of expenditure on public goods etc. favour the reversal of real wages. And the downsizing in Labour Market.

SUMMARY AND CONCLUSION

The foregoing analysis revealed that the impact of globalisation on the organised and unorganised workers in India is more of warning signals. The supply of labour to the organised and unorganised sectors would expand further in the present context of new economic reforms. This would lead to imbalance in the labour market due to excess supply of labour and low demand for labour leading to low real wages and low level of income. This process of change was getting reflected in the low levels of real wages and its trends of organised and unorganised workers. This situation would affect the social and economic conditions of the deprived working population. The labourers will be in the highly disadvantageous position as there would be a shift in the technology from labour to capital intensive and use of unskilled to skilled workers. To conclude, it can be argued that the impact of globalisation on the labour market in India would be disequilibrium leading to deplorable conditions of the labour.

Hence, along with globalisation, efforts should be initiated towards the welfare of the workforce population. So that they would also benefit in that process on the one hand, and on the other, contribute towards the success of globalisation.

REFERENCES

Alternative Survey Group (1998): Alternative Economic Survey : 1991-1998, Rainbow Publishers Limited, Delhi.

--------------(2000) : Alternative Economic Survey: 1998-2000, Rainbow Publishers Limited, Delhi.

Borkakoti J. and Milner C. (1997): International Trade and Labour Markets, Macmillan Press Ltd., London.

Chakraborty, Debashis and Prabal Kr. De (2001) : "Economic Reform and the Emerging Trends in Employment" The Indian Economic Association 84th Conference Volume, Vellore, 2001.

Dalip S. Swamy (1997): "The World Bank and Globalisation of the Indian Economy" in George KK, Sankaran Nair, V and Jose Jacob (1997) : Economics, Development and the Quest for Alternatives, *Concept Publishing Company, New Delhi*

Das, Bhagirath Lal (1998): An Introduction to the WTO Agreements, Eartheorm Books Pvt Ltd. Chennai.

Das Keshab (1998) : "The Unorganised Sector" in Alternative Survey Group (1998): Alternative Economic Survey: 1991-1998, Rainbow Publishers Limited, Delhi

Dutt Ruddar (2001) : "Economic Liberalisation and its Implications for Employment in India." The Indian Economic Association 84th Conference Volume, vellore, 2001.

Edwards, A. C. and Edwards, S (1997): "Trade Liberalization and Unemployment : Policy Issues and Evidence from Chile" in Borkakoti J. and Milner C. (1997): International Trade and Labour Markets, Macmillan Press Ltd, London.

Government of India, *Economic Survey 1998-99 and 1999-2000.*

Government of India, Ministry of Labour, *Annual Report 2000-2001*

Irani Dutta Medhi (2001), "Employment Scenario in Organised and Unorganised Sector of India in the liberalisation Period" The Indian Economic Association, 84th Conference Volume, Vellore 2001.

James Petras and Henry Velmeyer (2001) : Globalisation Unmasked, Madhyam Books, Delhi. Kunhaman M (2002): Globalisation: A Subaltern Perspective, Centre for Sabaltern Studies, Thiruvananthapuram.

Ngaire Woods (2000): The Political Economy of Globalisation, Macmillan Press, London.

Neeraj (2001): Globalisation or Recolonisation, ELGAR, Pune.

Rao K. V and Rao M. K. (1994): "Restructuring Indian Economy and Its Impact ion Labour " in Rao M. K. Growth of Urban Informal Sector and Economic Development, Volume 1, (Edited) Kanishka Publishers distributors, Delhi.

Shridhar Pandy and J. S. Tiwari (2001) "Economic Liberalisation and Employment in India". The Indian Economic Association 84th Conference Volume, Vellore, 2001

Unni, Jeemol (2001): Gender and Informality in Labour Market in South Asia, Economic and Political Weekly, Vol. 36(26).

Wood, Adrian (1997): "How Trade Hurt Unskilled Workers" in Borkakoti J. and Milner C. (1997): International Trade and Labour Markets, Macmillan Press Ltd, London

LABOUR MARKET IN ORGANISED AND UNORGANISED SECTORS

Dr. S. Kannan, M. Com. D.G.T., Ph. D.
Reader in commerce,
Kamaraj College, Tuticorin, Tamilnadu
Prof. A Padrakali M. Com. M. Phil
S. G. Lecturer in Commerce,
A.P.C. Mahalakshmi College for Women,
Tuticorin

INTRODUCTION

The changing scenario in the World Trade has resulted in many changes in India's socio, economic, and political policies. The changing policy from mid 1980s onwards has serious implication for the institutions and the members involved in the process of industrialization. The labour market is no exception. This paper attempts to reflect on the changes in the employment in organised and unorganized sector by the changes in the policy of the Government.

The Economic Reforms of 1991 were essentially based on the World Bank approach to development. The fundamental changes as part of the reforms include

a) Industrial licensing has been abolished

b) Large business houses are no longer required to take separate permission for investment and expansion.

c) The list of industries reserved for public sector has been reduced

d) Equity in public enterprises is being divested

e) Access to foreign capital and technology has been made freer

f) Quantitative restriction on imports have been virtually abolished

g) Import duties have also been significantly reduced[1]

All these changes made to labour policy, somewhere have an overwhelming consideration of the needs of market in the background. To put it in the right perspective, it is argued that neo-liberalism is returning to neoclassical economics, eliminating the foundation of development economics and the notion that developing economies represent 'a special case'. According to the neoliberal view, there is no special case. What matters is to "get the prices right" and make the market forces do their work. Development in the sense of government intervention is anathema. For it means market distortion. The central objective economic growth, is to be achieved through structural reform, deregulation, liberalization, privatisation all of which are to roll back government and reduce market distorting intervention and in effect annual development[2]

It is argued that the colonial legacy of "forced commercialization has rendered labour pauparised with post-independence period witness endemic underemployment and unemployment[3]

POTENTIAL LABOURERS IN INDIA

With its second largest population and good natural resources, India ought to be the leading country among the G7 countries. During the last 50 years, India has only achieved self-sufficiency in food production

EMPLOYMENT

It is estimated that among the employment opportunities 64% of employment are in agriculture, 15% are in Industrial sector and 21% of employment are in service sector. More than 590 million people depend on the unorganized sector. Further 16 million people are added annually to the pool of economically active man-power.

AGRICULTURE SECTOR

Intrinsic to globalisation is industrialisation of agriculture. As per GATT agreement, 3 per cent of a year's consumption is to be imported even when the country is self-reliant. India imports 714 agricultural products including cotton, tea, rubber, oil seed, mil products and coconut. The import of milk products threatened Indian dairy industries and drove 90 lakh farmers living on dairy industries to unemployed sector.

IMPLICATIONS OF ECONOMIC REFORMS ON LABOUR MARKET/ORGANISED SECTOR

Labour in Public sector

India has developed its economy as Industrial economy. But now it tends to reduce its level to the mere marketing agents. Govt introduced provisions in labour law by amending Industrial Dispute Act, that would make 'hire and fire policy' easier. Of the 149 National Textile Corporation mills, 71 have closed down; 5 are running on profit, and the rest are either loss making or referred to Board for Industrial and Financial reconstruction (BIFR).

The Govt of India closes the public sector units running at loss and sells the profit earning units at a fraction of the price that they would earn in the market. As a result the employees in public sector are reduced from 21.79 lakhs during the year 1990-91 to 18.54 lakhs during the year 1999-2000.

Labour in Private Sector

Global village opens market for MNC products. The very purpose of Restricted Trade is denied under Free Trade Policy. Indian Industries are not able to face international competition. Industrial sickness is becoming worse than ever before. As a result employment in private sector is in question. Labour intensive methods of production are to be replaced by capital intensive methods of automation. In 1991 when liberalization was formalized the number of private sector industries came down to 6 million. To day the work force in formal sector is around 28 million. For every job lost in the formal sector, several are lost in the informal sector. ILO estimates that 8 million jobs have been lost in India since 1991-96.

Labour in Service Sector

Table 1.1

Population and Employment

Year	Employment	Percentage to total population
1993-1994	23.9 crores	2.04%
1999-2000	23.6 crores	0.98%

(Source : Indian Labour Department Annual Report 2000-2001)

Every year 20000 to 40000 new jobs will be generated in the Bank. The Banking Service Recruitment Board is closed as the Government has decided that there will not be any addition in the Banking Service Industry. Since 1984, there has been no appointments in the postal Department Since 1990, no appointment has been made in the central Government

Downsizing the Government

The Government has decided to retrench the present employees. Every year 10% of people employed will be removed from service. Thus, the government has targeted to give up the manpower utilized at present, that is retrenching 4.25 lakhs employees within 5 year.

Unorganised labour in Small Scale Industries

Self employment is being suggested whenever unemployed manpower claims employment. Under LPG Polices, 1429 products restricted previously are freely imported. A basic norm of liberalization is that the economy of the poor county should be globally competitive. Unable to compete with MNC products, 4 lakhs small-scale units are closed. 70 lakhs employees engaged in the small scale industries are forced to remain unproductive. In Tamilnadu, 30 lakhs employees engaged in 6 lakh small scale units are at a crossroads. 1.5 crores of people involve in industries ancillary to small-scale industries. They are left with no direction.

LABOUR MARKET IN TAMILNADU

In Tamilnadu 60% of people are employed in agriculture,textiles industrial estates and small and medium scale industries.

ORGANISED SECTOR

In Tamilnadu Public sector provides more employment than private sectors.

Table 1.2 highlights the employment in Public sector and private sector during the 1995-2000

Table 1.2

Employment in Public Sector and Private Sector in Tamilnadu

Year	Public Sector	Private Sector	Total
1995-96	16,45,473	8,31,699	24,77,172
1996-97	16,52,312	9,30,794	25,83,103
1997-98	16,25,439	9,41,981	25,67,420
1998-99	16,30,002	9,15,968	25,45,970
1999-2000	15,97,240	9,27,233	25,24,473

(Source: Indian Labour department Annual Report 2000-2001)

PUBLIC SECTOR

Public sector industries play a vital role in generation of income and employment. As per 1997 estimate, there were 81 public sector enterprises. At present there are only 59 public sector enterprises. Recently the Govt of Tamilnadu has attempted to privitise the transport corporations. This may result in the retrenchment of 34,000 employees.

SMALL SCALE INDUSTRIES

Small-scale industries account for 40% of total production and 35 per cent of export from Tamil Nadu. It provides 80 per cent of employment.

Since the implementation of economic reforms (1984-1997) 177 industries were closed and 44,000 labourers have lost their jobs.

INDUSTRIAL ESTATES

Industrial estates provide employment to lakhs of people through medium and small-scale industries.

The Ambattur Industrial Estate, the largest in Tamilnadu was established in 1500 acres. 1600 enterprises were operated which provided 2 lakh employments. But at present more than 40 per cent of enterprises in the Industrial estate, has been closed. The reason for these changes is the free trade policy imposed by the Govt., Unable to meet the competition Indian enterprises were closed.

In Guindy Industrial Estate, more than 700 units were operated providing employments to 60000 people. But at present only 15000-20000 people alone are employed in this Estate[4]

Kummudipoondi Sipcot Industrial Estate that provided 12000 employments with 163 industries, at present provides only 3000 employments with 26-30 enterprises.

AGRICULTURE SECTOR

In rural Tamilnadu, only 34 per cent of the people own lands and 66 per cent of people are landless informal workers. These workers get employment hardly for 100 days in a year.

UNEMPLOYMENT

According to National Sample Survey Organisation, it is estimated that more than 1 crores of people are unemployed in Tamilnadu. The proportion of unemployment in Tamilnadu is worked out to be 11.78% where as the proportion of unemployment in India is worked our to be 7.1%.

Table 1.3

Registration in Employment Exchanges in Tamilnadu

Year	No of Employment Exchanges	Registration	Employment	Total No of Unemployed at the end of the year
1995	37	5,03,453	16,893	34,78,637
1996	35	6,11,397	25,046	38,60,244
1997	37	7,43.212	34,785	39,23,818
1998	38	7,70,506	24,688	41,49,265
1999	38	6,45,000	24,000	43,65,753
2000	34	6,22,462	18,239	49,23,296
2001	34			50,57,420
2002	34	4,33,544	10,354	50,20,346
2003 Feb	34			

Source : National Sample Surey Organisation, 2003

DIRECT INVESTMENT IN TAMILNADU AND EMPLOYMENT

Tamilnadu proudly announces that TN occupies third rank in achieving direct investment from MNCs. The direct investment in Tamil is estimated to be Rs. 23,470.30 crores.[5] It is expected that Globalisation and direct investment could generate employment and hence it is beneficial to the country. Table 1.4 throws light on number of employments made in few MNCs.

Table 1.4

MNCs and Employment

MNC	Investment	Employment
Hundai	15,615 million	1465 persons
Ford	1,700 crores	900 persons
Indian Companies		

Hindustan Motors		15,000 persons
Ford		2,224 persons

CONCLUSION

Economics is under the control of politics. The present political policies of the Govt have resulted in serious distortions in labour market and crisis in the entire sphere of economy. Economic reforms and Globalisation yielded enrichment of the few and the impoverishment of the majority. Crisis offers an opportunity for creativity, innovations, and newer initiatives. The people affected may discover newer ways to tide it over and use their new found discoveries for ending it. India should not adopt the policies followed by other countries where the population is very low. It should design policies which can provide employment to large section of the society. Let the arms of Indians be engaged in productive work and be used at optimum level.

REFERENCE

1. Chanduri, Sudip, Economic Reforms and Industrial structure in India, Economic and Political weekly, January 2002
2. Pieterease, Jan Nederven, Development Theory, Reconstructions/ Reconstructions, Sage publications, New Delhi, 2001 p.6
3. Patnaik, Srish Chandra, Industrial Development in Backward Region, Dynamics of Policy, Ashish Publication House, New Delhi, 1990.
4. K. V. Kanagambaram, Business line November, 2002
5. Financial Express 23rd December 2002.
6. Indian Labour department Annual Report 2000-2001
7. National Sample Survey Organisation, 2003

RURAL LABOUR FORCE AND ECONOMIC REFORMS : AN ANALYSIS

*Dr. A. Balakrishnan

INTRODUCTION

Rural labour consisting one of the largest work force in India remaining the most backward, unorganised, disadvantaged and deprived section of society. Rural labour force is engaged in agriculture and non-agriculture occupations. They are mainly labour households, basically comprising wage labourers and self -employed petty cultivators who are half-peasants, and half-labourers. The process of socio-economic development over the last five decades or so, has largely bypassed the rural labour.

The rural force, whether in agriculture or non-agriculture, has been growing at a faster rate than the population growth in rural areas. The main impact of globalisation on labour markets in developing countries has been on the growth of informal sector employment. Faced with declining employment opportunities in the formal sector, most new entrants to the labour force are forced to work in the informal sector.

DEFINITION OF RURAL LABOUR

"A person who is living and working in rural area and engaged in agricultural and/or non-agricultural activities requiring physical labour and getting wages or remuneration partially or wholly, in cash or kind or both during the year or such own-account workers like small farmers and artisans who are not usually hiring in labourers but are a part of the petty production in rural areas" (GOI, 1991, P. A-3) (NCRL 1991).

* Senior Lecturer, Department of Applied Research, Gandhigram Rural Institute (Deemed University), Gandhigram. - 624 302

STATUS OF RURAL LABOUR IN INDIA

The rural labour families have very little access to the minimum needs like primary education, health care, potable water, food grains from the fair price shops, etc. Further, rural labour is denied most of the social security benefits like old age pension, maternity and sickness benefits and compensation for accidents. The benefits from the meagre allocations made, in our country for social security accrue largely to the well organised urban workers who constitute a small fraction of the total work force in the country. It is now widely recognized that the degradation of environment has impacted more severely on the rural poor, particularly women and children among them, on account of the shortages of drinking water fuel-wood and fodder.

Thus, even though there are some signs of improvement in the levels of living during the eighties, the rural labour has been largely bypassed by the processes of socio-economic development over the last five decades, despite its immense contribution to the development of agriculture and of rural areas in general.

Assetlessness and high population growth are the two major causes for the increase in the number of people offering themselves as wage labour in rural areas under unfavourable terms.

II. DIMENSIONS OF RURAL LABOUR

According to the Planning Commission's estimates, our country's labour force was of the order of 340 million in the year 1995. This figure itself has been questioned since a large number of women who, in fact, do work in various kinds of jobs outside their homes, are not counted as part of the labour force. According to the 1991 census, the total number of workers in the country was about 305 million, of which 242 million, that is that about a third of them are women. In contrast, less then 10 per cent of urban workers are women. The significance of this is that in considering the conditions and problems of rural workers the special problems of women workers have to given importance commensurate with their proportion.

Workers in organised and unorganised Sector in 1999-2000.

S. No.	Activities	Total	Organised Sector	Unorganised Sector	Unorganised Workers in %
1.	Agriculture	190.94	1.39	189.55	99.3
2.	Mining & Quarrying	2.26	1.02	1.24	54.9
3.	Manufacturing	40.79	6.75	34.04	83.5
4.	Electricity, Gas Water Supply	1.15	1.00	0.15	13.0
5.	Construction	14.95	1.18	13.77	92.1
6.	Trade, Hotels and Restaurant	37.54	0.48	37.06	98.7
7.	Transport, Storage and Communication	13.65	3.15	10.50	76.9
8.	Finance, Insurance real estate and business service	4.62	1.65	2.97	64.2
9.	Community, Social and Personal services	30.84	11.49	19.35	62.7
	Total	336.75 (100.0)	28.11 (8.34)	308.64 (91.66)	91.66

Source: Compiled and computed from planning Commission, report of special group in Targeting Ten million Employment opportunities per year (2002) p.133 in Datt Raddur, Economic Reforms, Labour and Employment, (2003).

NATIONAL COMMISSION ON LABOUR

On 15th October 1999, the Government of India decided to set up the National Commission on Labour (NCL) with Mr. Ravindra Varma as the Chair Person indicating the following terms of reference.

i) to suggest rationalisation of existing laws relating to labour in the organised sector; and

ii) to suggest an 'umbrella" legislation for ensuring a minimum level of protection to the workers in the unorganised sector.

The Resolution of the government setting up the Commission desired that the Commission should take into account the new environment generated as a consequence of globalisation of the economy and liberalisation of trade and industry. At the same time, it urged up on the National Labour Commission to take into account the need to ensure a minimum level of protection and welfare to labour, to improve the effectiveness of measures relating to social security, safety at places of work, occupational health hazards; to pay special attention to the problems of women workers, minimum wages, evolving a healthy relation between ways and productivity; and to improve the protection and welfare of labour. The commission submitted its report to the government on June 1, 2002.

ECONOMIC REFORMS AND IMPACT ON LABOUR

Economic Reforms in India were introduced in 1991 by the Congress (I) Government led by Mr. P. V. Narasimha Rao. Now, the reforms process has completed twelve years and this cannot be considered as too short a period to assess the impact of economic reforms. India is not the first country to have embarked upon economic reforms aimed at macroeconomic stabilization and structural adjustment. Several countries with widely differing initial conditions, and indeed with varying socio-economic systems, have been experimenting with such reforms.

The most glaring and disquieting consequence of these reforms in several countries is the significant rise in unemployment rates and poverty levels and the decline in the social expenditures by the governments (Veltmeyer, 1993). Also, the increase in inequalities in income have given rise to the phenomenon of the new poor emerging from the middle or lower middle-income groups. Economic reforms, among other things, by freeing the factor markets are expected to bring the prices of factors of production, such as capital and labour in alignment with factor endowments. This implies that in the Indian rural setting, where capital is scarce and labour is abundant, the relative prices of these factors would be such that there would be incentive to employ more labour in relation of capital. This, in conjunction with higher rate of investment expected in the economy as a result of economic restructuring should result in growth of employment. However, such a reasoning overlooks the emerging nature of demand for goods and services unleashed by the market forces in a society where the distribution of income and wealth are highly unequal and where economic inequalities

A review of Industrial relations in the pre-reform period (1981-90) reveals that as against 402.1 million man days lost during the decade (1981-90) i.e., in the pre-reform period, the number of mandays lost declined to 230.1 million during (1991-2000) the post-reform period. Looking at the aggregate level, it may be stated that the loss of mandays in the aggregate declined and this can be treated as the index of improvement of industrial relations in the post-reform period . The loss of mandays is more during pre-reform period than in the post reform period. It have resorted much less to strikes fearing the wave of privatisation and liberalisation, employers' militancy has become much more pronounced in the post-reform period. All these have in reased the proportion of casual labour in total employment in the post-reform period. Growing casualisation of labour adversely impacts on the income of the labour. Consequently, workers are being pushed from the organised to the unorganised sector from secure to insecure employment.

DETERMINING FACTORS OF RURAL LABOUR ABSORPTION IN NON-FARM SECTOR

Decentralised development of the rural economy is brought about by many factors. Rural labour plays an important role in such development, no doubt, the fact that the non-farm sector has been increasingly absorbing the rural labour. Absorption of rural labour in the non-farm sector is neither solely due to distress diversion nor solely due to natural absorption. It is stimulated by several factors like literacy rate, inter–sector as well as rural –urban linkages, urbanisation, poverty level and above all prosperity of the farm sector.

In the context of the decentralised development of rural India employment of female has declined during the reform period 1993-94 to 1999-2000. This is presumably due to the fact that will the decentralised development of the rural India various types of activities particularly non-farm activities are generated which has resulted in an increasing demand for female labour. Also, interstate disparity arises in respect of utilisation of rural female labour. Employment in non-farm sector for female has increased in almost all the states excepting Andhra Pradesh, Gujarat, Karnataka, Maharastra and West Bengal at the cost of farm employment. Thus among the states, only in West Bengal utilisation of rural female labour has deceased in the non-farm activities during the reform periods.

Employment in Secondary and tertiary sector has risen in India and almost all the constituent states at the cost of primary sector, though its share has all through been the highest. Also, we not that the job opportunities for rural female have been expanded in most of the states due to rural industrialisation during the globalisation period. There has been a steep decline in the proportion of self employed households in agriculture. It appears that the continued sub-division of holdings among the small and marginal farms is rendering some of the self-employed labour force redundant on the families who are joining the ranks of wage labour. In non-agriculture, employment, particularly of females, in certain household industries has been declining under the impact of the technologically efficient and modern industries. These facts indicate the rising need for employment generation in rural areas.

RURAL FEMALE LABOUR AND ECONOMIC REFORMS

In the decentralised development of the rural female labour is utilized in alternative sectoral activities: (a) Primary Sector, (b) Secondary Sector, (c) Tertiary Sector.

More the non-farm activities, more the growth of secondary sector and tertiary sector and expectedly more the rate of utilisation of rural female labour in the non-farm activities. It is thus expected that with the share of the farm sector in total rural female labour would decline, resulting in a rise in the percentage share of the non-farm sector during the reform period.

RURAL FEMALE WORK PARTICIPATION IN INDIA AND ITS CHANGES

With structural transformation of the rural economy in the context of decentralised development employment of rural female labour is expected to decline over time. Employment of female has declined during the reform period 1993-94.

Indian States have exhibited wide variation in rural female labour. It is expected that more and more a state is economically and educationally backward, more and more is the utilisation of rural female labour in the state.

Rural Female Work Participation Rate in Indian States per 1000 Female

States	1993-94	1999-2000
Andhra Pradesh	462	443
Assam	86	87
Bihar	131	132

Gujarat	254	311
Haryana	56	33
Himachal Pradesh	363	281
Karnataka	326	354
Kerala	152	159
Madhya Pradesh	301	331
Maharashtra	404	393
Orissa	210	203
Punjab	37	40
Rajasthan	299	272
Tamilnadu	405	401
Uttarpradesh	131	122
West Bengal	84	116
India	238	231

Source : NSSO, Government of India

Estimates reveal that rural female Work Participation Rate has declined in India and is almost all the states expecting Assam, Bihar, Gujarat, Karnataka, Kerala, Madhya Pradesh, Punjab and West Bengal during 1993–1999. State wise analysis shows that rural female Work Participation Rate was lowest in Punjab in 1993–94 and in Haryana in 1999-2000. It was highest in Andhra Pradesh in both 1993-94 and 1999-2000. Thus among the states only Andhra Pradesh, has utilised more rural female labour in the globalisation era.

STABILISATION MEASURES AND RURAL LABOUR

For assessing the possible impact of the ongoing economic reforms on the livelihood of rural labour in our country, it would be useful to distinguish the effects of stabilisation measures from the impact of structural adjustment, although effort is on to proceed simultaneously on both the fronts, In any case, hardly any reforms of a structural nature affecting agriculture has yet been introduced. [It is, nevertheless, true that rural labour cannot remain unaffected by the structural adjustment measures undertaken in non-agriculture.

The rural labour, particularly in the less developed areas, is affected by stabilization measures in two fundamental ways. One is the reduced rate of public investment in agriculture and the sectors like minimum needs including primary education, health care, drinking water, etc.

The other important consequence is the rise in the prices of essential commodities like food grains. This has acted more hrashly on the poor. The stabilization measures appear to have had a granter effect is slowing down the growth of rural employment then in bringing down the prices of essential commodities.

STRUCTURAL ADJUSTMENT EFFECTS ON RURAL LABOUR :

The processes of structural adjustment under way is the economy have a direct as well as indirect bearing on the rural poor. It created a thread of "new entering the labour market. Therefore, reconciling the efficiency goals with considerations of social justice is the foremost challenge facing the on-going process of economic reforms.

CONCLUSION

Economic reforms not yielded the expected result in growth of employment. The income distribution and consumption patterns are changed drastically as a result of liberalization and marketisation, the prospects for labour use may not be as encouraging due to relative factor price. It is common knowledge that there is aversion to manual labour even among small farmers who also taken to economies on wage labour. So, the impact of ongoing economic reforms on the livelihood of rural labour has affected in agriculture and measures undertaken in non-agriculture.

REFERENCES

1. Datt Rnddar, Economic Reforms, Labour and Employment, New Delhi : Deep & Deep publications, 2003. Pp3-150.
2. Radha Krishna and Sharma (Ed) Empowering Rural Labor in India, New Delhi : Institute for Human Development, 1998, Pp.
3. Somashekar, Development and Environmental Economics, New Delhi New Age International, 2003.
4. Sudhir. M. A. and Balakrishnan. A. (Eds), Empowerment of Rural Women Labour force, New Delhi; Anmol Publications, 2002.
5. Balakrishnan, A Problems of Rural Landless labourers in Dindigul district, GRI, Gandhigram, 2003, (Unpublished thesis).

LABOUR MARKETS IN INDIA : BEFORE AND AFTER LIBERALISATION

T. Raj Pravin*

The Indian labour market is undergoing great changes after the inception of 1990 liberalisation reforms from being a closed economy dominated by public sector undertakings, to a new open economy by active participation of private corporation, multinational corporations and so on. This transition process has resulted in Indian economy emnating itself as a "knowledge based economy" satisfying, the service area needs of developed economies. Information today is becoming a vital resource and quick transfer of information to the targeted audience is expected to bring about prosperity and sustainable development. So information technology coupled with changes in manufacturing sectors like automobiles, construction industry has infuxed a large quantum of human resource to satisfy their demand. This process has resulted in total organisational sector employment numbers going up every year from 263.53 lakh in 1990 to 282.45 lakh in 1997. In other words there was about 19 lakh new jobs being created in organised sector which covers all private establishments employing 10 or more persons. However the later years has seen a dip in the organised employment market as shown in Table 1.

Table :1

(In lakh persons)

Total organised sector jobs

Years	Public Sector	Private Sector	Total	Manufacturing
1980	150.79	72.27	223.06	58.62
1985	172.69	73.09	245.78	61.83
1990	187.72	75.82	263.53	63.27

* Research Schools, Department of Agricultural Extersion and Rural Sociology, TNAU, Constructure-3

1991	190.57	76.76	267.33	63.33
1992	192.10	78.46	270.56	64.27
1993	193.26	78.51	271.77	63.96
1994	194.45	79.30	273.75	64.14
1995	194.66	80.59	275.25	66.21
1996	194.29	85.12	279.41	66.58
1997	195.591	86.86	282.45	71.29
1998	194.18	87.48	281.66	68.52
1999	194.15	86.98	281.13	67.43
2000	193.14	86.46	279.60	66.15
2001	191.38	86.42	277.89	64.43

Note: Figures are for end-March

[Source The Hindu-Business line]

From the Table 1, it could seen that every single year from 1998 to 2001 has saw organised job markets shrink in lakhs.

A recent statement made by the union ministry for the year ending 2002 has recorded a further drop of 4.2 lakh making a consecutive fifth year of decline in the organised market. However the reason for this great reduction in organised sector is attributed to the following causes.

INTERNATIONAL MARKETS AS NEWER GROWTH AREAS

All corporates have seen sending their produce to different destinations of the world as a emerging opportunity to garner good revenues. This has made them to be internationally competitive with high quality produce to be offered at cheaper prices. So many corporate both in public and private sector like Bajaj auto, Tata steel and SAIL undertaking has made manpower reduction through voluntary retirement scheme

(VRS) or by phasing out additional manpower at regular basis. This has made many losing up jobs in the organised market depriving many unskilled labourers there jobs.

MANUFACTURING TECHNOLOGY ADVANCEMENTS

The growth in technological advancements has resulted in creation of few skilled jobs rendering many jobless. At Present all sectors concentrate their efforts on improving technology employing less labour. Even American economy is facing this problem as the increase in productivity from 3.6% to 4.2% in manufacturing sector has rendered millions losing their jobs (Prabhat Kumar, 2003). So this phenomenon of technological advancements has reduced jobs in organised sector.

TRADE WITHOUT BARRIERS : A NEW PROBLEM

The free trade agreements (FTA) with neighours like Srilanka and SAARC nations has played a negative role in many sectors like plantation sector. The removal of restrictions for all products except in the negative list of both counties by free trade agreements has resulted in import of many plantation products like rubber, coffee, tea and so on. This has resulted in plantation industry facing stiff competition from neighbours in both domestic and international markets. Organised jobs in this sector faces threat with less remuneration for millions of labourers employed in this sector. Southern states of India like Tamilnadu, Kerala, Karnataka which have greater share on plantation sector incure huge job loses.

AGRICULTURAL GROWTH REDUCTION A MAJOR IMPEDIMENT

The Agricultural growth has been on a decline with many states like Rajasthan, Orissa , Tamilnadu suffering under the vagaries of monsoon. This has resulted in replenishing the sugar stocks of food corporation of India godowns. However the onset of good South west monsoon this year has resulted in judging the economy at a positive mode (Nagaraj, 2003). The absence of uniform rains in decan pleateau, reduction of water storage levels in major dams are also features that need to be considered on the side of agricultural productivity there has been a steady decline from 1990s (compared to 1980s) with reduction in public infrastructure investment for the past 15 years. This is well illustrated by the decline in power generation from 8.9% in 1980s to 3.4% in 1990s. Thus reduction in agricultural growth has affected organised and unorganised sector in agriculture and other related fields.

CHANGES IN LABOUR LEGISLATIONS

The Government of India has initiated the process of change in labour simplifying procedures under the laws for special economic zones (SEZs). This will facilitate creation of jobs on a fixed term basis however the social security aspect of pension, insurance is yet to be addressed. SEZs at present are exempted from payment of statutory dues such as contribution to employees provident fund, state insurance for a five year period. Exemptions have already come into existence with Gujarat becoming the first state to implement it. Many state governments are developing SEZs to increase exports. This recent phenomenon is going to reduce job security, social security to a large group of labour community rendering them jobless after productive years of employment.

STRATEGIES FOR IMPROVING LABOUR MARKETS

India has to be international competitive to garner more exports and improve its share in the international market. The following efforts need to be undertaken in a quick and phased manner in improving labour markets.

* The Ministry of Labour need to bring about Amendment to Contract Labour (Regulation & Abolition) act, 1970 to incorporate all social security benefits to labour community as all corporates, public undertakings are resorting to use of casual labour.

* Plantation products in free trade agreements need to be moved to limited quota access to restrict dumping by neighbouring countries. This will save millions of workers in plantation sector.
* Investments in public infrastructure need to be undertaken as this create the needed infrastructure for industrial and agricultural growth.
* Policy changes need to be advocated to bring in technological advancements to employ more labour, as India needs job opportunity to millions of population.
* Small scale industries, Tiny and cottage industries need to be encouraged in rural sector to give greater employment to skilled or unskilled labourer of agricultural sector during lean season and in years of monsoon uncertainties.

CONCLUSION

The world today is becoming a market with producers competing to sell their produce at competitive price. India, as a nation cannot stand away in isolation from this open economy are need to be internationally competitive to satisfy the growing needs of our raising population. Policy planners, administrators, researchers need to concentrate their efforts to evolve structural and institutional framework to benefit our labour market as millions of Indians livelihood is dependent on it.

REFERENCES:

Harish Damondharan & Ambarish Mukherjee (2003), Organised sector job shrink 5 consecutive years (1988-2000), The Hindu Business line dated 19th December.

Change in labour laws (2003), The financial express dated 7th November.

Prabhat Kumar (2003), Is China stealing American jobs?, The Economic Times 2nd December.

Trade without barriers (2003), The Financial Express dated 3rd December.

Nagaraj (2003), Judging the economy, The new Indian express dated 20th December.

EMPLOYMENT IN ORGANISED AND UNORGANISED SECTORS : EMERGING ISSUES AND FUTURE PERSPECTIVES

Dr. V. Anbumani*
T. Lingamurugeshwari**

INTRODUCTION

Employment is the most natural and best way to achieve the objectives of economic growth, poverty eradication, social justice, social stability and peace. To have gainful and creative work is the basic need of and an imperative for man.

In India, since the beginning of the planning progress, the magnitude and seventy of the unemployment problem have been posing a serious challenge to the planners and policy makers.

The absolute size of the unemployed to the total population swells because of the following reasons.

- The population has been growing at a rapid rate when compared to the snail pace in the growth of employment opportunities.
- The production process in the formal sector mostly based on imported technology, external capital inflow and foreign collaboration, which have a negative impact on the demand for labour force.
- The continued predominance of agriculture as the source of employment to more than 65% of the total population which comprises mainly marginal farmers, landless labourers and disguisedly unemployed.

* Faculty, Department of Economics, Bharathiar University, Cbe46

** M. Phil Research Scholar, Department of Economics, Bharathiar University, Cbe-46

ESTIMATE OF EMPLOYMENT AND UNEMPLOYMENT:

On the basis of NSS data, the number of unemployed to be of the order of 26.58 million in 1999-2000 as against 20.13 million in 1993-94 (current daily status basis). The growth rate of unemployed persons work out to be 4.74% per annum for the period, 1993-94 to 1999-2000, as against decline in the number of unemployed persons during the period 1983-1994.

This only underlines the fact unemployment rate, which was 8.33% in 1983, declined to 5.99% by 1993 but increased to 7.32% in 1999-2000.

Table-1

	1983	1983-84	1999-00	Employment Growth rate (% per annum)	
	Million person			1983–1993–94	1993–94 to 1999–2000
All India					
(1) Population	718.20	894.01	1003.97	2.0	1.95
(2) Labour force	261.33	335.97	363.33	2.43	1.31
(3) work worce	239.57	315.84	336.75	2.7	1.07
(4) No. of unemployed	21.76	20.13	2658	-0.08	4.74
(5) Unemployment rate(%)(4,2x100)	8.33	5.99	7.32		
Rural					
Population	546.65	658.83	727.50	1.79	1.67
Labour force	204.18	253.38	270.39	2.15	0.96
Work force	187.92	241.04	250.89	2.40	0.67
No. of unemployed	16.26	14.34	19.50	-1.19	5.26
Urban					
Population	171.59	234.98	276.47	3.04	2.74
Labour force	57.15	80.60	92.95	3.33	2.40
Work force	51.64	74.80	85.84	3.59	2.32
No. of unemployment	5.51	5.80	7.11	0.49	3.45
Unemployment rate (%)	9.64	7.19	7.65		

Source : Planning Commission (2002) Report of special group on targeting Ten million Employment Opportunities per year.

Special group report S. P. Gupta mentioned that the raising unemployment is primarily an outcome of a declining job creating capacity of growth observed. Since 1993-1994. The employment growth fell to 1.07% per annum (between 1993-94 and 1999-2000) from 2.7% per annum in the past (between 1983 and 1993-1994) in spite of acceleration in GDP growth from 5.2% between 1983 and 1993-1994 to 6.7% between 1993-1994 and 1999-2000.

The organized sectors employment generating capacity (measured in terms of employment elasticity) came down near to zero and has been negative in most cases in the public sector.

Table -2 : Interstate Employment Scenario

State	Unemployment Rate	
	1993-94	1999-00
Kerala	15.51	20.97
West Bengal	10.06	14.99
Tamil Nadu	11.41	11.78
Assam	8.03	8.03
Andhra Pradesh	6.69	8.03
Orissa	7.30	7.34
Bihar	6.34	7.32
Maharashtra	5.09	7.16
Haryana	6.51	4.77
Gujarat	5.70	4.55
Karnataka	4.94	4.47
Madhya Pradesh	8.56	4.45
Utter Pradesh	3.45	4.08
Punjab	3.10	4.03
Rajasthan	1.31	3.13
Himachal Pradesh	1.80	2.96
All India	5.99	7.32

Source : Report of the Special Group (2002)

The inter-state employment rates show greater regional disparities in 1999-2000 as compared to 1993-1994. In 1999-2000, the employment in Kerala was 20.97% of the labour force and the lowest rate of 2.96 % was observed in Himachal Pradesh.

In 1999-2000, the states which show higher unemployment rates than the national average of 7.32% are Kerala (20.97) West Bengal (15.0%), Tamil Nadu (11.78%) and Asam and Andhra Pradesh (8.03%) on the other extreme are states which show low unemployment rates including Uttar Pradesh (4.08%) Punjab (4.03%) Rajasthan (3.13%), Himachal Pradesh (2.96%).

ORGANISED AND UNORGANISED SECTOR EMPLOYMENT:

Employment in the organised sector has been hardly 8.34% of which the public sector accounts for 5.77% and private sector only for 2.57% in the total employment generated during 1999-2000.

Table-3

	Total	Organised Sector			Unorganised Sector 5 as % of 1	
		Public Sector	Private Sector	Total		
	(i)	(2)	(3)	(4)	5=1–4	
1. Agriculture	190.94	0.52	0.87	1.39	189.55 (61.4)	99.3
2. Mining & Quarrying	2.26	0.93	0.09	1.02	1.24 (0.4)	54.9
3. Manufacturing	40.79	1.57	5.18	6.75	34.04	83.5
4. Electricity, Gas & Water Supply	1.15	0.96	0.04	1.00	0.15 (0.0)	13.0
5. Construction	14.95	1.11	0.07	1.18	13.77 (4.5)	92.1
6. Trade, Hotel & Restaurants	37.54	0.16	0.32	0.48	37.06 (12.0)	98.7

7. Transport, Storage and Communications	13.65	3.08	0.07	3.15	10.50 (3.4)	76.9
8. Finance, insurance, real estate and business service	4.62	1.30	0.35	1.65	2.97 (1.0)	64.2
9. Community, Social & Personal services	30.84	9.79	1.70	11.49	19.35 (6.3)	62.7
Total	336.75 (100.0)	19.42 (5.77)	8.70 (2.58)	28.11 (8.34)	308.64 (100.0)	91.66

Source : Compiled and computed from Planning Commission, report of special group on targeting Ten Million Employment opportunities per year (2002) P.133.

The organised sectors is dominated by the public sector which accounts for 70% of the total employment in this sector. This is mainly in the areas of (i) Mining (ii) electricity and water, and (iii) community and social services. These three collectively constitute nearly 60% of the public sector employment figures and unfortunately all of them show negative employment elasticity. This is only underlines the fact that the public sector contributed to a very small extent in total employment generation during 1993-1994 to 1999-2000. This implies that the public sector has growth virtually jobless growth.

PRESENT EMPLOYMENT SCENARIO IN INDIA :

The main source of employment generation is the unorganized sector of the economy including self-employment and small business wherein the present contribution is as high as 92% of the total employed labour force. Its means employment generating activities are

a) agriculture and allied activities

b) trade restaurants and hotels including tourism

c) some social sectors like education and health

Table 4

	Current Daily Status			Employment Growth Rate		GDP Growth Rate (% per annum)		Employment elasticity	
	1983	1983-1984	1999-2000	1983-1993 1994	1993-94 1999-2000	1993-2000	1993-94 1999-00	1983- 1993-94	1993-94 1999-00
	1	2	3	4	5	6	7	8=4/6	9=5/7
1. Agriculture	151.35 (63.18)	190.72 (60.38)	190.94 (56.70)	2.03	0.02	2.9	3.1	0.70	0.01
2. Mining and quarrying	1.74 (0.73)	2.54 (0.80)	2.26 (0.67)	3.66	-1.91	6.2	4.7	0.59	0.33
3. Manufacturing	27.69 (11.56	35.00 (11.08)	40.79 (12.11)	2.28	2.58	6.0	7.8	0.38	-0.52
4. Electricity, gas and Water Supply	0.83 (0.34)	1.43 (0.45)	1.1 -(0.34)	5.29	-3.55	8.4	6.8	0.63	0.82
5. Constructions	7.17 (2.99)	11.02 (3.99)	14.95 (4.44)	4.21	5.21	4.9	6.2	0.86	0.62
6. Trade, hotels and restaurants	18.17 (7.58)	26.88 (8.51)	37.54 (11.15)	3.81	5.72	5.6	9.2	0.68	0.63
7. Transport, storage & Communication	6.99 (2.92)	9.88 (3.13)	13.65 (4.05)	3.36	5.53	6.1	8.7	0.55	0.64

d) small and medium enterprises mainly in the rural non-farm sector and

e) transport and construction.

It may be noted that small and medium enterprises account for nearly 80% of the manufacturing employment and their employment elasticity is 3.8 times higher than that of organised sector. Thus in order to achieve a more favourable effect on employment what is needed is a shift in the percentage, composition of manufacturing in favour of small and medium enterprises.

Agriculture is another source of employment generation as it accounted for 57% of India's total employment in 1999-2000. Between 1983 and 1993-1994 its employment elasticity was as high as 0.70, but in the post-reform period (1993-1994 to 1999-2000), its employment elasticity has declined to 0.01.

The other employment generating areas identified in the unorganized sector are trade, restaurants and tourism and information technology (IT), they are witnessing a high growth of above 9.0% per annum and have very high employment elasticities. The transport, construction and other service sectors are also equally equipped for high growth and employment intensiveness.

8. Finance, Insurance, real estate & business services	2.10 (0.88)	3.37 (1.07)	4.62 (1.38)	4.54	5.40	10.1	8.4	0.45	-0.25
9. Community, social & personal Services	23.52 (9.82)	34.98 (11.08)	30.84 (9.16)	3.88	-2.08	5.7	8.4	0.68	0.16
All	39.57 (100.0)	315.84 (100.0)	336.75 (100.0)	2.70	1.07	5.2	6.7	0.52	0.16

The appropriate organised sector, especially its public sector component has a rather low employment generating potential, being handicapped as it is by a negative employment elasticity with the exception of the financial sectors and potentiality in certain parts of the social sector like education health etc. But these two have a low weightage of 3.3% to the total employment. Community and social services need a major change in composition in favour of health, education etc, and only then can they substantial contribute to the growth. Already a significant increase in the weightage of this sector in this group is in sight. It was 25.8% in 1993-94 and has gone-up to 33.3% now. These two sub-sectors to gather show a growth rate of around 4.5% per annum as compared to this sector's growth of 0.2% per annum between 1993-94 and 1999-2000.

FUTURE STRATEGY:

On the Basis of data collected and analysed by the Special Group, it was found that in the unorganized sector the employment elasticity was as high as 0.213 in 1999-2000. Whereas in the organised sector it was as low as 0.066 i.e., almost a jobless growth. Moreover in the year 1999-2000, the total contribution to employment by the organised sector was only 8% of which the private sector segment's contribution was hardly 2.5% The balance 92% came from the unorganized sector.

Table - 5

	Organized Sector				
	Total	Public Sector	Private Sector	Unorganised Sector	Grand Total
	1	2	3	4	5
Value– added GDP (Rs. Crores at 1993-1994 prices)					
1993-1994	2,56849	1,80,843	76,006	4,41,143	6,97,992
	(36.8)	(25.9)	(10.9)	(63.2)	(100.0)

1999-2000	4,18,920 (41.1)	2,66,519 (26.1)	1,52,401 (15.0)	6,00,425 (58.9)	1,019,345 (100.0)
Growth rate (Per cent)	8.80	6.68	12.30	5.27	6.62
Bank Credit (Rs.000 crores)					
1993-1994	80.8 (46.0)	28.1 916.0)	52.7 (30.0)	94.9 (54.0)	175 (100.0)
1999-2000	247.4 (62.9)	66.8 (17.0)	180.6 (45.9)	145.9 (37.1)	393.3 (100.0)
Growth Rate (Per Cent)	20.5	15.5	22.8	7.4	1.4
Employment (millions)					
1993-94	27.18 (8.6)	19.30 (6.1)	7.88 (2.5)	288.66 (91.4)	315.84 (100.0)
1999-2000	28.11 (8.35)	19.42 (5.77)	8.69 (2.58)	308.64 (61.65)	336.75 (100.0)
Growth Rate (Percent)	0.56	0.10	1.64	1.12	1.07
Employment Elasticity labour	0.066	0.015	0.133	0.213	0.165
Productivity growth (pe. compe. annum)	7.88	6.67	8.38	4.10	5.38
Relative labour intensity (Organized/ unorganized) 1999-2000	0.1345				

Source : Compiled and computed from the Planning Commission (2002), report of the special group on targeting ten million employment opportunities per year.

The data provided in the table reveals that in 1999-2000, the unorganized sector contributed nearly 59% to the GDP, but its contribution to exports was also substantial. But of late, because of the opening up of the economy, with the resultant deregulation and market orientation including the withdrawal of several key subsidies, the unorganised sector in general and some of its components in particular are facing growing sickness and a slowing down of activities. During 1993-94 and 1999-2000, as a consequence of the policies of liberalization, the flow of bank credit of scheduled commercial banks increased significantly towards the organised sector from 46.2% in 1993-94 to 62.9% in 1999-2000, where as in the unorganized sector, it fell from 53.8% in 1993-94 to 3.71% in 1999-2000. This was despite the fact that the unorganized sector continued to provide employment to 92% of the work force in the economy. This trend affect the growth rate and efficiency of the unorganized sector and needs to be reversed.

To scene up the employment strategy for the future, to meet the plan's employment goals one has to encourage the use of labour intensive and capital saving technology in general and the rejuvenate the growth of the unorganized sector in particular which at present accounts for 92% of the country's employment and enjoys more than seven times labour intensity per unit of production, as compared to the organised sector.

The total employment generation by the private organised sector in barely of the order of 2.58% of the total. On account of its low employment base and low employment elasticity, even if it grows at the rate of 30% per annum over the tenth plan period, its contribution to the total employment will increase from 2.58% to 3.5% of the total employment by end of tenth plan.

It has been argued by the Task Force on Employment Opportunities that the present Industrial Disputes Act (1956) should be amended to enable the employers to have complete freedom to hire and fire employees. Such a change in legal conditions will make the organised sector more employment–

friendly and the employment generation in this sector can be improved. But the fact reveal that the organised sector (especially the public sector) is already carrying excess labour, the immediate effect will be more of firing than hiring.

CONCLUSION:

The organised sector is dominated by the public sector which accounts for 70% of the total employment in this sector. But the public sector contributed to a very small extent in total employment generation. The unorganised sector's employment elasticity was as high as the organised sector. The total contribution to employment by the organised sector was only 8% the balance 92% came from the unorganised sector. Because of opening up of the economy with the resultant deregulation and market orientation including the withdrawal of several key subsidies the unorganised sector in general and some of its components in particular are facing growing sickness and a slowing down of activities.

There fore, the unorganised sector needs to be made more productive in order to sustain itself against domestic and international competition by proper choice of programme and policies compatible with India's economic reforms.

REFERENCES

B. P. Chandramohan — "Economic Growth and Employment in India", Southern Economist, May 1997.

Ruddar Dutt & K. P. M. Sundharam – Indian Economy.

L. M. Bhole & P. Dash–employment–Unemployment in India–The Indian Journal of Labour Economics, Apr-June 2002.

EMPLOYMENT GENERATION PROGRAMMES IN RURAL AREAS OF COIMBATORE DISTRICT

N. Rajeswari
Ph. D. Research Scholar,
Department of Economics
PSG CAS Coimbatore

INTRODUCTION

The Programmes of Rural Developments initiated by Government of India have been playing an important role in the socio-economic development. The focus on generation of employment opportunities both wage employment and self-employment programmes and poverty alleviation were the need of the hour. The number of unemployed in the rural areas is swelling and the people below the poverty line (BPL) also has not declined significantly.

In this context a brief analysis on the various employment generation programmes implemented at a micro level (Coimabatore District) would help to understand their progress and performance. A brief note on various employment programmes is given in the first part. In the second part, with the help of available secondary data, the performance of rural employment schemes in Coimbatore district has been analysed.

WAGE-EMPLOYMENT PROGRAMMES

In the category of programmes for wage employment the Sampoorna Gramin Rozgar Yojana (SGRY) is most important. The programme was announced by the Prime Minister on 15th August 2001 and was launched in September 2001. Before the launching of the SGRY, Jawahar Gram Samridihi Yojana (JGSY) and Employment Assurance Scheme (EAS) were two major infrastructure development oriented on giving wage employment programmes for the rural poor at the village block, district and panchayat levels respectively with effect from 'April 2002'.

The primary objective of SGRY is to provide additional wage employment opportunities to the rural poor and thus to provide food security and improve nutritional levels of the rural poor. The secondary objective is the creation of durable community social and economic assets as well as infrastructural development in rural areas.

Any wage employment programme including SGRY is generally self-targeting i.e. the programme is open to all (poor) who are in need of wage employment and willing to work at a prescribed minimum wage. In terms of providing wage employment, however, the programme is envisaged to give preference to women, members of SC/ST and parents of child labour withdrawn from hazardous occupation

SELF-EMPLOYMENT PROGRAMMES

Poverty alleviation programmes have been in operation for several years. The specifically designed programmes for generation of self-employment and wage employment in rural areas have been redesigned and restructured to improve their efficiancy impact on the poor. An outlay of Rs.965 billion has been provided in 1999-2000 (Budget Estimates) as against Rs. 934 billion in 1998-99 (Revised Estimates).

In terms of resource allocation, the budget has proposed a marginal increase of Rs 400 crores, or nearly three percent in the central plan outlay for the Ministry of Rural Development over previous year's budget. Thus the Ministry will have at its disposals Rs. 14070 crores in 2003—2004 against Rs. 13670 crores provided in last years budget, However, the proposed allocation falls short of the revised budget estimate for 2002—2003 by Rs.4306 crores or over 23 per cent. The revised estimate of actual expenditure during the gone–by fiscal year has been put at Rs.18736 crores.

INTEGRATED RURAL DEVELOPMENT PROGRAMME (IRDP 1978)

IRDP is the biggest ,poverty removal and employment programme introduced in 1978. The objective of IRDP was promoting self-employment to the poor households by providing them with assets and inputs so that they can earn incomes that help them to cross the poverty line. Employment opportunities are to be generated through small scale industries and other suitable economic activities.

TRAINING OF RURAL YOUTH FOR SELF -EMPLOYMENT (TRYSEM 1979)

Training of Rural Youth for Self Employment was launched in August 1979. It helps to remove unemployment with requisite skills and techniques. Thus the youth can take up vocations that lead to self-employment.

NATIONAL RURAL EMPLOYMENT PROGRAMME (NREP 1980)

The Food for Work Scheme has been adopted as part of the National Rural Employment Programme since August 15,1980. It provided employment for the labour force; they received their wages in the form of food grains.

Integrated Rural Development Programmes Training of Rural Youth for Self-Employment Development of Women and Children in Rural Areas (DWCRA) and Million Well Schemes (MWS) have been restructured into a single self employment programme called the Swarnjayanti Gram Swarozagar Yojana (SGSY).

JAWAHAR GRAM SAMRIDHI YOJANA (JGSY)

Jawahar Rozgar Yojana (JRY)-(Jawahar Village Enrichment Programme-Jawahar Employment Programmes) has been restructured and streamlined with effect from April 1999 and has been renamed as JGSY. The primary objective of JGSY is creation of demand driven village infrastructure including durable assets at the village level to enable the rural poor to increase the opportunities for sustained employment. The secondary objective is generation of employment to below the poverty line (BLE) families.

THE EMPLOYMENT ASSURANCE SCHEME (EAS)

The Employment Assurance Scheme (EAS) launched on October 2, 1999 in 1772 identified back ward blocks situated in drought -prone, desert, tribal and hill areas has been restructured as a single wage employment programme from April 1999 with fixed annual outlay. The primary objective of the EAS is creation of additional wage employment opportunities during the period of acute shortage of wage employment through manual works for the rural poor living below the poverty line. The creation of durable community social and economic assets to sustain future employment and development.

EMPLOYMENT SCHEMES UNDERTAKEN IN COIMBATORE DISTRICT

The employment schemes that were taken up in the district include EAS and SJGSY and EAS was renamed as SGRYS Stream 1 and 2 and Special from 2002-2003 onwards.

During the year 2000-2001 the number of EASs taken up were 247 and all of them were completed by spending Rs. 199.07 lakhs. During the next year 562 schemes were taken up and completed at the cost of Rs. 647.34 lakhs.

The three scheme put together, taken up 1641 scheme during 2002–2003 and 1638 schemes were completed at an outlay of Rs.1716.35 lakhs. In the next year (2003-2004), the coverage of the schemes increased tremendously: 6682 schemes were completed out of 10762 undertaken at a cost of Rs. 3883.96 lakhs.

Table 1

Employment Scheme undertaken in Coimbatore District

(Rs. in Lakhs)

S. No.	Name of the Scheme	2000-2001			2001-2002			2002-2003				2003-2004			
		Taken up	Compl.	Fincl	Taken up	Compl.	Fincl	Taken up	Comp.	Bal	Fincl up	Taken	Compl	Bal	Fincl
1.	EAS	247	247	199.07	562	562	647.31			0				0	
2.	SGRY Stream 1							556	553	3	766.21	655	207	448	669.48
3.	SGRY Stream 11							981	981	0	687.16	2388	965	1423	796.23
4.	SGRY Special							104	104	0	263.01	7719	5510	2209	2418.25
5.	SJGSY	25	25	34.05	24	24	53.74	11	9	2	31.93	6	2	4	15.28

EAS – Employment Assurance Scheme

SGRY Stream I – Sampoorna Gramin Rozgar Yojana Stream 1

SGRY Stream II – Sampoorna Gramin Rozgar Yojana Stream II

SGRY Stream (Special) – Sampoorna Gramin Rozgar Yojana Special

SJGSY – Swarna Jeyanthi Gram Swarozgar Yojana

Table 2

Housing Schemes under taken in Coimbatore District (Rs. in Lakhs)

S. No.	Name of the Scheme	2000-2001			2001-2002			2002-2003				2003-2004			
		Taken up	Compl.	Fincl	Taken up	Compl.	Fincl	Taken up	Comp.	Bal	Fincl	Taken up	Compl	Bal	Fincl
1.	CCS	118	118	47.20	50	50	5.00	0		0	600.96	0		0	
2.	IAS	1559	1559	498.8 8	1552	1552	496.64	1875	1875	0	600.96	1840	40	1800	586.00
3.	IAY-UG	766	766	76.60	766	776	77.60	947	947	0	101.44	308		308	98.56
4.	PMGY-(RH)				310	310	99.20	313	313	0	101.44	308		308	98.56

CCS – Credit cum Subsidy
IAS – Indira Awaaz Yojana
IAY–UG–IAY – Up- Gradation
PMGY –(RH) – Pradhan Mantri Grameen Yojana (Rural House)

Under SJGSY scheme 60 projects were completed out of 66 proposed at an outlay of Rs. 135 lakhs during the period 2000–2001 to 2003–2004.

HOUSING SCHEME

The Housing Schemes that were taken up in the district include

i. Credit Cum Subsidy

ii. Indira Awaaz Yojana

iii. IAY–Up Gradation

iv. Pradhan Mantri Grameen Yojana

Table-3

Bio-gas and Chulah under taken in Coimbatore District

(Rs in Lakhs)

S. No.	Year	Bio Gas			Chulah		
		Taken Up	Completed	Financial	Taken Up	Completed	Financial
1.	2000–01	150	150	3.45	3100	3100	3.41
2.	2001–02	175	175	4.03	3000	3000	3.30
3.	2002–03	150	150	3.45	750	750	0.75

During 2000–2001two schemes (IAY, IAYU) together undertaken and completed 2325 schemes at an outlay of Rs. 575.48 crores. In the following year (2001–02) 2611 schemes were completed out of 2638 schemes under the three programmes (IAY, IAYU & PMGY)

During the year 2000–01 the number of credit cum subsidy schemes taken up and completed were 118 by spending Rs. 47.20 lakhs. During the next year 50 Schemes were taken up and completed at the cost of Rs.5.00 lakhs. During the years 2002–2003 and 2003–2004 no scheme was taken up.

Table 4

Other Schemes under taken in Coimbatore District

(Rs.Lakhs)

S. No.	Name of the Scheme	2000-2001			2001-2002			2002-2003				2003-2004			
		Taken up	Compl.	Fincl	Taken up	Compl.	Fincl	Taken up	Comp.	Bal	Fincl	Taken up	Compl	Bal	Fincl
1.	MPLAD	369	369		328	328	735.98	260	250	10	741.21	154	20	134	443.04
2.	PMGSY			776.32	24	24	467.26	17	17	0	420.08			0	
3.	Village Self Sufficency Scheme				148	148	289.80	33	29	4	207.55	5	1	4	23.28
4.	MLACDS	873	873	1106.97	609	609	1054.78	629	555	74	976.38	231	48	183	585.29

VSSS – Village Self Sufficency Scheme

The three schemes put together taken up 3135 schemes at on outlay of Rs. 803.84 lakhs in the next year (2002–2003). In the next year (2003–2004), the coverage of the schemes increased tremendously: number of schemes taken up were 2456 but only 40 were completed by spending Rs.783.12 lakhs.

BIO-GAS AND CHULAH

The two schemes put together taken up 3250 schemes and completed than during 2000–2001 at on outlay of Rs. 6.86 lakhs. During the next year 3175 schemes were taken up and completed at a cost of Rs. 7.33 lakhs. During the year 2002–2003 900 schemes were taken up and all of them were completed by spending Rs. 4.50 lakhs.

OTHER SCHEMES

The other schemes that were taken up in the district include MPLAD, PMGSY, Village Self Sufficiency Scheme, and MLACDS.

During the year 2000–2001 the number of MPLAD taken up were 369 and all of them were completed. During the same year the number of MLACDS taken up were 873 and all of them were completed by spending Rs. 1106.97 lakhs. During 2001–2002 all the four schemes put together taken up were 1109 and all of them were completed at a cost of Rs. 2250.82 lakhs. During the next year 934 schemes were taken up and out of that 851 were completed by spending Rs. 2346.22 During the following year 390 schemes were taken up and only 69 were completed at the cost of Rs.1051.61 lakhs.

CONCLUSION

Employment generation programmes are schemes implemented for the upliftment of the rural poor. Employment generation programmes in Coimbatore District though led to improvement of the economic conditions of the families living below the poverty line their coverage seems to be very low.

Such schemes have to be increased to bring about an upliftment of the masses living below poverty line so that all the rural poor can be benefited from such programmes.

REFERENCES

1. Daff, Gaurav (1998) Poverty in India and India States : An update *Indian Journal of Labour Economics* vol. 41(2)
2. Dev. S. Mahendra etal (1992) Rural Poverty in India: Incidence, Issues and Polices, Asian Development Review vol. 10 No.1
3. Dev. S. Mahendra (1999) Persisting Poverty and Social Insecurity in Kirit Parikh (ed) Indian Development Report 1999–2000, Oxford University Press
4. Narain U (1998) Resources Degradation and Cooperation Working Paper, Department of Agricultural and Resource Economics, University of California
5. Nayyar Rohini (1995) An Assessment of Wage Employment Programme JRY and EAS, *The Indian Journal of Labour Economics*, Vol. 38 No.3
6. Papola. T. S. and A. N. Sharma (1996) Structural Adjustment Poverty Employment and safety Nets. The Indian Experience *The Indian Journal of Labour Economics*
7. S. SP. Sharma (2003) Development Programmes, Environment ad Rural Poverty in India, *Journal of Rural Development* vol.22 (2), April–June 2003
8. Sri Kara Naik & Sukvir Singh, North Eastern States A Rural Development & Poverty Alleviation Perspective", *Yojana* vol. 47(3)
9. Surinder Sud (2003) "Focus on Consolidating Rural Development Programmes; *Kurukshetra* vol 51 (6) April 2003 pp. 32–35
10. G. Srinivasam, "Rein forcing commitment to all round Rural Development," Kurukshetra vol.51 (6) April pp. 36-38.

EMPLOYMENT AND OUTPUT GROWTH IN A SELECTED MANUFACTURING COMPANY IN COIMBATORE DISTRICT

*S. Gandhimathi

INTRODUCTION

The main goals of development planning in India over the past five decades were to generate more work, output and income. The goal to provide full employment through planned investment, particularly in the context of rapidly increasing population, still remained unreaslized (Sailabala Debi and Gyana Chandrasekar, 1995).

As the provision of work opportunities during the ninth plan period concenred, an additional 50.32 million jobs were to be created, i.e., an increase in job opportunities from 389.7 million in 1997 to 440.02 million in 2002. Out of which 24.16 million would be added by the primary sector, 8.10 million by the secondary sector and18.06 million by the tertiary sector. It means that agriculture would accounted for about 48.1% of the additional job opportunities, the secondary sector for 15.95% and the tertiary sector for 35.95%. Thus, the tertiary sector accounted for a considerably large proportion of income and employment not only in the developed countries but also in India. (Bishwanath Singh, 2000).

Among the share of various industries in the total employment of organized public sector, the share of community, social and personal services was the highest. The share of community, social and personal services increased from 73.55 lakhs in 1981 to 97.71 lakhs in 2000. In the organized private sector employment, the share of manufacturing stands at the

* Lecturer in Economics, Avinashilingam Deemed University, Coimbatore 641 043

top and next to it was the community, social and personal services sector. In the private organized sector, employment in the community social and personal services increased from 12.22 lakhs in 1981 to 17.23 lakhs in March 2000. The share of manufacturing sector stood at 45.54 lakhs in 1981 and increased to 52.33 lakhs in 1998. But it started to decline to 50.85 lakhs in 2000. The share of manufacturing sector employment had declined not only in private sector but also in public sector. The statistics in organized public sector employment shows that he share of manufacturing sector employment declined from 18.7 lakhs in 1990 to 15.31 lakhs in 2000. (Economic survey 2000-2001).

Thus it shows that though manufacturing sector stands as an important source of providing employment opportunities, the growth of employment in the organised manufacturing sector in India started to decline. Also, in the manufacturing sector, the growth of employment was less than the growth of output. Between 1950-94, employment in the organized manufacturing sector grew at an estimated average rate of 3.7 % per annum and declined to 2.05 per annum and declined to 2.05% between 1994-2000. But the gross domestic output in the organized manufacturing sector grew by an estimated rate of 8.2% per annum. In this background, only few studies (Ghose 1997) attempted to analyse the relationship between the output growth and employment growth. These few studies were at macro level.

Thus the preset study attempted to analyse the "Employment and output growth in selected manufacturing company in Coimbatore District" with the following objectives by fulfilling the above gaps in the previous studies.

OBJECTIVES

1. To estimate the output growth and employment growth of the selected manufacturing unit for the period of 1992-2002.

2. To study the relationship between labour productivity growth and output growth, between employment growth and output growth and also to test the relationship between employment growth and labour productivity growth.

METHODOLOGY

Since Coimbatore district is an industrially advanced district and the investigator aimed at studying the employment performance in the manufacturing sector, the study was conducted in this district. Among various manufacturing units in Coimbatore district, Salzer Electronics Limited is one of the manufacturing company producing cam operated rotary switches, accessories for CAM operated rotary switches, star delta starter, dies and tools etc., It involved in this production from the year 1985 onwards. It is an organized manufacturing electronic company with sizable organized labour force as compared to other manufacturing companies in Coimbatore. Thus Salzer Electronics Limited was purposively selected to analyse the employment growth and output growth.

The study was based on secondary data compiled from the annual reports and balance sheets of the company for the period of 1992-2002. To investigate the employment growth and output growth, the following analytical tools were used in the study.

a. Deflated index.

b. Annual growth rate.

c. Regression analysis.

A. DEFLATED INDEX

To eliminate the impact of the fluctuations in the money value of the production, productivity, wages and salaries for the period of 1992–2002, they were deflated by taking the year 1992 as the base year.

B. ANNUAL GROWTH RATE

To analyse the output growth, employment growth and growth of salary and wages, the annual growth rates were calculated by using the following formula

$$\text{Annual growth rate} = \frac{P_1 - P_0}{P_0} \times 100$$

P_1 = Current year value of the variable analysed.

P_2 = Last year value of the variable analysed.

C. REGRESSION ANALYSIS

To analyse the impact of growth of output on growth of labour productivity and growth of employment, the Kaldorian model of growth used was,

$$Lp = \alpha_0 + \alpha_1 QG + U$$

$$G\varepsilon = \alpha_2 + \beta_2\, QG + \Sigma$$

Where,

Lp = Growth in labour productivity

$$\text{Labour productivity} = \frac{\text{Total production}}{\text{Total labour force}}$$

$Q\varepsilon$ = Growth in output

$Q\varepsilon$ = Growth in employment

U and ε are the error terms

To study the impact of growth in employment on growth in labour productivity, Rowthornian model of growth was carried out. The linear form of the model was,

$Lp = \beta_3 + \beta_3\, G_\varepsilon + V$, where

Lp = Growth in labour productivity

$G\varepsilon$ = Growth in employment

RESULTS AND DISCUSSION

In the Indian manufacturing sector, the growth of employment was less than the growth of output. The output grew faster than the employment. Thus to examine the above fact at micro level, the growth of output, employment, wages labour productivity of Salzer Electronics Limited and the relationships between the employment growth and output growth were analysed under the following heads.

A. Trends and growth of production (1992-2002).

B. Trends and growth of employment of Salzer Electronic Limited (1992-2002).

C. Trends and growth of wages and salary.

D. Trends and growth of labour productivity.

E. The relationship between employment growth and output growth.

A. TRENDS AND GROWTH OF PRODUCTION (1992-2002)

To analyse the growth in the production of the company, time series data were compiled from the annual reports of the company the production data for the selected time period were deflated by taking the year 1992-1993 as the base year and the results are shown in table-1

Table -1

Trends And Growth Of Production (1992-2002)

Year	Production Value (in Rs.)	Production Index (deflated values) (in percent)	Annual growth rate (in percent)
1992-1993	31557460	100.000	
1993-1994	36401232	115.349	15.349
1994-1995	58948364	186.796	61.939
1995-1996	63100460	199.954	7.044

1996-1997	69948322	221.653	10.851
1997-1998	80043062	253.642	14.432
1998-1999	82224484	260.554	2.725
1999-2000	78744845	249.528	-4.231
2000-2001	94601585	299.775	20.136
2001-2002	125756536	398.500	32.935

Table -1 Shows that there was continuous increase in the production value index from 100 in 1992-93 to 260.554 in 1998-99. It implies that the production of the company during 1998-99 had grown more than two times of the production in 1992-1993. The annual growth rate was observed to be 2.725 in 1998-1999. This was due to the higher demand and orders form the customers, they liked the products of the company and there was no delay in the supply. The company had extra provisions to meet the extra demand. But in 1999-2000, there was a bad business mood towards the products of Salzer Electronics Limited. In 2000-2001, it had recovered, it produced Rs. 94601585 value of the products. The production index showed 299.775 per cent in 2000-2001 and reached 398.500 percent in 2001-2002. It was nearly four times of the production in 1992-1993. It shows the good production performance of the company.

B. TRENDS AND GROWTH OF EMPLOYMENT OF SALZER ELECTRONICS LIMITED (1992-2002)

Salzer Electronics Limited had a sizable labour force consisting of both permanent and temporary employees and workers. Trends and growth of employment of Salzer Electronics Limited consisting of permanent labour force was analysed and given in table-2

Table -2
Trends And Growth Of Employment (1992-2002)

Year	Employment (in Number)	Annual growth rate (in percent)
1992-1993	28	-
1993-1994	34	21.43
1994-1995	50	47.06
1995-1996	71	42.00
1996-1997	88	23.94
1997-1998	99	12.50
1998-1999	92	-7.07
1999-2000	98	6.52
2000-2001	126	28.57
2001-2002	175	38.89

From the table-2 it can be observed that there were only 28 workers and employees during 1992-1993. As the size of the plant expands, the employment had also been increased, it reached 99 during 1997-1998. Both the production and employment had grown simultaneously, but the growth of employment was greater than growth of output in many of the years.

C. TRENDS AND GROWTH OF WAGES AND SALARY (1992-2002)

Wages and salary is an important component of the total expenses of the company. It determines the demand and supply of labour force and productivity. Thus it was analysed and given in table-3.

Table -3

Trends And Growth Of Wages And Salary (1992-2002)

Year	Salary and wages (In Rs.)	Salary and Wages Index (deflated values in percent	Annual growth rate (in percent)
1992-1993	2694315	100.000	-
1993-1994	3259534	120.978	20.978
1994-1995	4744493	176.092	45.557
1995-1996	6761735	250.963	42.518
1996-1997	8415005	312.324	24.450
1997-1998	9485665	352.062	12.723
1998-1999	8775221	325.693	-7.489
1999-2000	9364444	347.563	6.714
2000-2001	1238796	446.822	28.558
2001-2002	16717912	620.488	38.866

It can be observed from the table-3 that there was continuous increase in the wages and salaries index except during 1998-1999. During 1998-1999 negative annual growth rate was observed in relation to wages and salaries. It was due to the fact that decline in the total labour fore. But from 1999-2000 onwards the company recovered in its production performance, thus employment, wages and salaries had also grown. In the year 2002, wages and salaries grew at the rate of 38.866 per cent.

D. TRENDS AND GROWTH OF LABOUR PRODUCTIVITY (1992-2002)

Labour productivity shows the efficiency of labour in production. It was calculated by dividing the level of out put produced by the total labour force. The results of labour productivity is shown in table-4

Table -4

Trends And Growth Of Labour Productivity (1992-2002)

Year	Production index (deflated values)	Employment (in number)	Labour productivity (in percent)	Annual growth rate (in percent)
1992-1993	100	28	3.571	–
1993-1994	115.349	34	3.392	–5.012
1994-1995	186.796	50	3.735	10.112
1995-1996	199.954	71	2.816	–24.605
1996-1997	221.653	88	2.518	–10.582
1997-1998	253.642	99	2.562	1.747
1998-1999	260.554	92	2.832	10.538
1999-2000	249.528	98	2.546	–10.098
2000-2001	299.775	126	2.379	–6.559
2001-2002	398.500	175	2.277	–4.287

The table-4 shows that there was slight increase in the labour productivity between the period of 1994-1995. However from 1995 onwards, there was deterioration in labour productivity of the Salzer Electronics Limited except during the year 1997-1998 and 1998-1999. The annual growth rates were observed to be negative in all the years except during 1992-1993, 1994-1995, 1997-1998 and 1998-1999. It shows the declining efficiency of the labour force. During 1998-1999 the growth rate of labour productivity was found to be maximum, which had grown at the rate of 10.538 per cent. But in the next year suddenly declined to -10.098 percent, which shows the greater inefficiency on the part of the labour force.

E. THE RELATIONSHIP BETWEEN EMPLOYMENT GROWTH AND OUTPUT GROWTH

To analyse the relationship between output growth and labour productivity growth and between the output growth and growth of employment, specified by the Kaldorian model, regression analysis was carried out. The results of the analysis is given in table-5

Table -5

Results Of Kaldorian Model

Kaldorian Specification			
Dependent variables	Constant	Outpur growth	R^2
Labour productivity growth	-18.115867 (-2.288)	.928151 (4.684)	.73278 F=121.93793**
Employment growth	9.693347 (1.733)	.830493 (5.932)	.81475 F=35.185332**

Note (i) Figures in the parentheses are T-values for co-efficients

(ii) ** Denotes significance at 1% level

It is observed from the table-5 that the out put growth had the significant impact on the labour productivity growth. The output growth alone explained 73 percent of the variation in the growth of labour productivity. The relationship was statistically significant. The positive sign of the co-efficient reveals that there were positive relationships between the output growth and the labour productivity growth and the output growth and the employment growth. It shows that when the growth of production increased, the growth of employment and the growth of productivity of labour force would also increase. Thus Kaldorian specification hold good empirically in Salzer electronics Limited.

To test the Rowthornian specification of the relationship between growth of employment and labour productivity growth, regression analysis was carried out. The result of the regression analysis is given in table–6

Table–6

Results Of Rowthornian Model

Rowthornian Specification			
Dependent variables	Constant	Employment growth	R^2
Labour productivity growth	-20.991920 (-1.767)	.864049 (3.050)	.53760 F-9.30108**

Note (i) Figures in the parantheses are T-values for co-efficients

(ii) ** Denotes significance at 1% level

The labour productivity function explained 54 per cent of the variation in the labour productivity. That is the growth of employment alone explained 54 percent of the variation in the labour productivity. The employment growth had significant positive impact on the labour productivity growth. It shows that when the growth of employment increased the growth of labour productivity would also increase. Thus the Rowthornian model hold good in the empirical analysis of employment performance of Salzer Electronics Limited

CONCLUSION

To sum up, though the output and employment in the company had grown in the study period, the growth rate of output was less than the employment growth in many of the years. Thus from 1995 onwards, there was a deterioration labour productivity except in the period of 1997-1998 and 1998-1999. It shows the declining efficiency of the labour force. It was due to the inadequate technological improvements in the production process. In the employment and production relationship it was observed that the increase in the production growth would increase the labour productivity growth and employment growth. Similarly, the increase in the employment growth increased the labour productivity growth. Thus by increasing the growth of output, both the growth of employment and the labour productivity could be increased.

SUGGESTIONS

1. The company did not have adequate technological improvements in production process. It was also one of the reasons for lowest growth of output. Thus it should spend huge amount on research and development and frame measures to update its technology to modernise its production process. It will improve the production and output performance of the company.
2. The company can increase its production by the effective use of labour force. The company should take measure to increase the productivity of the labour force by giving proper training and work related education. The inefficient employees and workers should be identified, they should be given a special training and education

REFERENCES

1. Sailabala Debi and Gyara Chandrasekar (1995), "Employment Generation in Industrial Sector, A Study of Orissa", Southern economist, Vol. 30, No.4 Pp 39-41.
2. Economic Survey 2000-2001, Government of India Publications, New Delhi, Pp. 52-53.
3. Ghose, B. N. (1997), "Labour Productivity, Employment and Output Growth in the Malaysian Manufacturing Sector", Indian Journal of Economics, Vol. LXXVII, No. 306, Pp. 427– 433

4. Bishwanath Singh, (2000), "Employment Growth in Organised Manufacturing Sector in India", Economic and Political Weekly, Vol. 35, No. 14 , Pp 1191-1194.

EMPLOYMENT IN LEATHER INDUSTRIES : EMERGING ISSUES AND FUTURE PERSPECTIVES

Dr. L. Rathakrishnan
Reader in Rural Industries
and Management
Gandhigram Rural Institute
Gandhigram -624 302

INTRODUCTION

Leather industry is one of the oldest and tradition cottage industry in India. It's an indigenous industry endowed with all the necessary raw materials, manpower, machinery, and equipments. Indian leather industry has made rapid strides during last three decades, especially after liberalisation. As the industry produce a host of finished goods such as industrial gloves, footwear, leather garments, wallets, wrappers, bags, belts and many other accessories, it has wide national and international markets demand.

Leather industry has tremendous potential to provide gainful employment to tens and thousands of people. It has a distinctive feature of providing employment to the weaker sections of the community. It provides full time and part time employment to a large number of people. The major portions of work force belong to depressed classes such as scheduled castes. It is largely export oriented and its scope for earning foreign exchange is almost unlimited.

Tannery industry, a subsidiary unit of leather industry produce large quantities of toxic effluent polluting the air, land, and water. As the industry has changed the processing technology from vegetables to chrome tanning, it spoil the air, land, water bodies crop yield, damage to livestock, damage the building of the neighborhood. Not only flora and fauna but men, women and children were also affected severely due to tannery pollution. Nevertheless, the tannery sector also provide substantial employment opportunities to the rural poor.

II. EMERGING ISSUES

In view of the above background the following issues were raised for further analysis.

(i) How far the larger availability of livestock population helps for the growth of the industry?

(ii) Does value addition industry demand higher labour?

(iii) Is it helps the depressed classes society by providing employment?

(iv) What is the further prospect of these industries in terms of new environmental regulation?

III. OBJECTIVES AND METHODS

The major objective of the study is to analyse the growth pattern of leather industry, its impact on employment, wage structure, and efficiency. The study is based on secondary data. The secondary data was collected from Central Leather Research Institute, Council of leather experts, Chennai and Tannery Association, Dindigul. The secondary data covers 25 years, from 1974-1975 and 1988-89. The period is sufficient enough to include the gestation period of the manufacturing units and to notice any effects on employment.

Cobb - Douglas production function is used to analyse the relation between investment, output, and labour employed in the industry.

$$Q = A X_1^{\alpha} X_2^{\beta}$$

Where, Q = the output; X_1 = Volume of capital invested, and X_2 = Volume of labour employed.

When it is transferred into log linear from it is expressed as

$$\text{Log } Q = \text{Log } A + \alpha \text{ Log } X_1 + \beta \text{ Log } X_2$$

Where

α = the exponent, represents the partial elasticity of output with reference to capital

β = the exponent, represents the partial elasticity of output with reference to layout.

In order to analyse the labour share, both money wage and real wage have been estimate. The average money wage has been estimated by dividing total emolument by total number of employees, working in the leather industry, namely :

Mw = TM/TE

Where, TM= total emoluments; TE= Total employees, and Mw = money wage.

Consumer price index (1996=100) has been taken into account to estimate the real wage as follows :

Rw = [Mw/CPI]x100

Where, Rw= real wage; Mw= money wage, and CPI = consumer price index.

Further, assess to the competitive advantage of the industry in terms of labour cost, the Keynesian efficiency wages has been estimated by taking the relative movement of money wage and labour productivity. In order to trace the movement in the relationship adopting the Kaldorian approach the index of money wage is divided by the index of productivity as

Ew = index (Mw)/index (AP_1)

Where, Ew = efficiency wage; Mw = Money wage, and AP_L= average productivity of labour.

The efficiency wage acts as the indicator of competitive advantage. Rise in efficiency wage implies that the layout productivity rises at a lower rate than the money wage of the workers engaged in the industry.

IV. ANALYSIS AND INTERPRETATION

The art of tanning originated before the dawn of recorded history. Pre-historic man used the hides and skins of the animal to wrap up his body. It was in the east that the art of manufacturing leather developed to a considerable extent. The Egyptians, the Chinese, and Indians had attained a high degree of proficiency in making leather. As time move fast the process of tanning become complex, in which chemical, physical and biological principles are involved. Whatever may be the technological development, tanning is considered an art.

4.1 GROWTH OF LIVESTOCK POPULATION

The growth rate of cattle and sheep population has been marginal. Populations of buffalo and goat have registered significant annual growth rates. The annual rate of growth of buffalo's worked out at 1.86% during 1961-1992. This is about 3.5% times that of growth rate of cattle. An increasing demand for meat of buffaloes in global trade is promoting the rearing of the animal. Compared to cattle population, the growth of buffalo population is greater, Nevertheless, a steady growth was found in cattle and buffalo population. Goat population has increased from 47 million heads in 1951 to 115 million heads in 1992. It is projected that population of goat may increase to 162 million by the year 2005. The annual growth rate of goat during 1961-1992 has been 3.11%. Nearly one in four goat skins processed in the world is processed in India. Although the rate of slaughter is nearly 60% of the stock, the reproductive rate of goat is such that there is a net 3.1% increase reared all over the world. The rate of growth of sheep in India works out to the 0.5% per annum. Even though the sheep population has a low rate of growth, red hair sheep skin offers a vast untapped opportunity for leather section. Sheep is prone to number of epidemic diseases. Some of them affect the quality of skin and lead to the loss of value in material. Implementation of animal health care practices can lead to significant economic benefit to the farmers.

Table 1

Growth Of Livestock Population in India

(in million)

Year	Cattle	Buffalo	Goats	Sheep
1951	153.3	43.4	47.1	39.1
1956	158.6	44.9	55.4	39.2
1961	175.6	51.2	60.9	40.2
1966	176.2	52.9	64.6	42.0
1972	179.0	57.9	68.0	40.4
1977	180.1	62.1	75.6	40.8
1982	194.4	69.7	95.3	48.1
1987	195.8	76.0	99.0	44.8
1992	204.5	83.5	115.3	50.7
1996	207.3	89.7	129.7	50.8
1997	208.4	91.3	133.3	52.0
2000	211.6	96.0	144.1	52.8
2005*	217.0	103.7	162.0	54.1

Source : Census of India, Chennai.

*Estimated.

4.2 RAW HIDES AND SKINS SCENARIO

Table 2 show the availability of hides and skins in India. The cattle hides is increasing from 141.21 lakh pieces in 1951 to 247.70 lakh pieces in 2002. In other words a growth of 106.49 lakh pieces was noticed within a half-century. During the last two decades the annual growth in availability of cattle hides has fallen to 0.5%. Buffalo hides increased from 47.68 lakh pieces to 206.90 lakh pieces during the same period, thus registering a growth of 159.22 lakh pieces. The annual growth of population of buffalo continues to remain at 1.7–1.8% during the last 45 years. Goat skins increased from 212.52 lakh pieces to 1037.90 lakh pieces, recording an increase of 824.38 lakh pieces during the reference period. Sheep skins availability increased from 154.66 lakh pieces to 308.10 lakh pieces, registering a growth of 153.44 lakh pieces during the same period. There is a quantum jump in availability of buffalo hides and goat skins during 1950-2000. The preference of small farmers and consumers for meat and diary products from buffalo and goat is favouring such a trends.

Table 2

Availability of Raw Hides and Skins in India

(in lakh pieces)

Year	Cattle hides	Buffalo hides	Goats Skins	Sheep Skins
1951	141.21	47.68	212.52	154.66
1961	175.44	56.21	288.01	189.88
1972	214.00	86.13	405.10	199.91
1982	209.92	144.39	647.11	290.25
1992	235.20	172.00	805.80	283.90
1997	241.40	189.50	921.80	296.00
2002	247.70	206.90	1037.90	308.10

Source : CLRI, Adyar, Chennai-20.

4.3 GROWTH PATTERN OF THE LEATHER INDUSTRY

Table 3 explains the growth of leather manufacturing units in India. In the year 1974-75 there were 667 units in total , out of which 478 units were leather tanning, 129 units of foot wear manufacturing and the rest of the units were leather goods and garments. Within the span of 25 years the units have increased 947 and 371 in tanning and footwear sectors respectively.

The table also shows the indices computed for tanning, footwear sector and the leather industry. The Indexes for both the sectors including the industry have increased over the period with few exceptions. The index of units of tanning and footwear manufacturing has increased to 198.14 and 287.59 respectively. The number of units of footwear manufacturing has increased proportionately more than that of tanning and the leather industry as a whole. This is due to the added emphasis and liberal policy of the government for export more value added products than raw hides.

Table 3

Growth of Leather Manufacturing Units in India

(industries in Number)

Year	Tanning	Index	Footwear	Index	Leather	Index	Total	Index
1974-75	478*	100.00	129*	100.00	60*	100.00	667	100.00
1975-76	490	102.51	121	93.80	59	98.33	670	100.45
1976-77	539	112.76	123	95.35	65	108.33	727	109.00
1977-78	542	113.39	138	106.98	82	136.67	762	114.24
1978-79	561	117.36	142	110.08	112	186.67	815	122.19
1979-80	615	128.66	166	128.68	81	135.00	862	129.23
1980-81	596	124.68	201	155.81	89	148.33	886	132.83
1981-82	605	126.57	199	154.26	95	158.33	899	134.78
1982-83	623	130.33	176	136.43	81	135.00	880	131.93
1983-84	663	138.70	215	166.67	64	106.67	942	141.23
1984-85	649	135.77	185	143.41	95	158.33	959	139.28
1985-86	701	146:65	187	144.96	111	185.00	999	149.77
1986-87	665	139.12	193	149.61	118	196.67	976	146.33
1987-88	686	143.51	221	171.32	167	278.33	1074	161.02
1988-89	731	152.93	270	209.30	194	323.33	1195	179.16

1989-90	746	156.07	284	220.15	208	346.67	1238	185.61
1990-91	779	162.98	297	230.23	311	518.34	1387	207.95
1991-92	783	163.82	301	233.33	457	761.68	1541	231.04
1992-93	807	168.84	311	241.08	471	785.03	1589	238.24
1993-94	816	170.72	321	248.83	493	821.00	1630	244.39
1994-95	866	181.19	337	261.23	509	848.37	1712	256.69
1995-96	894	187.05	341	264.33	521	868.37	1756	263.29
1996-97	912	190.82	350	371.31	533	888.37	1795	269.16
1997-98	934	195.42	363	281.39	547	911.70	1844	276.49
1998-99	947	198.14	371	287.59	569	948.37	1867	282.94

Note : 1974-75 as the base year =100

Source : Annual Survey of Industries, CSO. Government of India.

* Industry

– Leather making units

4.4 EXPORT PERFORMANCE

India is no more an exporter of raw hides and skins, as was in the past. Today, it exports of leather and wide range of leather products with latest sophistication in style and design, creating to the needs of the changing world market, since 1974-75 exports of leather and leather products have made an impressive growth and today, it has emerged as a leading sector, exporting traditional and nontraditional goods, ranking fourth among other export oriented sectors of the Indian economy.

Table 4

India's Export Performance Of Leather And Leather Products

(Rs. in Crores)

Year	Semi Finished Leather	Finished Leather	Leather Footwear	Footwear Compo-ments	Leather Goods	Leather Garm -ents	Manufac-turing & sports goods	Total
1975-76	144	55	19	1	8	1	4	232
1976-77	150	105	26	6	10	3	9	300
1977-78	122	108	19	15	11	6	11	292
1978-79	111	192	23	18	19	8	16	387
1979-80	113	321	30	37	21	8	23	553
1980-81	51	227	34	45	25	5	24	411
1981-82	54	226	30	77	29	7	21	444
1982-83	46	210	29	87	26	10	26	434
1983-84	52	235	31	122	32	12	27	511
1984-85	65	361	45	175	49	22	31	748
1985-86	68	334	41	224	59	28	25	779
1986-87	59	408	69	229	71	69	38	943
1987-88	56	538	123	295	108	120	49	1289
1988-89	30	650	140	381	130	182	67	1580
1989-90	16	729	199	439	195	360	100	2039
1990-91	13	799	303	573	253	557	127	2625
1991-92	11	717	425	700	391	761	168	3173
1992-93	–	808	555	602	555	1044	194	3758
1993-94	–	753	803	659	594	1009	180	3998
1994-95	–	1201	1000	652	743	1224	293	5113
1995-96	–	1241	1103	814	1013	1387	370	5928
1996-97	–	1065	1212	833	1123	1545	@	5778
1997-98	–	1097	981	888	1607	1584	83	6240
1998-99	–	1132	1238	1040	1973	1573	-	6956

Note : @ Included in Leather Goods.

Source 1. Monthly Statistics of the Foreign Trade of India (Volume 1), exports & Re-exports, March 1976 to 1996, D. G. I. S., Calcutta.

2. Compiled by Economics Research Division, C. L. R. I., Chennai–20.

The volume of India's total export and export of leather and leather products for the period 1975 to 1998-99 were represented in Table 4. The export sector of leather industry has undergone significant changes during the period under reference. India, since independence was an exporter of raw hides and skins and the UK was the major trading partner. Though ban was imposed on export of raw cattle hides, buffalo hides, and calf skins of all types in the year 1951, export of goat and sheep skins continued on the basis of restricted quota imposed by the government of India from time to time. The export of semi-finished leather has been drastically reduced after the Seetaramaiah Committee report (1972-73). Since April 1990 the export of semi-finished leather has been totally banned. The export of semi-finished leather has decreased from 144 crores in 1975-76 to 11 crores in 1991-92. But the exports of finished leather played role in the world market. In 1975-76 the export value of finished leather was 55 crores. It accrued one third of total export of leather product. In 1998-999, the export value was 1132 crores. The exports of leather footwear in terms of money increased from 19 crores to 1238 crores in 1998-99. During 70's and 80's earning of foreign currencies by leather and leather products were very low. After liberalisation the level of export earning of leather and leather products increased gradually. During 1998-99 the level of leather export earning was 6956 crore rupees.

4.5 TREND IN EMPLOYMENT GENERATION

In a country like India with vast unemployment the industries are expected to create more gainful employment opportunities. In the year 1951, it was estimated by the national income committee that 0.763 millions of people were employed in the leather industry and their total earning was about Rs. 600 million. At present it employees 12 lakhs working forces in cottage, small, and large scale sectors. However, the present study attempts to examine the growth of employment in registered manufacturing units of leather industry. Table 5 depicts indices of employments generation in tanning, footwear and leather industry in total. Up to the year 1998-99 the employment generation in tanning and footwear sectors and in the leather industry has been increasing with wide fluctuations. The respective indices in the terminal year are 290.97, 246.83 and 375.39 for the tanning sector, footwear sector and the leather industry. The rate of growth of employment in leather sector during the span of 25 years is 7.18 T and it is 4.25 % in case of tanning sector. Even though, index numbers show that there has been more of employment over the years but it is much higher in the tanning sector. Since, the rate of growth of employment generation is only 4.25 % in footwear sector, the growth of employment in the leather industry as a whole has been reduced to the level of 5.77% in an average.

Table 5
Growth of employment in Tannery, Footwear and Leather Industry

(in Number)

Year	Tanning Industry	Index	Footwear Industry	Index	Leather Industry	Index
1974-75	21296	100.00	21405	100.00	44858	100.00
1975-76	21574	101.31	7138	33.35	30668	68.37
1976-77	27240	127.91	19566	91.41	48716	108.60
1977-78	26642	125.10	21776	101.73	50377	112.30
1978-79	28146	132.17	17665	82.53	49270	109.00
1979-80	32222	151.31	25713	120.13	60765	84.00
1980-81	30457	143.02	24808	115.90	58227	135.46
1981-82	32295	151.65	25557	119.40	60927	129.80
1982-83	31173	146.38	28081	131.19	62443	135.82
1983-84	31518	148.00	28036	130.98	62694	139.76
1984-85	36041	169.24	29388	137.30	69169	154.20
1985-86	37082	174.13	31052	145.07	72023	160.56
1986-87	34677	162.83	30593	142.92	70739	157.70
1987-88	35897	168.56	33683	157.36	76389	171.29
1988-89	40753	191.36	41166	192.32	91002	202.87
1989-90	77558	223.32	42492	198.51	102902	229.39
1990-91	48931	229.77	43471	203.08	98941	220.56
1991-92	55372	260.02	43698	204.14	99871	222.63
1992-93	53478	250.03	46917	219.18	112810	251.47
1993-94	51305	240.93	48113	224.77	129117	287.82
1994-95	54480	255.84	48996	228.90	146715	327.05
1995-96	58354	274.03	49631	231.87	139991	312.06
1996-97	58973	276.94	50606	236.43	154718	344.89
1997-98	61894	290.66	51617	241.15	157799	351.76
1998-99	61961	290.97	52833	246.83	168397	375.39

Source : Economics Research Division, C. L. R.I, Chennai

4.6 MONEY AND REAL WAGE

Here, it is intended to analyse the trends in money and real wage efficiency and find out their relationships with labour productivity in leather industry. It is clear from Table 6 that the index number of money wage in tanning sector have risen sharply except some setback. It has increased from 100 to 418.67 in the terminal year. Similarly, money wave in footwear sector has increased from 100 to 272.60.

The rate of rise of money wage in the tanning sector is more than that of footwear manufacturing. In the leather industry, including all sectors, the trend in money wage has been found to be rising throughout the period except certain years. In the year 1998-99, it is noticed that the money wage has increased 4 times in comparison to 1974-75. This increase may be due to rise in consumer price index.

On the other had, real wages in both sectors and in the leather industry have been fluctuating over the years. Between the two sectors namely, tanning and footwear, index of real wage has gone up to 117.56 and 76.33 respectively in the terminal year. Like money wage, real wage in tanning sector has increased proportionately more than that of the footwear sectors. It is also evident that the real wage in the leather industry grows more than the foot wear sector but less than the tanning sector. The highest growth of the real wage was achieved in the year 1978-79 in all industries.

Table 6

Money and Real Wage Efficiency

Year	Tanning Sector				Footwear sector				Leather Industry				
	Money Wage	Money Wage 1	Real Wage	Real Wage1	Money Wage	Money Wage 1	Real Wage	Real Wage1	Money Wage	Money Wage 1	Real Wage	Real Wage1	Consumer Price Index 1986=100
1974-75	3615.70	100.00	5623.18	100.00	5951.88	100.00	9256.42	100.00	4665.83	100.00	7256.35	100.00	64.30
1975-76	4083.62	112.94	6430.90	114.36	4819.28	80.97	7589.41	81.99	4193.30	110.47	66023.62	91.00	63.50
1976-77	4350.22	120.31	7131.51	126.82	6485.74	108.97	10632.36	114.86	5154.36	116.57	8449.78	116.45	60.99
1977-78	4143.83	114.61	6307.20	112.16	7214.36	121.21	10980.77	118.63	5438.99	137.89	8278.52	114.09	65.69
1978-79	4942.09	136.68	7365.26	130.98	9606.57	161.40	14316.79	154.67	6433.94	137.84	9588.58	132.14	67.10
1979-80	5167.28	142.91	7078.46	125.88	8377.09	140.75	11475.46	123.97	6413.33	153.05	888.05	121.41	73.00
1980-81	6303.97	174.35	7753.96	137.89	8489.20	142.63	10441.82	112.81	7141.02	154.64	8783.54	121.05	81.30
1981-82	6329.15	175.05	6917.11	123.01	8600.38	144.50	9399.33	101.54	7215.19	168.63	7885.46	108.67	91.50
1982-83	7179.29	198.56	7288.62	129.62	8917.06	149.82	9052.85	97.80	7869.98	201.25	7986.79	110.08	110.99
1983-84	7954.18	219.99	7165.93	127.44	11356.83	190.81	10231.38	110.53	9390.05	216.19	8459.51	116.58	118.10
1984-85	8229.52	227.60	6968.26	123.92	12790.94	214.91	10830.60	117.01	10086.89	229.64	8540.97	117.70	118.10
1985-86	9020.55	249.48	7176.25	127.62	13171.45	221.30	10478.48	113.20	10714.63	257.14	8523.97	117.47	125.70
1986-87	10583.38	292.71	7736.39	137.58	13329.85	223.96	9744.04	105.27	11531.12	281.75	8429.18	116.16	136.80
1987-88	11382.57	314.84	7634.18	135.76	15847.76	266.26	10628.95	114.83	13145.87	258.41	8816.82	121.50	149.10

1988-89	11577.06	320.19	7111.22	126.46	13081.18	219.78	8035.13	86.81	12056.88	301.36	7405.94	102.06	162.79
1989-90	13104.00	362.42	7557.09	134.39	16132.45	271.05	9303.60	100.51	14060.95	346.18	8108.97	111.75	173.40
1990-91	14269.07	394.64	7944.92	141.29	16068.18	269.97	8946.65	96.66	16152.05	346.18	8993.35	123.93	179.60
1991-92	12863.9	355.78	7002.67	124.53	15966.4	268.26	8691.57	93.90	17453.51	374.07	9501.10	130.93	183.70
1992-93	13234.53	374.33	7056.59	125.49	14956.19	251.29	7797.81	84.24	16754.72	359.09	8735.52	120.38	191.80
1993-94	14575.57	403.12	7291.43	129.67	15259.9	256.39	7633.77	82.47	15961.49	290.14	7984.74	110.03	199.90
1994-95	14871.51	411.28	7309.67	129.99	16231.93	272.72	7978.34	86.19	15249.29	277.19	7495.35	103.29	203.45
1995-96	14461.73	399.95	6799.13	120.92	15548.74	261.24	7310.18	78.97	16043.17	291.62	7542.63	103.29	203.45
1996-97	15208.65	420.61	6966.86	123.90	16118.64	270.82	7383.72	79.76	16041.44	291.59	7348.35	101.27	218.30
1997-98	14767.18	408.40	6537.04	116.26	16322.14	274.24	7225.39	78.05	17074.25	310.36	7558.32	104.16	225.90
1998-99	15138.55	418.67	6610.73	117.56	16224.7	272.60	7066.51	76.33	17050.77	309.93	7426.30	102.34	229.60

Source :Handbook of Industrial Statistics. Labour Burear, Government of India, New Delhi.

Table –7
Efficiency of Wage in Leather Industry

(in number)

Sl. No.	Year	Tanning EW_T	Footwear EW_F	Industry EW_L
1.	1974-75	1.00	1.00	1.00
2.	1975-76	1.34	0.84	0.85
3.	1976-77	1.55	1.21	1.25
4.	1977-78	1.34	1.48	1.32
5.	1978-79	2.19	2.17	1.93
6.	1979-80	2.21	1.91	1.93
7.	1980-81	3.15	1.97	2.36
8.	1981-82	2.82	1.66	2.01
9.	1982-83	2.97	1.50	1.99
10.	1983-84	2.18	2.26	2.05
11.	1984-85	2.63	1.87	2.10
12.	1985-86	3.96	2.19	2.73
13.	1986-87	4.70	2.12	2.89
14.	1987-88	4.08	2.36	2.87
15.	1988-89	3.76	2.42	2.67
16.	1989-90	4.60	2.46	3.02
17.	1990-91	4.82	2.97	3.70
18.	1991-92	4.13	2.59	4.19
19.	1992-93	4.04	2.28	4.04
20.	1993-94	4.21	2.23	3.34
21.	1994-95	4.31	2.51	3.34
22.	1995-96	3.99	2.19	3.26
23.	1996-97	1.16	2.37	3.01
24.	1997-98	3.79	2.34	3.40
25.	1998-99	3.70	2.36	3.47

Note : EW_T = Efficiency of wage in tanning sector;
EW_F = Efficiency of wage in footwear sector, and
EW_L = Efficiency of wage in Leather Industry as a whole.

Source : Centreal Leather Research Institute, Chennai

Table 7 results in efficiency of wage in leather industry. The efficiency of wage in tanning has tended to rise more rapidly than the leather industry as a whole. Thus, it implies that the wage cost has increased or in other words, the competitive advantage for the industry has declined. In simple terms, it can be put that wage has increased more than proportionately without any corresponding rise in productivity over the period. The efficiency wage in tanning is 3.70 in 1998-99, 2.36 for footwear and 3.47 in leather industry as a whole.

4.7 PRODUCTION FUNCTION

The most widely used production function in economics is the Cobb – Douglas as compared to other production functions. The only reason is that they are relatively simple.

Table 8

Results of Cobb-Douglas Production Function: Tanning Industry

Predictor variables	Co-efficient	Student's T
Constant	-2.7044	-4.09
LK	0.3482(α)	1.65
LE	1.3009(β)	1.47

Note: LK = Log of capital in tanning; LE = Log of labour in tanning.

Degree of Freedom = 22 Adjusted R^2 = 0.9601

R^2 = 0.9634 Durbin-Watson Statistics = 2.0562

Using exponential form of Cobb-Douglas production function, the derived equations.

$$\text{Log } Q_T = \text{Log } A_T + \alpha_T \text{ Log } Z + \beta_T \text{ Log } Z_4$$

$$\text{Log } Q_T = -2.7044 + 0.3482\ Z_2 + 1.3009\ Z_4$$

The result of the function shows as follows:

0.3482 and 1.3009 are represent the partial elasticity of output with reference to capital and labour. It is observed that the sum of $\alpha+\beta$ is 1.64 which is significantly different from unity. It implies that the tanning industry is operating under increasing returns to scale. In other words output does not responds proportionately to the sector. Under t-distribution, the calculated values of inputs are 1.65 and 1.47, which exceeds the table value. So it is significant at 1% level [1t1 + 0.01]. This shows that 96% of variation in value added is explained by labour and capital.

Table 9

Results of Cobb-Douglas Production Function: Footwear Industry

Predictor variables	Co-efficient	Student's T
Constant	-4.4742	-1.05
LK	0.4673(α)	1.75
LE	1.6391(β)	1.45

Note: LK = Log of capital in tanning; LE = Log of labour in tanning.

Degree of Freedom = 22 Adjusted R^2 = 0.8184

R^2 = 0.8227 Durbin-Watson Statistics = 2.0568

Under footwear industry, the exponential form of Cobb-Douglas production function is

$$\text{Log } Q_F = -4.4742 + 0.4673Y_2 + 1.6391\ Y_4$$

The sum of partial elasticity of output with reference to a capital and labour is 2.1 (0.4673+1.6391). So footwear sector is operating under increasing returns to scale. Under t-distribution, the calculated value, namely 1t1, [1.75 and 1.45] which exceeds the table value. So it is significant at 1% level (e.i.)1.75 and 1.45 is greater tan 1.321. The estimated values of R^2 and R^2 are 0.8227 and 0.8184 respectively. So 81% to 82% variations in value added is explained by labour and capital.

Table 10

Results of Cobb-Douglas Production Function: Leather Industry

Predictor variables	Co-efficient	Student's T
Constant	–0.1129	-0.05
LK	0.7977(α)	2.45
LE	0.6422(β)	1.49

Note: LK = Log of capital in tanning; LE = Log of labour in tanning.

Degree of Freedom = 22 Adjusted R^2 = 0.8110

R^2 = 0.8267 Durbin-Watson Statistics = 2.0845

In the case of leather industry as a whole the production function is

$$\text{Log } Q_F = -0.1128 + 0.7977\ X_2 + 0.6422\ X_4$$

The sum of partial elasticity of output (ie) $\alpha + \beta$ with reference to capital and labour is 1.43 which is greater than unit, so leather industry in India is operating under increasing returns to scale. At present, India got 4th place in leather and leather product export in the world. The calculated value of t–distribution (2.45 & 1.49), exceed the table value 1t1>+0.01. So it is significant at 1% level. A degree of freedom for all sectors is 22. The estimated value of R^2 and R^2 are 0.8267 and 0.8110 respectively, so 81% to 82% variation in value added or output is explained by labour and capital.

From the above discussion of the production function, the level of contribution of labour is more than capital because of the labour intensive technique. In the above case, the value of d in Durbin–Watson statistic more or less equal to two, so there is no auto correlation prevail between the successive value of estimates.

V. MAJOR FINDINGS OF THE STUDY

- Leather goods and garments are almost entirely produced in cottage and small–scale sector. Major production centres for leather goods are Calcutta, Mumabi, Chennai and Delhi.
- There has been a gradual but slow rise in the growth of total number of units in tanning, footwear sector and the industry as a whole during the period of reference.
- The growth rate of output as well as values added are found to be highest in case of footwear manufacturing. All selected parameters of growth have increasing proportionately at a higher rate than that of tanning and the industry.
- Cobb- Douglas production function estimates show that the tanning, footwear, and industry as whole are operating under increasing return to scale. The sum of $\alpha + \beta$ for tanning, footwear and the industry are 1.6, 2.10 and 1.43 respectively.
- Employment of labour in both the sectors and the industry are in rising trend during the period of reference.
- The money wage and real wage in sectors and in the industry have increased very significantly. The rise of money wage and the real wage is comparatively more in case of tanning sector in comparison to footwear sector.
- The efficiency of wage in tanning and footwear sectors and in the industry on the other hand, has registered a rising trend.

- The export sector of the leather industry has emerged as one of the thrust sectors for foreign exchange earnings. The exponential growth rate for leather exports is higher than the growth rate of total exports of the country. Hence, the export potential have to be geared up with the help of suitable policy.

VI. CONCLUSION

India has vast scope for exporting leather products to the world market. Already, this sector ranks fourth position in terms leather product export in the world market. As this industry is labour intensive it has high potential in providing employment to rural non-farm sector. But the marginal labour productivity is low due to bad living condition of workers and adaptation of primitive technology. Policy changes may greatly help the industry to grow fast and do better to the poor people as well.

REFERENCES

Bagaram Tulpule and R. C. Data (1989), , "Real Wages and Productivity in Industry : A Desegregated Analysis", Economic and Political Weekly– Vol. 24 No. (34) : M4–102.

Beri G. C. (1962), Measurement of Production and Productivity in India Industry with Special Reference to Some Methodology Aspects. Asia Publication, Bombay : 85-94.

Bhagwat M. K. (1975), "Leather industry, its growth, and future". Industrial Bulletin. Vol. 14.No. (6): (6).

Choudhury G. R. (1979), "Standardization and Quality Control for Export of Leather and Leather Manufactures",, ISI Bulletin, Vol. 23(10): 105-108.

Gupta A. R. (1979), "Leather Industry in India and Marketing Problems of Small Units", Journal of industry and Trade, Vol. 29. No. (3) : 45-48.

Kumar N. C. (1985), "Export Strategy for Leather Products: Some Suggestions in Foreign trade and India's Export Policy", Deep & Deep Publication, New Delhi: 246-53

Kuyvehnhoven Aire, "Technology, Employment and Basic Needs in Leather Industries in Developing Countries". Discussion Papers No.51, Centre for Development Planning, Rotterdam; 107-111.

Majurrdas D. (1980), "Leather Manufacture. An Employment Oriented Industry", Indian Journal of Commerce, Vol. 40 (15) : 38.40

Notsale R. T. (1980), "Problem of Leather Industry as a Problem of Labours", Indian Worker, No. (14) : 4-5.

Singh S. D. (1959), Export Challenges to Leather Industry in India, Indian Journal of Commerce, Vol. XLII (160): 67-69.

Sinha S. and Sinha S. (1991), "Leather Exports an Illusory Boon", Economic and Political Weekly, Vol.26 (35) : M 111-116.

Srinivasan N. R. (1971), "Promoting Implementation of Indian Standards for Footwear and Leather Industries", ISI Bulletin, Vol. 23 (10) : 38-47.

Usha P. (1985) "Mechanization and Labour Utilization Leather Industry in Tamil Nadu". Economic and Political Weekly, 20(4) : 167-171.,

POULTRY FARMING AND EMPLOYMENT OPPORTUNITIES

Dr. A. Annadurai*

India is primarily an agricultural country. About 70 per cent of the country's population seeks employment opportunities from agriculture with a contribution of 26 per cent of Gross Domestic Product (GDP) as compared with advanced countries i.e., in UK only 2 percent; in USA it is 3 per cent.; in Canada it is 4 per cent ; in Australia it is 5 per cent and so on. In terms of area, India ranks seventh in the world, while in terms of population it ranks second. With a total area of 32.87 crore hectares absolute size, India is a big country. At present, the land utilisation figures are available for about 92.7 per cent of the total geographical area, that is for 30.5 core hectares. But , even then, we are not free from the issues.

We, in India, are facing twin persistent issues namely, poverty and unemployment. It is really pathetic condition of our planning process that even after half a century of planned development, almost all the plans have given top priority for solving these issues. Unfortunately, we were not able to solve these issues fully.

The ever growing population is also responsible for this. On account of over-population in agriculture, considerable disguised unemployment exists in this sector. In an underdeveloped economy, not only the per capita income is low but the capital per head is also very little. Due to widespread poverty, most people have virtually no ability to save and whatever accumulation is done, it remains highly concentrated in the hands of people whose values are not conducive to investment in industry or agriculture. Most of the people spend major portion of their income on food and necessities, and thus food grains remain the principal wage good,. Trade and Commerce are generally limited as like credit facilities.

Our country is located with different agro-climatic conditions in nature. Due to the gambling nature of the monsoon, we are not able to receive normal rain in time. The peculiar situation in our country is that there is floods in some areas and heavy drought in other areas.

Another, problem that we are facing today is the impact of WTO which adds fuel to these issues. The rate of job creation has in all probability halved, and after some years of decline the number of job seekers on the live register has increased by more than once. When we look at the picture of unemployment both in the pre and post economic reform periods, the problem of unemployment is on the increase.

When we look at the number of unemployed it has (on CDS basis) declined from 21.61 millions in 1983 to 19.58 millions in 1993-94 but rose to 26.44 millions in 1999-2000. The annual growth rates of unemployed in India for the period, 1983 to 1993-94, has turned out to be -0.62 per cent, while in the same period, 1993-94 to 1999-2000, it was as high as 4.55 per cent.

When we see rural-urban distribution of unemployed in all-India in the year 1983, the number of rural employed was 16.18 millions, which has declined to 14.3 millions in 1993-1994. However, the number of rural employed has increased significantly to 19.31 millions by the year 1999-2000. The growth of rural employed in all-India is estimated to be as high as 5.13 per cent per year during the period, 1993-94 to 1999-00 which is alarmingly high as compared to negative growth rate of unemployed (–1.16 per cent per year) observed during the pre 1993-94 period. As far as share of rural unemployed in the total number of unemployed persons in all-India, in the year 1999-00, nearly 73 per cent of unemployed in all-India have been from rural areas .

The number of unemployed in urban areas has increased tremendously for the last two decades and that the number of urban unemployed in all-India was 5.4 millions in 1983, which has increased to 5.94 millions in 1993-94, and further to 7.12 millions in 199-00. The growth rate of urban unemployed in all India for the period, 1983 to 1993-94, was 0.85 per cent, which has increased to 3.07 per cent durign thc last decade (1993-94 to 1999-2000).

We may also look at the sex-wise distribution of the number of unemployed in all-India. The numbers of both male and female unemplyed in all India declined between 1983 and 1993-94, but increased during the period, 1999-2000. It is also observed that in 1983, of the total employed in all India ,nearly 71 per cent were males, and their share has increased gradually over the years. In the year, 1999-2000, the share of males in total unemployed was found nearly 74 percent. The growth rates of males and females unemployed both of these were negative durign the period, 1983-11993-94, but turned out to be quiet high and positive during 1993-94 to 1999-2000. During the period, 1993-94 to 1999-2000, the growth rate of male unemployed in all-India is estimated to be 4.96 per cent per year and it is the same for female unemployed (3.46 per cent).

The foregoing facts and figures clearly show that the employment opportunities for the people are scarce and facing unemployment crisis are growing pre and post economic reforms that too in pre economic reforms period growth rate so high either rural or urban. Therefore, We in India are forced to find out the employment opportunity for our survival. This is right time to search for employment opportunities with the available resources and with less investment.

The reasons put forth above justify that poultry farming business is the right type of venture suited to our people.

Poultry Farming has transformed itself from a backward activity into an organised, sophisticated and medium scale industry. The productivity of layers and broilers has improved to be on par with developed countries. India has 12 pure-line research and breeding farms with over 300 hatcheries.

India is the 5th largest egg producer in the world and the 22nd largest broiler producer. The sector provides livelihood to 1 lakh farmers and direct and indirect employment to about 1.5 million people. It contributes Rs.7,5000 crore to the national income. With the emergence of the fast growing poultry industry and the consequent enormous demand for high quality layer chicks in large numbers leading to the subsequent emergence of the Hatchery industry with its links abroad with foreign counter parts, the Indian Council of Agricultural research (ICAR) felt that it was the right time to step to act as balancing factor to ensure interrupted supply of the required chick stock to the industry.

Despite the fact that the growth rate of the paultry industry has been much higher than that of other livestock segments, the per capita consumption of eggs 32 and poultry meat 1100 gm in our country is for below the World Health Organisation (WHO), Nutritional Advisory Committee (NAC) and Indian Council Medical Research (ICMRC) recommends 180 eggs and 8 kg poultry meat per person per year. It is estimated that an increase in the per capita consumption by one egg or 50 grams of poultry meat can create employment for about 25,000 people.

The present commercial poultry industry has given risen to a number of supporting industry like feed compounding units, poultry processing equipments and machinery, pharmaceuticals and biological etc. With the emergence of the fast growing poultry industry and the consequent enormous demand for high quality chicks in large number leading to the subsequent emergence of the Hatchery industry with its links abroad with foreign counterparts, the Indian Council of

Agricultural Research (ICAR) felt that it was the right time to step in to act as a balancing factor to ensure uninterrupted supply of the required chick stock to the industry.

While the poultry sharks are largely concentrated in and around urban areas the vast rural scenario remains untouched for smaller operations lived happily. While the urban operators contribute around 60 percent of eggs the rural group can make up remaining 40 per cent. This small scale sector of poultry can generate lot of employment to the educated unemployed and also contribute effectively to the food security system. Appropriate technologies and plans have to be formulated and effective training programmes of pragmatic nature have to be launched quickly without further loss of time. Poultry being a livestock industry, it requires certain infrastructural facilities which can help storage, distribution, marketing and import. The sheer volume in international trade is too large to be ignored. Export prospects of the country's poultry are bright, because most favourable agro- climatic conditions and its manpower cost is the lowest in the world. The proximity to major world markets like West Asia and Far East. The Gulf countries, Bangladesh, Maldives and the Philippines are potential importers. There is a wide scope to explore newer markets in South-East Asia and Japan .

The current poultry revolution is bound to maintain its growth rate . With low requirement of land, relatively low capita requirements, simplicity of operations and fast returns and poultry sector can create contribute significantly to the solutions of unemployment in the country.

This is a golden opportunity to act quickly and make the best use of this powerful tool, Solving unemployment problem, elimination of poverty and protein hunger from rural; masses by spreading germaplasm of these poultry stocks for adverse environments on a wide scale.

SELECTED READINGS

1. Krishna Rao, "Dynamics of the Poultry Industry in India" *Poultry line.*
2. Satya Sundram. I, "Poultry. Pressure on Profits " *Facts for you* July 2003 p.13 & 14.
3. Krishnaswamy. V," High Costs put Poultry Farmers in the Soup" Alive August 2003 P.81 & 82
4. Panda. A. K. Et. all, "rural Poultry Production -A key approach to Alleviate Protein Hunger from India" *Poultry Line* June 2002 p.24-26.
5. Bhaummik. S. K., "Unemployment in India in the Post Liberalisation Era" *The Indian Journal of Labour Economics* Vol: 46, No.1 Pp 72 & 73.

TOURISM INDUSTRY — NEW VISTAS FOR EMPLOYMENT

Dr. (Mrs.) B. Shyamala
Prof. & Head of Dept. Of Economics
Fatima College, Madurai -18 Tamil Nadu

Recognising the right to work of every citizen the main thrust of the new Government will be 'Berozgaari Hatao' (eradicate unemployment). As against the present trend of jobless growth we will measure growth by generation of gainful employment. Jobless growth is socially unacceptable. We have to create a 10 million jobs a year and aim at every family having at least one of its members in regular employment. The trend is clear that the relative share of primary and secondary sector to GDP has been declined and is hovering around 26.8% and 22% in 1998-99. Services sector however continued to contribute increasingly to the GDP which was about 41% in 1980-81 and it increased to 51% in 1998-99.

Services comprise economic activities like transport, trade, tourism, communication, banking and insurance, real estate, education and public administration. To this can now be added newer activities like software development and other activities related to information technology. In the next 10 years the number of unemployed persons is going to rise at an explosive peace. So from where can new jobs come? The answer is services sector.

There is a phenomenal rise of the services sector in India in the share of employment. There is a noticeable shift in the sectorial share of employment. Certain sub sectors within the services sector are growing even faster. Tourism industry has got a shot in the arm from 1998 budget. Coupled with the improving scenario of transport and communication set in motion by the economic reforms, there is a positive opportunity for growth. The employment generation potentiality of tourism industry is much more than that of other industries in the services sector. Therefore tourism can fit in ideally for an area with unemployed and unsophisticated population.

The general objective of this paper is to discuss the performance of services sector in contrast with primary and secondary sectors in generating employment. The specific objective of this paper is to study the employment aspect of Tourism industry in India. It would be worthwhile to discuss the magnitude of employment and the nature of employment created in this industry.

EMPLOYMENT IN SERVICES SECTOR

The decline in the share of agriculture in GDP and increase in the share of services is the same. India appears to be shifting directly from an agricultural economy to one dominated by services of about 18.6 million additional jobs generated during post reform period 1992-93 to 1995-96 nearly half (9.03 million) has been in agriculture. The manufacturing sector comes third in employment generation (3 million) next to services.

This is clearly given in the Table - 1

Table 1

Sectorwise Employment In Organised Sector

(In Percent)

	Public Sector					Private Sectors				
Sectors	1976	1986	1991	1994	1998	1976	1986	1991	1994	1998
Agriculture	2.69	2.97	2.92	2.80	2.65	12.08	11.5	11.61	11.14	10.22
Industry	25.22	26.84	25.74	25.22	25.87	64.56	63.32	61.14	60.80	58.32
Services	72.08	70.19	71.35	71.98	71.48	23.36	25.55	27.25	28.06	31.46
Total	100	100	100	100	100	100	100	100	100	100

Source : Centre for Monitoring Indian Economy, India's Social Sector.

EMPLOYMENT IN TOURISM INDUSTRY

The most significant features of the tourism industry is its contribution to employment generation. Taking all segments together, in the tourism sector the ratio is 47.5 jobs which is still higher than other industries. Besides the time lag between investments in this sector and the actual generation of job is minimal. Nearly 3 per cent of the total population in India is employed in this industry. Tourism generated employment may be classified under three heads – (1) Direct employment in business that sell goods and services directly to the tourist e.g. hotels restaurants, shops etc. (2) Indirect employment stimulated by tourist expenditure in activities that supply goods, services to the tourism business and (3) Investment related employment in construction and other capital goods-industries.

There are many limitation in studying the effects of employment generation in the tourism industry. The lack of coherent statistical apparatus remains serious obstacle to proper evaluation of tourism employment creation effect. Employment statistics usually consider only employees and omit those working as employers or self-employed. Moreover the seasonal nature of tourist activity leads to fluctuations in the numbers employed.

There are many studies related to labour intensiveness and its measurement in tourism industry.

— The labour intensiveness of tourism industry could be better appreciated if one considers the employment–capital ratio in tourism industry. The job creation can be estimated as 4.35 per $ 10,000 expenditure in tourist industries compared with 1.90 per $10,000 generally. Though this applies to the U.K. the same situation would be very much true in India.

— The degree of labour intensity of tourism can also be measured in terms of employment./output ratio, i.e. the number of workers employed divided by the contribution of tourism to N. I.

— According to one estimate an investment of Rs.10 lakhs creates 89 jobs in the hotel and restaurant sector, key component of tourism as against 44.7 jobs in agriculture and 12.6 in manufacturing industries.

The British Tourist Authority has shown that the employment attributable to tourist spending increases employment. The employment attributable to tourist spending the U. K. was estimated at 1.5 million in 1982 both direct and indirect employment.

From the above studies it is arrived at the conclusion that substantial employment is generated by tourism in both developed and developing countries and the cost of job creation in tourism industry is less than the traditional industrial sector.

The data set out in the table II indicates clearly the Government expenditure on tourism, tourist arrival, foreign exchange earning and the number of employment created during the period 1951-2002 covering all the Five Year Plans. The data for Nineth plan is only an estimated value. Table III gives an idea about the seasonal arrival of foreign tourist in India.

Table - 2

A profile of Indian Tourism 1951-2002

Five year Plans	No. of Employ ment generated (in Million)	Foreign Exchange Earning (Rs. in Crore)	Govt. Expen-diture on Tourism (Rs. in Crore)	No. of tourist arrival (in Million)
First Plan	0.50 (0.82)	7.7 (0.07)	*	1.01 (3.56)
Second Plan	0.62 (1.02)	40.3 (0.37)	0.12 (0.007)	1.28 (4.53)
Third Plan	0.93 (1.53)	76.4 (0.69)	0.68 (0.05)	2.61 (9.21)
Fourth Plan	1.20 (1.97)	115.6 (1.06)	3.75 (0.25)	2.85 (11.12)
Fifth Plan	2.00 (3.28)	129.0 (11.18)	59.10 (3.93)	3.15 (11.11)
Sixth Plan	10.02 (16.44)	328.3 (2.99)	120.42 (8.01)	3.30 (11.64)
Seventh Plan	12.44 (20.41)	1978.2 (18.06)	140.89 (9.38)	4.24 (14.96)
Eighth Plan	15.81 (25.94)	3275.4 (29.19)	187.58 (12.62)	4.80 (16.94)
Ninth Plan**	17.42 (28.59)	5000.6 (45.66)	990.00 (65.88)	5.10 (17.99)
Total	**60.94** **(100)**	**10951.5** **(100)**	**1502.54** **(100)**	**28.34** **(100)**

** Estimated Value. No allocation in the First plan.

Source : Department of Tourism.

Figures in Paranthesis indicate percentage to total

Table 3

Quarterly Indices of Seasonality In Foreign tourist Arrival

Quarter	Index
January — March	107.8
April — June	77.8
July — September	96.0
October — December	118.4

Source : Department of Tourism

From this Table-3 it observed that seasonality may however contribute to fluctuations in the levels of local and regional employment.

An Attempt has been made in present study to examine the association between employment and Government expenditure on tourism, employment and the number of tourist arrival and employment and foreign exchange earnings. The correlation co-efficients are 0.7307, 0.8926 and 0.9019 respectively and are statistically significant at 5 percent level. This correlation analysis reveals that increasing trends in employment, tourists arrival, Public expenditure on tourism and foreign exchange earnings are positively associated. But a one to one correlation is not observed. Even this increase in employment over the years under study can not exclusively be attributed to the above mentioned variables because employment in this industry is a function of interaction of many factors in country such as power, telecommunications, information technology, transport, financial services, fiscal policy, tourism planning and tourism marketing.

POLICY IMPLICATIONS

It is estimated that by 2010 tourism can provide Indian economy substantial resources even by very marginal progress. Tourism in India will contribute another Rs. 5,000,00 Cr. to the G. D. P. , will create 8 million new jobs, will give rise to Rs.1,30,000 Cr. in capital investment and tourism will earn Rs.,1,60,000 crore in export earnings. For this to happen the country has to take pragmatic steps, most of which are well known. It can be listed in five categories. First tourism as a national priority. Second Liberalised economy open and competetive markets. Third, pursuing a policy of sustainable development. Fourth, removal of fundamental barriers to growth – incentives for infrastructure growth, rationalise taxes, remove disincentives. Fifth, professionalise human resource development.

While these trends suggest a rosy picture, tourism scene is also shadowed by seemingly endemic snags for which policies are suggested (1) Research is a pre-condition for planning in tourism and planning has to be done both at Central and State level. (2) There is a fierce competition in tourist generating markets from several nations for attracting a large share of traffic to their countries. It is therefore necessary for India to strengthen her promotional and marketing efforts continuously even to maintain its existing market share.

(3) For years, India was projected as a land of monuments, ancient temples, holiday ghats and varied culture. It is time to redesign many of our tourism packages and explore new areas. Adventure tourism is one of tourism package which can infuse new blood in the industry.

(4) Provision has been made in the New Tourism Policy for exempting all recognised tourism units from trade tax, entertainment tax, luxury tax for five years from the date of commencement. This provisions should be continued and the governments to come also should patronize this policy.

(5) Development of tourism should not be treated as the responsibility of Tourism Department alone. All other tourism related departments like Forest, Environment, Rural Development. Horticulture, Soil Conservation, etc. should also

contribute to its growth.

(6) Health is closely connected with travel and tourism. We have a system of Medicine which is closer to the nature. India with its long range of forests which are full of Medicinal herbs and mountain regions with stones of medicinal value is a ideal place for every tourist to become a part of the nature and rejuvenate mind and body.

CONCLUSION

On the threshold of a new millennium, the country is poised for a major breakthrough in infrastructural development. The growing spread of its power and telecommunications network is bringing its vast regions closer. The time is thus ripe for bringing its vast regions closer. The time is thus ripe for simultaneously giving a powerful thrust to tourism as well so that tourism industry can contribute through poverty alleviation and employment generation.

REFERENCES

Bhardwaj. D. S. and Manjula Chaudhary (1997) "Contemporary Issues in Tourism"

—Himalaya Publishing House

Bhatia. S. M. (1995) "Tourism marketing–Himalaya Publishing House".

—Sterling Publishers Limited.

Jha. A. K. (1991) "International Tourism –Fundamentals and Practices".

—Sterling Publishers Limited.

Kaul. R. N. (1992) The Dynamics of Tourism – (Three Volumes in one)

—Sterling Publishers Pvt. Ltd.

Kunal Chattopadhyay. (1995) Economic Impact of Tourism Development —An Indian Experience–

— Knishka Publishers Distributors. New Delhi.

Percy K. Singh (1998) Fifty years of Indian Tourism
— Kanishka Publishers Distributors. New Delhi.

Pran Nath Seth (1997) Successful Tourism Management.
— Fundamentals of Tourism vol. 1
—Sterling Publishers Private Limited.

Pushpinder S. Gill (1997) Tourism Economic and Social Development
—Anmol Publications Private Limited, New Delhi.

Sinha. P.C. (1998) Tourism : Issues and Strategies
—Anmol Publications Pvt. Ltd., New Delhi.

Tewari. S. P. (1994) Tourism Dimensions – Atma Ram & Sons, Kashmere Gate, New Delhi.

EMPLOYMENT GENERATION IN RURAL INDUSTRIES

Dr. Aroma G Sam.
Dean, Professor and Head,
Department of Social Sciences,
Tamil University, Thanjavur.

Rural systems rely on the balance of a set of values, many of which are not productive in the formal economic sense. In such a system of agriculture, agro based industries play an integral part, together with perhaps equally important elements like group acceptance, social interchanges and inactive leisure. Gunner Myrdal (1956) in his Asian Drama, has broadly supported Gandhiji's emphasis on village and cottage industries. He has observed that the development of industries would take work and tread away from millions with no immediate alternative source of employment or income. Again Gunner Myrdal (1956) has stated Industrialization and the growth of that part of the working population that is engaged in industry, is therefore a means of raising National Percapita. This paper makes an attempt to analyze the generation of employment by the Rural Industries in the central region of Tamil Nadu.

The composite Thanjavur district Now trifurcated as Thiruvarur, Nagapattinam, & Thanajvur districts in the granary of Tamilnadu. Dependence on agriculture has made it to be a backward district. Industrial development of district has been neglected to back seat. Agriculture is the main occupation of the region and rice is the staple food of the people. Paddy, pulses, soyabean tobacco, cotton, sugarcane, oil palm are main pursuits of the people besides fish farming and prawn culture. The trifurcated districts bear and inherit the same features and problems of erstwhile Thanjavur. Diminishing rainfall coupled with problems in sharing Cauvery Water between the states of Karnataka and Tamil Nadu for the last few years has suddenly woke up to the fact that the district miserably lagged behind in industrialization. Necessity has turned the attention of the people and administrators to look out for the possibilities of rapid industrialization. The clamour for exploring new venues for industrialization is vividly seen in the rural parts of the districts.

Data collected through an empirical study of undivided Thanjavur district by surveying 300 cottage and tiny rural industries is considered here for analysis and discussion. The surveyed industries are from eight selected backward Taluks of Thanajvur. They are the representative areas and rural industries specified. The 36 categories of rural industries functioning in the study area are classified into four groups (Table No.) 1 based on the products they produce. It is done for the practical purpose of conducting a survey and for analytical process. Only those industrial units located and functioning in rural areas are taken into consideration for the survey. Owner or Entrepreneur who holds the responsibility of running the unit and who bears the risks is interviewed personally with a questionnaire and their responses recorded.

Table No. 1 Rural Industrial Units

S. No.	Food Products Units	Agro Based	Metal & Chemical Units	Other
1.	Fruit Processing	Mat	Dobi-washing and Cleaning	Shoe Making Repairing
2.	Applam Product	Coir	Jewellery	Paper Flower Making
3.	Oil Grinding	Coconut Palmleaf	Soap Making	Tailoring
4.	Ice Cream	Honey	Candle Making	Rexin Product
5.	Backery	Cane Products	Perfumed stick Making	Photo Frame Making

6.	Pickle Products	Sandal Garland Making	Plumbing	Ink Pad.
7.	Masala Power	Pottery	Block Making	

Source : Compiled from Collected Data

Rural Industries are employment oriented. Apart from providing employment they also require less capital. With limited funds, such industries provide minimum employment, use local raw materials and cater to the needs of local market. The whole work and functioning of industry can also be carried out with available building. The members of the family can join together and do the work. As such, like agricultural this rural industrial work is done by all the members of the family. Therefore it provides employment to many people. The following Table No. 2 indicates the number of persons employed in different rural industries in the present study.

Table No.2

Generation of Employment by Rural Industries

S. No.	Number Employed	Number of Industries	Percentage
1	1	125	38.7
2	2	132	44
3	3	32	10.7
4	4	11	3.6
	Total	**300**	**100**

Source : Compiled from Collected Data.

Table No.3
Employment Potential of the Surveyed Rural Industries

S. No.	Category	Number of Labours Employed		Total	Percentage
		Men	Women		
1	Food Product	94	26	120	21.58
2	Agro Product	81	59	140	25.18
3	Metal and Chemical	180	41	121	39.75
4	Products Other Products	54	41	75	13.49
	Total	**409**	**148**	**556**	**100.00**

Source : Compiled from Collected Data

The Table No.3 clearly highlights the employment opportunities generated by the rural industrial units under study. It is clear that, number of men labourers employed in the rural industrial units have been found to be comparatively more than the women labourers absorbed. It has been observed that due to the nature of activities performed by the rural industries the number of labourers employed by the metal and chemical products happened to be more when compared to the other surveyed rural industrial units. the analysis also vividly states that, the rural industries have a large employment potential. The various rural industries taken for the study provide different levels of employment to the rural people. There are 116 works in which only one person is employed and 44 percent of the industries two persons are employed. / this shows that in Majority of the rural industries even though the work needs only one person, more than one person is employed, that is in 62 percent of the industries employment of labour is two and more than two. This clearly proves the employment oriented nature of rural industries.

Labour intensiveness of rural industries help the rural people to get employment in times of seasonal unemployment. Rural people are more attached to their houses and native villages and may hesitate to migrate to urban places. In such a situation transfer of labour from agriculture to other allied activities becomes a difficult task. If the chances of industrial employment is available in their villages itself, they will readily take up the job. This transfer will help in the effective utilization of available labour power in the country and increases productivity.

Rural industrial workers do not have any fixed time period of work. If they want to finish the work within a stipulated time period, then they do not consider the time of work. At the time of availability of raw material only they can do some work. So at such situations they work for long hours. Sometimes they have to even stop their work due to non-availability of raw material. This results in variation of working time within the industry and also between industries. The hours of work in different industrial units is given in Table No.4.

Table No. 4

Hourly working Time in Different Industries

S.No.	Working Hours	No. of Units	Percentage
1.	1-3	16	5.33
2.	4-6	57	19.00
3.	7-9	80	26.66
4.	10-22	147	49.00
	Total	**300**	**100.0**

Source Compiled from Collected Data.

Working time in different industrial units ranges between one and 12 hours. There are 147 units which work for 10 to 12 hours a day. This number is 49 percent of the total which shows that nearly half of the industrial units taken for the study work for 10 to 12 hours. Only in 24 percent the industries working hours happens to be less than 8 hours a day. When the workers work for more hours their leisure time is reduced and their power is utilized for productive purpose. The working time is less than 8 hours in some of the units because, these people take up the work on a part time basis. After all agricultural activities they do such work in the rest time to add to the family income. Since people in the agriculture sector share the work in land, they find time to carry out such allied activities. This in fact solve the problem of disguised unemployment and increases the earnings of the rural family.

Rural industrial units, even though they are too small and tiny, they generate employment opportunities in the villages where seasonal and disguised unemployment exist along with educated unemployment. Among the 300 rural industrial units studied 39 per cent of them are self employed units. Table No.3 shows that women are less attracted to the labour force in rural industries than men. Nearly 40 percent of the rural industrial labour are found in Metal and Chemical products units. Employment generated in food products units 22 percent, agro-products units 25 percent and 14 percent in other product units indicate the wide choices of employment opportunities in rural industrial sector. The working time schedule analysis of the rural industries reveal that they are not following stipulated working hours as they have to depend on agro-cultural raw material availability whcih is irregular and seasonal which again depend on monsoon and other agricultural inputs and constrains. The informal working time schedules help the surplus agricultural labour, the disguised unemployed and educated unemployed to be gainfully employed in rural industrial units and augment their income.

The policies of globalization liberalization and privatization since the 1990's and the consequent copy rights, properly rights and the pros and cons of the whole thing are still an academic and urban subject. It has not reached yet to the common knowledge of rural mass especially to be surprised, the rural entrepreneurs are not aware of the implications of this policy in the long run. None of the surveyed entrepreneurs of the rural industrial units entertained interest on them. They are aware of their poverty, and poor working and living condition and understand the great gulf that exist between themselves and follow humen in the urban and industrial region and elsewhere. They are reconciled to their lot and their conscience has been stirred to a certain extent only to the mounting government programmes of technical and financial help and advice.

WOMEN ENTREPRENEURSHIP IN TRADITIONAL AND MODERN MICRO ENTERPRISES

Dr. N. Manikekalai,
Reader,Dept. of Economics,
Bharathidasan University,
Tiruchirapalli

INTRODUCTION

Development of entrepreneurial skill among women is essential for the economic growth of a country. Entrepreneurs initiate, increase and sustain the process of economic development. The need for a broad based entrepreneurial class in India arises from the need to speed up the process of achieving the factors of production, leading to a higher rate of economic growth, dispersal of economic activities, development of backward and tribal areas, creation of employment opportunities, improvement in the standard of living of the weaker section etc. Women entrepreneurs are making significant impact in all segments of the economy which may empower the women and facilitate them to involve in decision making.

It is quite common to find women in labour occupation, professions like teaching, nursing etc. Women as Managers, as Executives or Entrepreneurs are very rare to see. As per the 1991 census, roughly 48 percent of the population is women. Of these, only 34% of them could participate in economic activities, in which more than 96% are in the unorganised sectors. The majority of them are self-employed in agricultural and allied activities. Hence, woman assuming self-employment in micro enterprise activity has been common from the traditional period but they have been remaining in such scale of operation permanently. This trend needs to be changed. It is observed by a study that there were 2,95,680 women entrepreneurs during 1995-96, which was 11.2 per cent of 2.64 million entrepreneurs in total. During the eighth plan, the number of SSIs were expected to rise from 1.7 million to 2.5 million adding 0.8 million in five year period. Among the total entrepreneurs, approximately 9% were women entrepreneurs. About 70% of the women entrepreneurs are still in traditional business, garment, food, leather , interior decoration, handicrafts, etc.

The factors which motivates or pushes a woman to entrepreneurship may be unemployment, untimely death of father or husband, desire driven by poverty/social injustice, NGO's encouragement, government's concessions, subsidies, use of traditional skill acquired, special training, previous experience etc. But these women whether pulled or pushed to assume such enterprises, remain micro in their scale of operation. They are micro entrepreneurs and the problems faced by them may include:

- Timely securing of funds,
- to keep a fine balance between the two roles which may otherwise leads to role conflict.
- Limited marketing, dependence on local customers, who do not have steady income
- Extending credit business, bad debt, hampering their growth.
- Lack of quality consciousness and economic use of inputs making the informal sector to be less competent with formal sector.
- Mostly self-employment ventures and handicapped by single person's show and unable to expand.
- Lack of systematic approach, planning, all contribute negatively to the growth of the enterprises.

Despite these problems the growth rate of women-owned

business in small and medium industries in countries like Japan, U. K., U.S.A, Germany, China, Korea and France, which is growing more than 40%, is maintained. However, in India it is only 7%, though Tamil Nadu is faring better than other states with 18%, in a way it stands in the first place in the country.

As V. G. Patel rightly observed that in a tough competitive market, it makes no difference whether the entrepreneur is a man or a woman, and as such women need not be given special incentives. But whether it is to be treated as a welfare measure for the underprivileged. As already mentioned, the women once assume entrepreneurial role, they behave like a typical entrepreneur and it does not make any difference in terms, skill, intelligence, capability.

RELATED STUDIES :

Studies suggest that it is more difficult for women to start and be in business due to [a] lack of previous opportunity to develop business skills; [b] expectations about entrepreneurship and women that influence the granting of business credit and [c] domestic responsibilities that make them feel a conflict of roles. It is thus concluded that female entrepreneurs want freedom to combine responsibilities for the family with a fair income i.e. they express need for flexibility that has not been found among male entrepreneurs. Nina Gunnerud Berg [1997], Glady L. Symons [1990], Hisrich and Brush [1983], Lavoid [1987], Watkins and watkins [1984], Gopffee and Scare [1985], Susan Marlow [1997] on the continuous existence of women in business suggest that it is more difficult for women to start and be in business, first due to lack of previous opportunity to develop business skills, second, expectations about entrepreneurship and women that influence the granting of business credit and third, domestic responsibilities that make them feel conflict of roles. It is thus concluded that female entrepreneurs want freedom to combine responsibility for family with a fair income i.e. they express a need for flexibility that has not been found among the male entrepreneurs.

Forje Lema Catherine [1998] observed that the women, running micro enterprises face long hours with low returns, often accumulate debts. In spite of their low returns, women's businesses are critical to the survival of their households through the current economic crisis, and as such are important for the national economy.

While analyzing the size determinants of women owned businesses, Nancy M. Carter and Katheleen R. Allen [1997] found that having capital to grow and expand the business operations through commercial business, loans and private sources in addition to a personal bank relationship and a focus on profit and growth, contributes significantly to the size of women owned businesses. The result suggested that support for the availability of financial resources is a major influence on attaining large size, overwhelming the effect of the entrepreneur's life style choice or intension. It suggests that women entrepreneurs must place more emphasis on financial aspect of the business and on building banking relationship. Helping women to gain access to bankers and others sources would increase the size of business.

Studies of N. P. Singh et. al [1986] of Delhi Women Entrepreneurs, Kohli Chandra [1987] of the beneficiaries of National Alliance of Young Entrepreneurs [NAYE] in Delhi, Kamala Singh [1992] of Haryana Women Entrepreneurs, Shah [1995] reveal certain diverse characteristics of women entrepreneurs in India.

It is found from these studies, which have been done in metros and others urban areas, that the women entrepreneurs are from business and non-business background, engage in both traditional and modern fields. Unlike the general belief that women entrepreneurs choose only to feminine nature of products, these studies revealed that they are found in manufacturing, trade and service industries of both feminine and non-feminine nature of products. Women entrepreneurs did not face any financial problems, and the domain of women entrepreneurs includes women with and without formal training. There is absolutely no role conflict with enterprise and family and women are much concerned with expansion, diversification and modernization.

H. S. Anitha and A. S. Laxmisha [1999] in their study observed that entrepreneurs are motivated by both pull and push factors, and evidenced that entrepreneurs are no longer born but they can be made. They suggested that in government and non-government organizations have to play a vital role.

K. Chidambaram and Thenmozhi. G [1998] analysed the various constraints faced by women entrepreneurs including social-psycho constraints, personal, economic, support system constraints and called for effective steps to mitigate the constraints.

Meera Bal [1998], observed that the community initiatives have been taking the issues of women in business seriously for the past ten years. She underlined that female entrepreneurs need psychological support designed to reinforce entrepreneurial spirit among women, technical assistance in the development of a business project, marketing support and guidance through the development phase, would improve the entrepreneurial base in the region.

A study on rural entrepreneurship in Bangladesh villages by David J. Lewis [1996] has identified the nature of rural entrepreneurship in the light of green revolution and argues that the processes of technological change under privatisation and structural adjustment have created new opportunities leading to the creation of new forms of technology-based enterprise in rural areas.

N. Manimekalai [1999] suggested that by conducting conferences by bringing entrepreneurs and bankers together, developing political skill and awareness, support networks to voice women entrepreneurs, assistance from male experienced entrepreneurs etc. women entrepreneurial base may be enhanced.

N. Manimekalai & G. Rajeswari [2000] observed that in Tiruchirapalli, women entrepreneurs are found in risk taking industrial activities requiring modern techniques of production. These entrepreneurs faced the problems of dual responsibility, but they were above to manage by delegating their responsibilities and duties without any detriment to the normal chore. The problems faced include, shortage of capital, lack of seed capital and the dependence of informal sources of credit, and lack of initiative to expand their scale of operations due to financial constraints.

Manimekalai and Ganesan on global women entrepreneurs [2001] found that women entrepreneurs who are emerging as a force in recent times, associate through net working which must be encouraged and supported both by government and family. It is observed that age is not a barrier to venture into business, for women. Majority of the women in the global context hailed form urban region, well educated technically and professionally. The motivational factors differed considerably between developed and developing countries, as it is more of non-economic factors for the former and economic factors for the latter.

Although women have entered every sphere, there are some which can have more success in the hands of women. Among these are beauty, fashion, clothes, accessories, catering, health and fitness centres, health resorts, restaurants and so on. But there is ever-widening scope and never ending opportunities. This study has attempted to analyse the nature and characteristics of women entrepreneurs in urban micro enterprises. It was further probed to make an analysis of the women micro entrepreneurs in a most traditional activity such as 'tailoring' and the most modern activity such as 'beauty clinics'.

OBJECTIVES

[i] To find out the socio-economic profile the sample women entrepreneurs in a traditional and modern micro enterprise activity in Tiruchirpalli district.

[ii] To identify the factors, performance and problems faced by women entrepreneurs in such enterprises and make recommendations to overcome the problems.

METHODOLOGY

For the purpose of the study, a census survey on women micro enterprises was conducted in Tiruchirapalli district of Tamilnadu. Since tailoring and beauty clinics were purposively selected as traditional and modern entrepreneurial activities respectively, all the units run by the women in the above two lines were completely enumerated. Accordingly a total of 230 and 93 units respectively were identified. Of these a sample of roughly around 20% of the units were chosen, at random, covering 45 tailoring and 18 beauty clinic units. Some of the units have not responded properly and they had to be eliminated. Primary data needed were collected from the entrepreneurs on the aspects of socio-economic profile, factors motivated and discouraged, nature of assistance, training availed, performance since the start up to the present, problems faced in business and family etc. Secondary data were collected from the offices such as District Industries Centre, District Rural Development Agency, Lead Bank, NABARD etc.

In this study, women entrepreneur is defined as a person who initiates, organises and conducts a business enterprise for profit. It may be a self-employed unit employing only the self or hire additional labourers.

Micro enterprise is defined in this study as those units which have investment in their plant and machinery or for their business ranging from Rs.10000 to Rs. 1 lakh. The entrepreneurs who run such enterprises are called as micro entrepreneurs.

Traditional activity in this study refers to the activity which have been assumed by women either as commercial activity or for self-use, from the traditional period. Modern activity refers to the activity which has recently been assumed by women as commercial activity.

SOCIO-ECONOMIC PROFILE OF THE SAMPLE ENTERPRISES:

In order to find out the characteristics of women who increasingly assume traditional and non-traditional activities, their Socio-economic background has been studied. In order to find out as to who does well, whether women running traditional or non-traditional activities, their performance analysis has been done.

SOCIO-ECONOMIC PROFILE:

Marital status of the women entrepreneurs indicated that majority of the women [95%] are married. Actually there is no change in the unmarried categories but some of the married became destitute either widowed or divorced. Such destitute status must have forced them to assume entrepreneurship.

Table 4.1

Educational Status of the Sample Women Entrepreneurs

Education	Tailoring	Beauty clinic	Total	Percentage
Illiterate	1	-	1	1.6
Primary	1	-	1	1.6
Middle	5	-	5	7.9
High School	24	3	27	42.9
Higher Secondary	6	5	11	17.5
Under Graduate	3	6	9	14.3
Post Graduate	5	3	8	12.7
Technical and Diploma	-	1	1	1.6
Total	45	18	63	100

The educational details of the sample women entrepreneurs explain that only one is an illiterate. Another 10% have only primary education. Of all the groups, majority had high school education. Only less than one fourth them have crossed graduation. The educational details indicates that the majority of the sample entrepreneurs were not able to go for higher education but still were able to become entrepreneurs. This further indicates that education is not determining factor but only a facilitative factor.

Table 4.2

Nativity of the Sample women Entrepreneurs

Location	Tailoring	Beauty clinic	Total	Percentage
With in the District	29	12	41	65.1
Other District	12	4	16	25.4
Other State	2	1	3	4.8
Other Country	2	1	3	4.8
Total	45	18	63	100

Table 4.2 brings out the details of nativity of the sample entrepreneurs.

Nearly two-third of them are from the same district and others are either from other district or state or country. The other country's entrepreneurs are mainly from Sri Lanka as refugees. It is true that the entrepreneurs who are from the same district may have a better networking compared to women who hailed from others districts or country. Studies have shown that the native entrepreneurs could perform better than non-native entrepreneurs due to better contract and networking in their native.

Table 4.3

Region of the Origin of the Sample Women Entrepreneurs

Location	Tailoring	Beauty clinic	Total	Percentage
Rural	15	6	21	33.3
Semi Urban	5	1	6	9.5
Urban	25	11	36	57.2
Total	45	18	63	100

The region of origin as to whether they are from rural or urban area has been analysed. It is observed that majority of the women originated from urban and nearly one-third of them were from rural areas. Their urban background and urban contacts have enabled these women to initiate and enterprise on their own.

Table 4.4

Community Background of the Sample women Entrepreneurs

Caste	Tailoring	Beauty clinic	Total	Percentage
OC	1	-	1	1.6
BC	40	14	54	85.7
MBC	2	4	6	9.5
SC/ST	2	-	2	3.2
Total	45	18	63	100

Religion wise information of the sample entrepreneurs revealed that nearly three-fourth of them belong to Hindus and the remaining are distributed between Christians and Muslims. This distribution is in line with the distribution of the population in this area.

Community background of the sample entrepreneurs has been enquired into, as the community plays a very important role in determining one's entry into business. It is true that the entrepreneurship has been observed among the vsyays who belong to economically and socially forward communities. Some new communities are emerging among the backward communities also, which is reflected in this study also. It is particularly true with the micro or very small scale of operation wherein the traditionally dominant business communities may not be represented much but the newly emerging communities tend to be represented more. In this study as high as 85% belongs backward community. Only a marginal percentage of them belongs to either Most Backward Community or Scheduled Caste and Scheduled tribe.

It is hypothesized generally that the women entrepreneurs with joint or extended families tend to concentrate more on business, as there are elders to take care of the family. On the other hand, the nuclear family may not be able to contribute positively in reducing the double burden of women so also in business performance. It is observed in this study that roughly 70% of the sample respondents are found in joint families and therefore able to enter into business and relieved from the double burden to certain extent. This was the case at the time of start up. The nature of family at present shows a slight change moving towards the joint families from 69% to 73% at present.

The average size of the family has been 4, which tells that the size of the family is well under control. Roughly 40 per cent of them have more than four members in their families, which may be joint families. The large size of the family also limits the contribution of the entrepreneurs to business to a great extent, as these women need to devote most of their time on household activities. Activity-wise, beauty clinics have lower size of the family than the tailoring activities.

Table 4.5
Age of the Sample Women Entrepreneurs

Age Group	Tailoring	Beauty clinic	Total	Percentage
Below 20	1	-	1	1.6
20-25	2	4	6	9.5
26-30	6	6	12	19
31-35	25	6	31	49.2
36-40	5	1	6	9.5
Above -40	6	1	7	11.2
Total	45	18	63	100
Average	36.5	32.11	35.25	

The age distribution of the entrepreneurs explains that the average age of entrepreneurs in the traditional activity has been slightly higher [36. yrs] compared to the modern activity of beauty clinic [32.11 yrs]. The overall average age of the sample women has been 35 years. This indicates that the women assume the entrepreneurial activity in the young age. This may be for two reasons. They might have been forced to assume due to poor economic conditions of the family. Another reason may be that these women entrepreneurs must have fulfilled the family requirements of child care and others and therefore, enter into business.

Table 4.6
Previous Experience of Sample Women Entrepreneurs

Experience	Tailoring	Beauty clinic	Total	Percentage
Below 5	8	7	15	23.8
5-10	17	9	26	41.3
11-15	5	1	6	9.5
16-20	7	1	8	12.7
21-25	9	-	6	9.5
26-30	-	-	-	-

Above -30	2	-	2	3.2
Total	45	18	63	100
Average	13.22	7.27	11.52	

Previous experience is one of the determinants of performance of entrepreneurship. It is found in this study that the average experience of the sample women entrepreneurs has been 11 and it is more among tailoring units than among the beauty clinic activities. It is true that the beauty clinic has been one of the recently emerged activities and hence the average experience of the activity has been seven years. Whatever may be the nature of activity, the prior experience has been positively contributing and also responsible for many of the women to assume separate concerns. Many of the sample women have put in equal number of years of service by working with other departments.

FACTORS RESPONSIBLE FOR ENTERING INTO ENTREPRENEURSHIP:

Only a few communities, which are traditionally doing business, may stick on to business for generations. Others are normally entering into this activity by accident or by force. It is found in this study that desire to be independent, to give their children a better life, to earn additional income were the three major factors which were responsible for the sample women to chose to entrepreneurship. All factors are distress factors and a few felt that they had chosen entrepreneurship to secure social prestige, to make themselves busy etc.

Table 4.7

Factors Responsible for becoming Entrepreneurs

Factors	Tailoring		Beauty clinic	
	Score	Rank	Score	Rank
Desire to be independent	190	I	78	I
To Earn More Money	53	VII	33	VI
Inherited Business	57	V	31	VII
More Challenging	16	X	11	IX
Nothing else to do	19	IX	5	XI
To have additional income	139	II	39	III
To secure social prestige	108	IV	37	V
To be able to give children a better life	119	III	47	II
To provide employment to others	37	VIII	25	VIII
To be busily occupied	54	VI	38	IV
To fulfill the ambition of partners	19	IX	8	X

Source : Compiled from primary data

Education and training, availability of time, attractive location, experience in the chosen line, regular order i.e. constant demand were the major motivational factors for the both tailoring and beauty clinics. Other factors as given in the table do contributed favourably to choose to entrepreneurship.

Table 4.8

Motirational Factors Responsible for Becoming Entrepreneurship

Factors	Tailoring		Beauty clinic	
	Score	Rank	Score	Rank
Education and Training Received	315	I	115	I

Friends and relatives in the field	76	VIII	24	IX
Government officials	88	VI	28	VIII
Availability of time	210	II	74	II
Desire to complete with others	16	VIII	9	XIV
To do some thing creative	48	XIII	31	VII
Potential demand for product	54	XII	19	XII
Regular order	95	V	36	III
Location	116	III	38	IV
Parents encouragement	54	XII	4	III
Govt. Incentives and concession	81	VII	24	IX
Personal enthusiasm in the activity & to prove oneself	61	X	22	X
Availability of managerial and Communication skills	28	XV	6	XV
To gain status	57	XI	11	V
Experience in this line	97	IV	29	VI
Less competition	47	XIV	20	XI
Sufficient resources	67	IX	11	XII
High demand for product	24	XVI	4	XIII

More than the encouraging factors, the entrepreneurs are forced normally to assume entrepreneurship either due to lack of employment, loss of husband or father who were looking after the enterprise. Such factors are called push factors, in which the entrepreneurs may really lack the interest and enthusiasm to assume any risk but compelled to remain in business.

Table 4.9

Copmpelling Factors to Choose To Entrepreneurship

Factors	Tailoring		Beauty clinic	
	Score	Rank	Score	Rank
Economic Compulsions	172	II	50	III

Education in the line	222	I	75	I
Expire/Inability of parent/ Husband/ Wife	59	VII	19	VIII
Lot of leisure time	142	III	57	II
Knowledge about the market and techniques of product	100	VI	30	V
Work experience	109	V	23	VII
Unemployment	140	IV	34	IV
Unemployment of Husband/wife	36	X	24	VI
On the job training	55	VIII	15	X
Do not know any other work	52	IX	16	IX
Others	7	XI	2	XI

It is found in this study that, education economic compulsion and lot of leisure time have forced both the group of entrepreneurs, in different order of preference. The other significant factors may include, unemployment, knowledge acquired on the enterprise, previous work experience etc.

BACKGROUND OF THE ENTERPRISES AND THEIR PERFORMANCE:

Table 4.10

Location Of The Sample Enterprises

Location	Tailoring	Beauty clinic	Total	Percentage
Urban	40	15	55	87.3
Semi Urban	5	3	8	12.7
Total	45	18	63	100
Percentage	71.4	28.6	100	

The location of the sample enterprises indicates that majority of the enterprises are in urban area [87.3%] and others were found in semi-urban areas referring to units located beyond the Corporation limit. It is quite true that in urban areas women are increasingly occupying with certain micro economic activity formally in shops or complexes.

Majority of the sample enterprises are proprietary concerns and only less than 5% of them are either partnership or family business concerns. It is very rare to see a woman running a small enterprise or more than this scale. In future this trend should change and women must assume a larger scale of operation and perform equally well like a male entrepreneur.

PERFORMANCE ANALYSIS

The performance has been done taking the investment, working capital requirement, employment, reinvestment, profit, capacity utilisation etc. the contribution of the income to the family by the women entrepreneurs has been taken to measure the level of dependency of the family on the income the sample women enterprises.

Table 4.11a

Investment Of The Sample Enterprises At The Start Up

[in. Rs.]

Size of the Investment	Tailoring	Beauty clinic	Total	Percentage
Below 50000	24	3	27	42.9
50000-1000000	17	7	24	38.1
1000000-150000	3	3	6	9.5
150000-200000	-	3	3	4.8
200000 and above	1	2	3	4.8
Total	45	18	63	100
Average	59717.78	109522.22	73947.62	

Table 4.11b

Investment Of The Sample Enterprises At Present

[in. Rs.]

Size of the Investment	Tailoring	Beauty clinic	Total	Percentage
Below 50000	12	2	14	22.2

50000-1000000	21	6	27	49.9
1000000-150000	7	2	9	14.3
150000-200000	1	5	6	9.5
200000 and above	4	3	7	11.1
Total	45	18	6.3	100
Average	87653.33	140277.78	102688.89	

It is observed that the average size of investment of the sample units has been Rs.73947 and it is little higher for beauty clinics compared to tailoring units. However, more than 40 per cent of the units have investment less than Rs.5000, which indicates how tiny or micro the scale of operation of the sample units are. The current investment size showed a slight increase with respect to both the sample group. As per the current investment size the average investment has increased to 1,02,688 and in fact the beauty clinics have more than this average investment. Another fact noticed is that, the units having less than Rs.50000 have declined from more than 40% to 22%. This implies that the expanding, modernizing etc.

The sample enterprises are mostly self-employed units and the average employment extended has been less than one as most of the sample entrepreneurs did not employ outside labourers.

Table 4.12a

Capacity Utilization of the Sample Enterprises at Start Up

[in. Rs.]

Capacity Utilization (in%)	Tailoring	Beauty clinic	Total	Percentage
Below 20	2	1	3	4.8
20-40	32	10	42	66.7
40-60	9	7	16	52.4
60-80	2	-	2	3.2
Total	45	18	6.3	100
Average	37.89	40.56	38.65	

Table 4.12b

Capacity Utilization of the Sample Enterprises at Present

Capacity Utilization (in%)	Tailoring	Beauty clinic	Total	Percentage
Below 20	2	-	2	3.2
20-40	20	5	25	39.7
40-60	18	8	26	41.3
60-80	5	5	10	15.9
Total	45	18	6.3	100
Average	46.24	55.56	48.91	

Activity-wise the average size of employment, has been very limited as most of the units are self-employed without extending employment to others. Nearly one third of units do not employ others and they are self-employed units providing employment to only self. Others and able to extend employment ranging from two to six, depending the size and nature of activities. Tailoring units are seem to be more labour intensive than beauty clinics. Beauty clinics are capital intensive, as it is observed that they have shown a higher average initial and current investment compared to tailoring units. On the other, the average employment has been higher with tailoring than beauty clinics. Countries like India, which is labour abundant, must encourage more labour intensive than capital intensive units.

Table 4.13a

Profit Of The Sample Enterprises At The Start Up

Profit (in%)	Tailoring	Beauty clinic	Total	Percentage
Below 20	22	-	22	34.9
20-40	22	-	22	34.9
40-60	1	6	7	11.1
60-80	-	12	12	4
Total	45	18	63	100
Average	24.33	65.44	36.08	

Table 4.13b

Profit Of The Sample Enterprises At Present

Profit (in%)	Tailoring	Beauty clinic	Total	Percentage
Below 20	13	5	18	28.6
20-40	17	5	22	34.9
40-60	13	3	16	25.4
60-80	2	1	3	4.8
80 and above	-	4	4	6.3
Total	45	18	63	100
Average	34.73	43.44	37.16	

The capacity utilization of the women enterprises has been 40 per cent on an average in the initial years and it is slightly higher for the beauty clinics in the initial years. When it is taken for the current year there has been an improvement for both the type of units. The improvement is higher with beauty clinics than tailoring units. It implies, on the one hand that [i] more women are going for beauty clinics and on the other [ii] the expansion of modern nature of enterprises is faster than traditional units, given that the competition is the same for both the type of units.

Profit in the initial years has been higher among beauty clinics earning as high as 70 percent whereas it was only less than 25% for the tailoring units. However, in the later stages, the trend has changed such that tailoring units has been making greater profit than the beauty clinics. Perhaps the stiff competition among the latter might have caused lower profit percentage.

Reinvestment of the profit would help in expansion and modernization of the enterprises. It is observed in this study that at the time of start up, the entrepreneurs revisit from 20 to more that 80% of their profit. The beauty clinics are more reinvesting than the tailoring units. Perhaps the commitments to meet the household expenses may be more pressing for tailoring units than beauty clinics. As regards the present condition, it is observed that there is an increase when compared to the previous period both in tailoring and beauty clinic units.

The average income earned has been slightly lower for tailoring units than beauty clinics. The overall average income per month from the enterprises has been Rs. 4923 which indicates the significance of the women's earnings to the household.

As far as the contribution of female income to the family is concerned, it is observed that the sample entrepreneurs family earn on an average Rs.1000. The beauty clinics earn slightly higher family income than tailoring units. It indicates that in terms of both the economic background and the earnings, the modern units in the sample are better placed than the traditional units.

Education wise the distribution of the income indicates that the enterprises owned by the less educated has been lower than the better educated. This is true up to the higher secondary level, as it is found that the average income has been increasing with the levels of education. However, undergraduates have been found to be earning more than post-graduates. Similarly, the technically qualified earns less than non-technically qualified. This implies that entrepreneurship requires certain minimum education but more than that, what is needed is experience not higher education.

Table 4.14

Mean Performance of the Sample Units By The Type Of Activity.

Variables	Tailoring		Beauty clinic		Overall	
	Startup	Present	Startup	Present	Startup	Present
Age [in yrs]	30.71	36.51	26.11	32.11	29.4	35.25

Investment [Rs]	59717.78	87653.33	109522.22	140277.78	73947.62	102688.89
Profit [%]	24.33	23.67	65.44	70.39	36.08	37.02
Reinvestment [%]	34.73	34	43.22	48.28	37.16	38.08
Capacity utilized [%]	37.89	48.24	40.56	55.56	38.65	48.91
Employment [nos.]	2.04	2.69	0.50	0.83	1.60	2.16

With respect to growth of profit, it is observed that there is marginal increase with the overall average but the tailoring units have realised a marginal decline in the percentage of profit earned form 24.73% to 23.67% whereas beauty clinic units are able to perform and show a positive growth.

Regarding the reinvestment of profit, similar trend has been observed with marginal decline in tailoring and slight increase with the modern activity namely beauty clinics.

However, over the period, there has been an increase in the capacity utilisation both in the traditional tailoring and modern beauty clinic activities. This indicates that there is expansion in the activities but the women entrepreneurs due to competition keep low margin of profit, which might have contributed for the decline in the profit margin.

As far as the employment is concerned, as already pointed out, the sample units are mostly self-employed units and therefore, it is quite obvious to find not much growth in employment. Tailoring units during seasons, employ additional labourers and therefore there is a slight increase and the beauty clinics are mostly self-employed and hence the employment numbers are in fractions.

On the whole, it is found that the beauty clinics which are labelled as modern units have done better than the traditional units run by the women in terms of investment, profit, reinvestment of profit, capacity utilisation etc.

PROBLEMS

The problems related to the women entrepreneurs are given

in table 4.28. It is true that entrepreneurs generally face some problems related to finance, marketing, competition etc. it is true in this study also. Apart from the problems faced by male, the female entrepreneurs face additional hurdles. They are more vulnerable than for male enterprises. Lack of exposure, lack of mobility, lack of society's confidence on women, lack of confidence of the self, etc., are the problems, which are specific to the women,. It is these women specific problems, which prevent the entire women community from assuming entrepreneurship.

In addition to the business related problems, the women also face problems in the family as they assume double role as housewives and as business women. Crossing all the boundaries, they successfully start an enterprise but still suffer from the problems of lack of co-operation form husbands and parents, dual role and its associated pressure, lack of time to concentrate on the business and failure or poor performance ultimately.

To sum up, the analysis of the data on the traditional and modern entrepreneurial activities run by the women entrepreneurs in a micro scale revealed that women are still predominantly engage in the activities which are traditionally done by women example being 'tailoring'. Another fact observed is that the women tend to assume remaining nature of activities and they find comfortable in dealing with the activities, which are female centered.

RECOMMENDATIONS :

There is a need to popularize and adopt modern methods to disseminate the information about the technologies and the consultancy facilities available for women entrepreneurs do face women intrepreneurs do face the problems of lack of confidence, lack of support or encouragement from family. If they cross all these stages, the bankers may have creditability problems. Hence the EDPs must address these issues and by way of personal counseling, they have to motivate strongly the enthusiastic women to become successful entrepreneurs.

In selecting the project women take long time as she has to see whether it is suitable or approved and encouraged by he family members, whether it would be viable, profitable etc. ?Similarly, marketing becomes a big problem if she does not read the demand for her goods. All these need to be counseled by the authorities who impart training.

It is also learnt that the women entrepreneurs in the initial stage of starting the enterprise will have credibility problems and hence she has to prove her ability by struggling hard, which of course require lot of courage and determination. Hence women must be very independent and must be from a strong business background also.

Infrastructure is a great hurdle for the women entrepreneurs. Man can move to any distance to establish his unit, but women are constrained to have their units close to home as they have to attend the family. Hence majority of the women failed to start the enterprises mainly due to non-availability of infrastructure or lack of mobility to occupy the infrastructure elsewhere.

Above all, the training institutions must have a follow-up action which should be one of the action plan of the courses as such. Many of EDP trained entrepreneurs whether male or female either remain non-starting or start and give up and only few become successful. Hence the follow-up action addressing the reasons for failure to start must be discussed and necessary action may be taken or it can be recommended to take up such issues in future courses.

It is to be emphasised that it is necessary to improve the performance of existing entrepreneurs; As the motive is to bring more and more new entrepreneurs, very often the existing entrepreneurs are ignored from further counseling on management or marketing etc. Even further development programmes to create awareness on new products, new techniques may be given, to protect them from falling sick or leave the industry etc.

Association of women entrepreneurs must be formed to place their demands and such associations can represent their problems to the state. Also these associations can bring out the case studies of successful women entrepreneurs to motivate the new and existing entrepreneurs.

REFERENCES

1. Anitha H. S. and Laxmisha L. S. [1999], Women Entrepreneurship in India", Southern Economist, Vol.38, June 15,11-13
2. Catherine Lema Forje [1998], "Are Women's Micro Enterprises profitable?, A case study of Cameroon women", Small Enterprise Development, Vol 9, September
3. Carter, Nancy, M [1997], "Size Determinants of Women Owned Businesses: Choice of Barriers to Resources", entrepreneurship and Regional Development, 9,220-21
4. Chidambaram K and Thenmozhi. G. [1998], "Constraints for Women Entrepreneurs", Social Welfare, Vol 45, No.1, April, 28-31,
5. David L. Lewis [1996], "Understanding Rural Entrepreneurship in a Bangladesh Village Individuals–roles or structures" Small Enterprise Development, Vol. 7, No.4
6. Gladys. L. Symons [1990], "women Occupational Carriers in Business, Managers, Entrepreneurs in France and Canada", ed. Nancy J. Alder Dufia N. Izraeli, Women in Management, Annie, Phizacklea.

7. Gunnerrud Berg Nina [1997], "Gender, Race and Entrepreneurship", and Regional Development, 9,209-268

8. Hisrich Robert D. [1998], "The woman Entrepreneur: Implications of family, educational and occupational experience; in John A Hormaday, Jelfry A. Thomans and Karl H. Vesper [ed], " Frontiers of Entrepreneurship Research" Boston College.

9. Manimekalai N [1999], " Nature and Characteristics of Women Entrepreneurs in India", in M. Soundarapandian [ed.], "women Entrepreneurship-issues and strategies", Kaniska Publishers, Distributors, New Delhi.

10. Manimekalai N. & G. Rajeswari [2000], "Nature of Women entrepreneurs in Tiruchirpalli", SEDME, 27[2], June, 69-86

11. Manimekalai N. & Ganesan R., "Global Women Entrepreneurs a Profile: An Analysis", Southern Economist, 40[6], 12-16. July.

12. Marlow, Susan [1997], "Self-employed Women—New Opportunities, Old Challenges", entrepreneurship and Regional Development, 9,1999-210

13. Meera Bal [1998], "Women Entrepreneurs in the European Union", Southern Economist, Aug. 13-14.

14. Patel V. G [1988] "Women Entrepreneurship Development". In Developing New entrepreneurs, EDI, Ahemadabad, Shaitya Mudranlaya Pvt. Ltd.

15. Patel V. G. 11986], "women Entrepreneurship Development, key note address at Fifth national Convention of Women Entrepreneurs, NAYE, Feb. 6-8 Ahmedabad.

16. Shanta Kohli Chandra [1997]," Development of Woment Entrepreneurship", Mittal Publications, New Delhi.

17. Singh, Kamala [1992], "Women Entrepreneurs", Ashish Publishing House, New Delhi.

18. Singh N. P. P, Shegal, Madan Tithani and Rita Sengupta [1986], "Successful woment Entrepreneurs— Their identity, Expectations and Problems", National Institute for Entrepreneurship and Small \Business Development, New Delhi.

19. R. Venkatapathy [2003], "Nurturing Woment Entrepreneurs: Process and Perspectives"., paper presented at Fifth Biennial Conference of Current Trends in Entrepreneurship Research, EDII, ahmedabad 6-8 Jan.

EDUCATED UNEMPLOYED WOMEN IN TAMILNADU

Dr. P. Ambiga Devi,
Prof of Economics,
Avinashilingam University,
Coimbatore-641043

Human beings are active agents who accumulate a capital, exploit natural resources, build social, economic and social organizations and carry out national development. A nation which is unable to develop and utilize its labour forces effectively will be unable to develop anything else. The process of planned economic development aims at giving employment to every one, besides achieving other socio economic goals. Employment is a social, economic, political and ethical necessity. All economic systems amply demonstrate the need and urgency of individuals getting employment according to their qualifications, caliber and resourcements. Unemployment is a notorious social giant, which if persists long, will become a potential danger to political stability. As the United Nations Report (1988) states, words such as 'unemployment' 'part time employment' anxiety' and 'survival' have become common in the life of young people in the current decade. Every 5th person in the world is in the age group 15-24 years but the world is wasting this healthiest and valuable resource. Widespread unemployment and under unemployment is a notable feature of many developing countries of the world. Many people are unemployed or under employed not because they prefer idleness but because there is insufficiency of co operant factors of production to them to work. Unskilled or semi skilled labour is also without work because the supplies of other complementary factors of production are inadequate.

Though creation of employment opportunities has been an important objective of development planning in India, there has been chronic problem of unemployment encircling almost all the organs of the society. The problem of unemployment, even after five decades of planning, still occupies the top most position among all other problems,. The annual growth rate of overall employment in both organized and unorganized sectors) declined continuously from 2.75 percent in 1977-78 to 1.77 percent in 1983-88, but increased to 2.37 percent in 1987-94 (Planning Commission 1997). Government has taken several steps to tackle the problem of unemployment in both rural and urban sectors. Economic survey (1995-96) states, "The government has accorded the highest priority to promoting sustainable, employment intensive growth in the economic reform policies". The basic medium term objective of these policy reforms, initiated in the last decade of the 20th century, was to lay the foundation of a sustained growth of output and employment in the context of increasing global competitiveness of the Indian economy. The figures available on employment showed that the growth of employment picked up to 2.47 percent during 1994-97 (Planning Commission, 1997). The Ninth Five Year Plan has expected the creation of about 54 million additional job opportunities during the plan period and by the end of the plan, the rate of open unemployment was expected to come down to 1.66 percent which was of the order of 8.33 percent in and 5.99 in 1993-94 and 7.32 percent in 1999-2000. (Planning Commission, 2002) However one could not be too much optimistic as the emerging trend in the employment elasticity of output especially in the organized sector has shown lower, fluctuating trends in recent years of economic reforms. The five year averages of employment elasticity which was 0.38 during 1981-85 had come down to 0.24 per cent during 1986-1990 and further to 0.17 percent during 1991-95 (Economic Survey, 1981-97). Further in the unorganized sector, the employment elasticity was 0.213 in 1999-2000, where as it was 0.066 only in the organized sector. (Planning Commission, 2002), almost a jobless growth. Besides, the total contribution of the organized sector was only 8.35 percent of which the public sector contribution was 5.77 percent and the private sector segments contribution was only 2.58 percent. The balance 92 percent had come from the unorganized sector. In public sector enterprises, and in the organised private sector with technology up gradation and competition the government is vigorously following the policies of voluntary retirement providing a golden hand shake and shedding its load of excess workers. A silent exit policy was followed in the organized private sector shedding its load of excess workers. All these policies resulted in contraction of employment with the labourers losing their employment opportunities. Nobel laureate Amartya Sen (1995) has revealed his anguish over the explosive situation of unemployment. He has said that peace and progression in the world is possible only when all efforts are made to implement 'employment oriented plans".

EDUCATED UNEMPLOYMENT

The first employment and unemployment data for India was collected in the 9th round of the NSS during May to August 1955. The unemployment rate was very low at 0.29 percent for rural and 1.99 percent for urban population, 0.59 percent for India as a whole. No break up of male female figures was available. The unemployment problem from the start has been that of educated and urban unemployment and the subsequent surveys reiterated the aggravating and increasing dimensions of educated unemployment. The earlier 8th round of the NSS gave the break down of the unemployment with educational levels as follows: urban unemployment was made up of 21.6 percent illiterate, 60.23 percent literate but below metric and 17.99 percent educated. The incidence of unemployment was particularly heavy among the females. NSSO Report on 1993-94 survey pointed out that the share of the educated unemployed among the total unemployed had risen progressively and most substantially from 39.9 percent to 62 percent during 1988-94. Further unemployment among the educated youth was 18.5 percent in 1993-94, 20.8 percent in urban area and 17 percent in rural area. This had shown a decline in 1999-2000 with 14.8 percent unemployment among the educated youth, 18.3 percent in urban and 12.5 percent in rural area. These dimensions pose a substantial challenge not only for man power planners but also for economic policy making as a whole since the unemployment problem cannot be viewed in isolation from movement of the economy as a whole. The following table 1 gives the unemployment rates by educational levels of education.

Table 1

Unemployment Rates by Level of Education

(as % of labour force)

Education	1987-88	1993-94	1999-2000
Illiterate	1.1	0.2	0.2
Primary	1.9	0.9	1.2
Middle	5.3	3.4	3.3
Secondary	8.7	6.2	5.5
HSC	-	8.7	7.8
Graduate & above	9.9	9.3	8.8
Secondary & above	9.0	7.7	7.1
All	2.7	1.9	2.2

Source : NSS Surveys, 43rd round (1987-88); 50th round (1993-94) and 55th round (1999-2000)

In the post economic reform period though unemployment rate had declined very marginally among the literates the disturbing fact is that for the educated in 1999-2000 the unemployment rate was more than three times the unemployment rate for the population as a whole. The number of persons on the live register of employment exchanges, i.e., the number awaiting employment gives an idea of the trend of unemployment among the educated subject to certain limitations. Registration with employment exchanges being voluntary, not all unemployed register their names in them. Further, some of the registrants who are already employed have registered themselves for seeking better employment. The employment exchange statistics reveals declining trend in the placements in comparison to the total registrations. In the year 1981, 62.77 lakhs registered in 592 employment exchange offices of the country. The vacancies notified were 897 but the number of placements was only 504. In 1991 the employment exchanges increased to 772, the number of candidates registered was almost stagnant with 62.36 lakhs but both the number of vacancies notified and also placements reduced considerably to 459 and 253 respectively. In 1998, the employment exchanges increased to 860 but the number of candidates registered decreased to 2.36 lakhs and the placement was only 150. (Report on Currency and Finance, 1997-98). The economic reforms have not diluted the problem of unemployment among the educated.

EDUCATED UNEMPLOYED IN TAMILNADU

The current work studies the level of unemployment privileging in the pre and post reform periods in Tamilnadu, through the number registered in the employment exchange in Tamilnadu. The data on the number of educated unemployed in Tamilnadu by educational level and faculty level for the pre reform period 1980-90 and for the post reform period 1991-96 are given in the following table 2

Table 2

Number Of Educated Unemployed In Tamilnadu By Educational Levels As Per Live Registers 1980-1996

Year	SSLC	Higher Secondary	Graduate	Post Graduate	Diploma	Total
1980	344337	98097	101576	14184	-	558194
	(61.68)	(17.57)	(18.19)	(2.5)		
1981	368621	11473	9590	16326	-	599280
	(61.51)	(19.15)	(16.62)	(2.72)		
1982	440593	143132	116880	21467	-	722072
	(61.01)	(19.15)	(16.62)	(2.97)		
1983	408493	157540	121779	23979	13706	7257
	(56.30)	(21.70)	(16.79)	(3.3)	(1.88)	
1984	464173	184913	19065	27904	16404	812459
	(57.13)	(22.76)	(14.65)	(3.4)	(.020)	
1985	567214	255192	141725	36646	21778	1022555
	(55.47)	(24.96)	(13.86)	(3.58)	(2.12)	
1986	697466	350436	176103	42698	28204	1294907
	(53.86)	(2.06)	(13.6)	(3.3)	(2.18)	
1987	772278	357187	186715	48253	34653	2399086
	(32.19)	(14.89)	(7.78)	(2.01)	(1.44)	
1988	919311	444721	208947	50162	49469	1672310
	(54.97)	(26.59)	(12.49)	(2.99)	(2.94)	
1989	951185	446982	272550	40661	48180	175538
	(54.06)	(25.40)	(15.49)	(2.31)	(2.74)	
1990	913359	476256	314130	44372	50031	1798148
	(50.79)	26.49)	(17.47)	(2.47)	(2.78)	
1991	1058416	561866	343246	39250	50157	2052945
	(51.56)	(27.37)	(16.72)	(1.92)	(2.44)	
1992	1068193	581287	402903	47277	65459	2165089
	(49.34)	(49.34)	(18.61)	(2.18)	(3.02)	
1993	1232564	610768	386403	60882	71408	2362027
	(52.18)	(25.86)	(16.35)	(2.58)	(3.02)	
1994	1125008	645420	395506	59717	74543	2300194
	(48.9)	(28.41)	(18.23)	(1.81)	(3.4)	
1995	1099666	64809	416491	41257	77702	2284025
	(48.15)	(28.41)	(18.23)	(1.81)	(3.4)	
1996	1104816	701736	400383	45166	87771	2339872
	(47.22)	(29.99)	(17.11)	(1.93)	(3.75)	

As can be seen from the table, the number of educated unemployed who had registered in the employment exchange was high among the SSLC candidates followed by higher secondary candidates, under graduates, diploma holders and post graduates. During 1980-90 the SSLC candidates who had registered in the employment exchange had come down from about 61.68 percent to 50.79 percent It had further declined to 47.22 percent in 1996. This was in the increasing side for the higher secondary graduates. It was 17.57 percent in 1990 and rose to 26.49 percent in 1996. For the other candidates the change was only marginal. The growth at which the number of educated unemployed who had registered in the employment exchange in Tamilnadu for the two periods 1980-90 and 1991-96 were calculated and are given in the following table.

Table 3

Growth Rates In Educated Unemployed In Tamilnadu (1980-1996) (%)

Educational level	1981-90	1991-96
SSLC	12.09	6.0
HSS	18.8	4.30
Graduates	12.19	2.50
Post Graduates	13.28	7.20
Diploma	22.50	10.0
Total	15.16	2.20

The above table provides the following results:

1. The rate at which the educated candidates had registered in the employment exchange had come down for all types of candidates in the post reforms period.
2. The diploma holders were found to form the highest growth in registering in the employment exchange during the pre and post reforms period.

3. During the pre reform period, the higher secondary graduates formed the second largest group in the rate at which they registered in the employment exchange office followed by the post graduates. This trend changed in the post reform period in which the post graduates had the second highest growth, followed by the SSLC candidates.

Faculty wise data on the number of educated unemployed graduates who had registered in the employment exchange are given in the following table 4.

Table 4

Number Of Educated Unemployed Graduates (Faculty wise in Tamilnadu) 1980-1996

Year	Arts	Sciences	Commerce	Engineering	Medical	Agri	Agri engi	Law	Education	Vet	Others	Total
1980	37089 (36.51)	33928 (33.40)	14265 (14.04)	2320 (2.28)	1323 (1.30)	275 (0.27)	-	250 (0.25)	11894 (11.71)	107 (0.11)	125 (0.12)	101576
1981	41710 (41.88)	35456 (35.60)	15248 (15.31)	1979 (1.19)	1185 (1.19)	485 (0.49)	-	417 (0.42)	12815 (12.87)	173 (0.17)	122 (0.122)	99590
1982	42096 (36.02)	39724 (33.99)	15104 (12.92)	2201 (1.88)	1326 (1.56)	396 (0.39)	-	485 (0.41)	14615 (12.50)	196 (0.17)	737 (0.63)	116880
1983	44488 (353)	38904 (0.05)	18514 (15.20)	1899 (1.56)	1902 (1.56)	175 (0.14)	-	611 (0.50)	14382 (11.81)	34 (0.03)	870 (0.71)	121779
1984	41004 (34.44)	38851 (32.63)	18742 (15.74)	1805 (1.52)	2279 (2.06)	172 (0.14)	-	614 (5.05)	13791 (11.59)	52 (0.04)	1755 (.47)	119065
1985	49044 (34.61)	45145 (31.85)	22277 (15.72)	2009 (1.73)	2453 (1.73)	526 (0.37)	-	862 (0.61)	18474 (1.25)	49 (0.03)	886 (0.63)	141725
1986	59150 (3359)	52491 (281)	28040 (15.92)	4902 (2.78)	2815 (1.59)	591 (0.28)	-	1547 (0.88)	25119 (14.26)	205 (0.12)	1343 (0.760	1761103
1987	66602 (35.67)	58539 (31.35)	29330 (15.71)	5012 (2.68)	2389 (1.28)	671 (0.36)	41 (0.02)	1353 (0.72)	21840 (11.69)	51 (0.03)	887 (0.48)	186715

1988	76393 (36.56)	63462 (30.37)	32233 (15.43)	6209 (2.97)	1849 (0.88)	918 (0.44)	168 (0.08)	1192 (0.9)	24194 (11.58)	75 (0.04)	2254 (1.08)	208947
1989	85096 (3122)	82658 (3033)	41243 (15.13)	9165 (3.36)	3722 (1.37)	956 (0.35)	113 (0.04)	8852 (0.68)	46045 (16.89)	242 (0.09)	1459 (0.52)	272550
1990	92029 (29.30)	82398 (26.23)	51869 (16.52)	14528 (4.62)	4097 (13.04)	1260 (0.40)	213 (0.06)	1150 (0.68)	60124 (0.11)	172 (0.05)	5287 (1.68)	341430
1991	90719 (26.43)	84493 (24.62)	46941 (13.68)	21738 (6.33)	7104 (2.07)	797 (0.23)	231 (0.06)	1538 (0.45)	78175 (22.78)	281 (0.08)	11229 (3.27)	343246
1992	101748 (25.25)	9911 (24.0)	59374 (14.74)	25462 (6.32)	4312 (1.07)	1088 (0.27)	329 (0.08)	1712 (7.004)	91884 (0.22)	412 (0.10)	1741 (4.34)	402903
1993	94002 (24.33)	90861 (23.51)	53190 (13.76)	28172 (7.29)	4423 (1.14)	1841 (0.48)	394 (0.09)	1889 (0.49)	100353 (24.91)	959 (0.24)	10364 (2.68)	386403
1994	10577 (2.57)	84916 (21.47)	60789 (15.37)	22670 (5.73)	2819 (0.71)	1754 (0.44)	360 (0.09)	2570 (0.5)	91762 (23.45)	709 (0.18)	24579 (6.21)	395500
1995	10658 (256)	97105 (23.3)	64397 (15.46)	27700 (6.65)	1284 (0.01)	358 (0.09)	387 (0.09)	1734 (0.41)	78407 (1.83)	687 (0.16)	37851 (9.09)	416491
1996	113206 (28.27)	78731 (19.66)	69689 (17.41)	25376 (6.34)	1179 (0.29)	363 (0.09)	281 (0.07)	115 (0.02)	78428 (19.59)	585 (0.15)	31428 (7.85)	400383

The number of educated unemployed in the arts group formed about 36 percent in 1980 which had come down to 29.30 percent in 1990. It was 28.27 percent in 1996. For the science group also there was a decline from 33.40 percent in 1980 to 26.23 percent in 1990 and 19.66 percent in 1996. Commerce had shown an increasing trend with 14.04 percent in 1980 to 17.41 percent in 1996. Again increasing trends were seen in the case of engineering graduates and in bachelor of education students. The rate at which the number who had registered in the employment exchange office had grown (faculty wise) are given in the following table 5.

Table 5

Growth Rates of Educated Unemployed In Tamilnadu-Faculty wise 1980-1996

FACULTY	1980-90	1991-96
Arts	9.90	-0.201
Science	7.11	20.15
Commerce	13.60	6.95
Engineering	21.42	2.34
Medical	11.43	-0.312
Law	22.08	-0.303
Education	15.83	-0.0156
Veterinary	15.0	15.0
Others	33.49	31.26

The table shows that the number registered in he employment exchange had considerably increased for the science graduates with the growth rate increasing from 7.11 percent in 1980-90 to 20.15 percent in 1991-96. In fact for the professional degree holders in medical, law and education, it could be seen that the growth rate was in fact negative. For the engineering graduates it had remarkably declined from 21.42 percent during 1991-96. For the veterinary science graduates, the growth rate was almost the same for the pre and post reform periods.

UNEMPLOYMENT AMONG EDUCATED WOMEN

No country can progress if half of the population is left with subsidiary function and subsidiary status in work participation. As of 31.12.2000, in Tamilnadu, the educated women job seekers accounted for 12.61 lakhs (41 percent) out of the total educated job seekers (30.97 lakhs) registered with the employment exchange. The following table gives the number of women job seekers buy their educational levels.

Table 6

Women Job Seekers By Educational Levels

Educational Level	As on 31.12.2000		
	Total	Women	% Share
SSLC	1336927	540452	42.9
HSC	882195	369536	29.3
Diploma	169388	51121	4.0
Graduates	567981	238732	18.0
Post graduates	140240	61419	4.9
Total	3096731	1261260	100.0

Source : Department of Employment and Training, Chennai.

It could be seen that among women, unemployment was high with those who have completed just SSLC by 1990 were selected from TVS Nagar in Coimbatore District. Among the selected women, 8 have completed SSLC, 16 have completed +2, 19 have graduate degree, 5 are diploma holders and 2 are professional degree holders. Of the 50 educated unemployed women, only

19 had registered in the employment exchange. The number of women who had registered in the employment exchange was high among the B. Sc candidates (26.32 percent), followed by HSS (21.05 percent), B.A. (15.79 percent), B. Com and SSLC (both 10.53 percent each) and diploma (5.26 percent), B.E. (5.26 percent), and M. Sc (5.26 percent) graduates.

In the selected sample, 26 (52 percent) were voluntarily unemployed and 24(48 percent) were seeking for jobs. To find out whether the type of unemployment prevailing among the women namely, voluntary and non-voluntary depends on socio economic conditions prevailing in the families of the selected families discriminant analysis was applied with the following variables: the total family monthly income (x_1), number of dependents in the family (x_2), educational level of the women respondents (x_3) and educational level of the husbands (x_4). The women were divided into two groups: Group 1 comprising of voluntarily unemployed women and Group II comprising of non voluntarily unemployed women. For educational level, the following criteria was applied.

With SSLC = 1; Diploma = 2; +2=3; U. G=4; P.G.=5 and B. E. =6.

The estimated canonical discriminant function using SPSS package was

$$Z=0.00013\ X_1-0..1267\ X_2+0.73347\ X_3-0.22106X_4$$

The first group was characterized with higher family income, lesser number of dependents, higher educational level of the women and lesser educational level of the head of the families. The importance of each of the variable in discriminating the two groups was found out using the formula

$$Ij= |\ Kj\ (Xj_1-Xj_2)\ |$$

Where Ij=importance of the Jth variable

Kj= unstandarised discriminant coefficient of the jth variable

Xj_1 = mean of the jth variable in the first group

Xj_2 = Mean of the jth variable in the second group

The relative importance Rj of the jth variable was calculated as follows.

Rj= (Ij/ΣIj) 100

The calculated Ij and Rj values are given in the following table.

Table 7

Relative Importance of the Variables

Variable	Ij	Rj
Family income	0.1332	30.55
Dependents	0.0005	0.11
Education-women	0.3009	69.01
Education-head	0.0014	0.32

The educational level of the women had the highest discriminating power of 69.01 percent in discriminating the two groups of women, followed by the total income of the family with a relative discriminating power of 30.55 percent. The other two variables had less discriminating power.

CONCLUSION AND FUTURE STRATEGY

To sum up, the following points had emerged from the study

1. Among the graduates who had registered in the employment exchange, there is a decline among the arts, science and commerce students from 78 percent in 1980-90 to 65.27 percent in the post reform period. It is not because that these students entering into these

subjects have come down or because the students have lost faith in the employment exchange registration.

2. Among the total registered, the engineering graduates formed about 3 percent in 1980-90 which increased to 6 percent in 1991-96. With an increase in the output of the engineering graduates– thanks to the record level growth of engineering colleges-the engineering graduates had started to taste the feeling of being unemployed. But with in the engineering graduates, the growth in registration had declined from 21.42 percent in the pre reform period to 2.34 percent in the post reform period-thanks to globalization-the creation of open employment opportunities with fascinating pay being offered by the MNCs.
3. Radical changes have to be made in the educational system so as to develop human resources properly to provide employment to all those who have received education.
4. Poverty and unemployment are related to each other. The ongoing employment and anti poverty programmes must be fully coordinated and monitored at the central, state, district, taluk and panchayat levels through massive support of the NGOs, central and state agencies.
5. The reduction in unemployment and ultimately ensuring gainful employment to the surplus labour force should constitute one of the key objectives of the second generation of the economic reforms.
6. A coordinated rural development plan and establishment of agro based centres will link rural-urban development and generate large employment opportunities for women

REFERENCES

1 Chauby P.K (2000, "Youth and Unemployment in Perspective: The Indian Context", the Indian Journal of Labour Economics, Vol. 43, No.4, pp.625-640

2. Damodar Gujarati (1999, "Essentials of Econometrics", Irwin McGraw Hill, New York)

3. Government of India, Census of India, 1971, 1981,1991

4. Government of India, Economic Survey, Various Issues

5. Government of Tamilnadu, "Tamilnadu An Economic Appraisal", Various issues.

6. NSSO, "Employment & Unemployment in India (1999-2000): Key results NSS 55th Round", Dec 2000.

7. Planning Commission, Five Year Plan Reports.

8. Planning Commission (2001), "Report of Task Force on Employment Opportunities"

9. Planning Commission (2002), "Report of Special Group on Targeting Ten Million Opportunities per year".

DEVELOPMENT OF WOMEN ENTREPRENEURSHIP THROUGH INDUSTRIAL COOPERATIVE SOCIETY

*Dr. Samwel Kakuko Lopoyetum
** Mr. R. Velu Raj

INTRODUCTION : AN OVERVIEW

In India, Village and Small— Scale Industries (VSSI) play significant role in developing the national economy. They provide independent as well as subsidiary occupation to a sizable proportion of the rural, semi-urban, and urban population. Even, time immemorial, the artisans and workers of country have excelled in certain directions such as handloom, tie and dye workers, calico — printing, hand— made papers, local shoes, glassware and bangles, pottery carving on metal etc. The advent of the British rule in India and the consequent ushering of the machine age resulted in a widespread deterioration of these villages and small — scale industries. These industries were stggering forwant of aded nate finance, dnality rawmaterials and technical guidanceand marketing facilities. The lack of interest on the part of the Government was the most important factor contributing to the decline of these industries. If some of the industries still flourished, it was due to large number of families engaged traditionally in the work, showed a high degree of skill and their goods continued to find a market place in the well-to-do sections of the society.

The importance of giving a distinctly co–operative bias to cottage and small-scale industries was suggested as early as 1918 by the Industries Commission. The Royal Commission

* Senior Post-Doctoral Research Fellow, Department of Cooperation. Faculty of rural Social Sciences, Gandhigram Rural University Gandhigram -624 302

** Lecturer - Department of cooperation, R. K. Shanmugam College of Arts & Cience, Kallkurichi—606 202, Tamil Nadu.

on Agriculture suggested the organization of village artisans on a cooperative basis for credit, raw materials and marketing. The 18948 Industrial Policy Resolution of the Government of India also reiterated the importance of development of cottage and village industries on co-operative lines.

Considering the importance of small industries organized on co-operative lines, Indian Constitution has laid down in Article 43. "The state shall endeavour to promote cottage industries on individual or co-operative basis in rural areas". The 1956 Industrial Policy Resolution again stressed the Government's intention to develop a steadily increasing proportion of the activities of the private sector along co-operative lines. Increasing importance has been given to he development of Village and Small– Scale Industries on co-operative lines in the successive Five Year Plans. As much as to give the importance of empowering women in recent years by the Government of India, it is realized that the type of industrial cooperative were started on the lines of development of women and weaker sections of the community. Empowerment of women entrepreneurs through co-operative ventures and enterprise is the need of the hour.

SIGNIFICANCE OF INDUSTRIAL COOPERATIVES AND EMPOWERMENT OF WOMEN ENTREPRENEURS

An industrial Co –Operative is an undertaking of craftsmen or skilled workers engaged in the cottage or small–scale industries to undertake production, purchases of supplies and raw materials, marketing of products and supplying other services to the members.

The cottage and small–scale industries occupied a key position not only form their potential for raising rapidly the existing levels of income and employment with relatively low capital outlays, but also from the need to ameliorate the economic conditions of some of the weaker sections of the Society.

Industrial co–operative have been organized with tow objectives in view, namely Social and economic. Among the social objectives, the most important are the safeguarding the interest of the poorer sections against exploitative trends and the diffusion and dispersal of wealth. The economic objectives of these societies are creation of employment opportunities, increase in production and productivity, competitive capability and acceleration in the rate of capital formation.

EMPOWERMENT AND DEVELOPMENT OF WOMEN ENTREPRENEURSHIP

The Federal and State Government organizations have empowered women through imparting education and enlightenment through training camps, seminars, conferences, workshop etc., from their educational facilities. They have been gaining more entrepreneurial skills and practical knowledge regarding the modern management techniques and methods. They can get confidence to control the management affairs of cooperative organisation. Women's participation would give an effective and efficient management and administration of the society in the new millennium.

Women are eligible to organise any type of cooperative society, subject to legal provisions of membership. They can form their own cooperative organization exclusively with women membership. Most of the women cooperative in India have been either sponsored or assisted by the Central or State Social Welfare Boards. Majorities of women cooperative were thrift and credit, encouraging the women to save and provide them with credit on easy terms. The industrial cooperatives and weavers cooperatives are next to none. The industrial cooperatives which are run by the women mainly engaged in activities such *as tailoring, knitting, preparation of pappad, jam pickles, masala powder garment making, etc.* Now–a–day, women contribute to about 80 per cent of dairy production and fish farming and share half of leading cottage industries.

The rural women cooperatives and entrepreneurs were involving in the handicraft, sericulture, floriculture, horticulture, poultry, bee-keeping, seed bank, sheep keeping, cultivation of flowers and medical plants etc. Such cooperatives have provided benefits to women as they get gainful employment leading to higher income and render services to the needy women sector.

The need to ensure active participation of women in the cooperative movement could be further highlighted and brought into the main stream of national life and national economy. Cooperative Institutions at all levels including those at base levels have the necessary infrastructure to take-up various promotional activities such as women and children welfare activities (child care), family welfare, nutrition, general education, adult education etc., in addition to their economic activities. In this context, Chinnasalem Food Manufacturing Women's Development Cooperative Society is manufacturing energy food for children. Cooperatives have given women greater opportunities to participate in the economic affairs of the community. While stating the role of women in cooperatives, the late Prime Minister Sri. Rajiv Gandhi said, "Involvement of women in cooperatives is a practical programme for raising the status of women in the society on a very large scale especially in those echelons of our society where help and assistance are needed more". Thus, the cooperatives provide many varied opportunities for women participation. No doubt their standard of living would improve and their family income and quality of life would be enhanced. Their children will be healthy by eating energy food manufactured by the Women's Industrial Cooperative Societies.

PROFILE OF THE SOCIETY

The Chinna Salem Energy Food Manufacturing Women's Development Cooperative Society was registered on 20-12-

1998 and commenced its business on 31-1-1989 under the Tamil Nadu Cooperative Societies Act 1983, which has been controlled under the Department of Social Welfare, Tamil Nadu government. The area of operation of the society have been confined to the entire Panchayat Union of Chinna Salem. The name and address of the Society is called as the Chinna Salem Energy Food Manufacturing Women's Developments Co-operative Society limited, S. W. 74, Chinna Salem post, Kallakurichi Taluk, Villupuram District. Out of 23 Cooperative societies functioning in the State of Tamil Nadu, this is the only society which has remarkably performed well and their objectives are achieved. It is moving towards success.

PRODUCTION AND MANUFACTURING OPERATIONS OF THE SOCIETY

(i) Purchase of Raw Materials

It is the duty of the Board of Directors of Special Officer to arrange for purchase of raw materials required by the society and get them converted into finished goods as per the specifications prescribed. As such, the society purchased the raw material of wheat from Tamil Nadu Civil Supplies Corporation and the rest of the raw material being purchased from a consumer society or any department or undertaking of the Government by inviting quotation or tender method. There is a link-up between consumers cooperative organizations with the cooperative manufacture organization.

The purchase committee is liable to administer the quotations or the tenders called for ordering raw materials to the society in order to carry out the manufacturing activities. The Committee is consisting of five members including the District Welfare Officer, the Special Officer of the Society, the District Project Nomination Officer and the rest of them are members.

The following table provides complete details of purchase of raw materials by the society made during the period of 1997—1998 and 2001-02.

Table 1
Position of Purchase of Raw Materials

(Rs. In lakhs)

S. No.	Years	Purchase of Raw Materials	
1.	1997-1998	34.72 (-)	(-)
2.	1998-1999	49.30 (41.99)	(41.99)
3.	1999-2000	44.68 (-9.39)	(-9.37)
4.	2000-2001	62.9 (40.78)	(40.78)
5.	2001-2002	118.00 (87.60)	(87.60)

(Figure in Parenthesis indicator Annual Growth Rates)

The study shows that the fluctuating trend is associated with the purchase of raw material during the study period. As on 31st March 2002, the total of purchase of raw material was Rs.118.00 lakhs. It is, therefore, understood that the requirement of manufacturing of energy food is inevitable on the part of the functions of the society and fulfillment of the welfare of the weaker sections (Child development by providing Energy foods) to the community as a whole.

(ii) Manufacturing operations

The society, in every month, has been getting orders for manufacturing of energy food from the Director, Department of Social Welfare and Energy Food Programme. In view of implementing the Integrated Child Development/Scheme in the State. This has been implemented with the help of programme officers of Cuddalore, Villupuram, Nallure and Kalvarayan Hills as may be ordered (Indent Method) as per every months' demand. The society manufactured the energy food and distributed the same to the concerned programme offices. The manufacture can equally be done by the member and each members can earn a salary on an average for Rs.500 per month.

The table below depict the specimen of indent method of Kalvarayan Hills during the month of January 2003.

Table 2

An Effective Indent Method -Kalvarayan Hills Under I.C.D., Scheme

S. No.	I. C. D. Scheme	Block and Quantities
1.	Name of the Block	Kalvarayan Hills
2.	Requirement For one day For 30 days	135. Kg 4050. Kg
3.	15 days Buffer stock	2025. Kg
4.	Total Requirement	6075. Kg
5.	Quantity supplied from 28th August, 2002 to 24th December, 2002	-
6.	Quantity consumed from 25th November, 2002 to 24th December, 2002	3242. Kg
7.	Stock at hands on 25th December, 2002	1505. Kg
8.	Deduct from 26th December, 2002 to 30th December, 2002 (Per day requirement)	673. Kg
9.	Balance Stock on hand as on 1st January, 2003 Col (9-10)	832 Kg
10.	Next Requirement Col (6-11)	3,975 Kg

The indent method of Kalvarayan hills is one of the example of Integrated Child Development Scheme. This method, is being following by all the programme offices located with in the area of operation.

PROCESSING AND MANUFACTURING OF ENERGY FOOD

The basic ingredients required for manufacturing of energy food are Wheat, Ragi, Maize, Jaggery, Bengal–grame dal and Pre Mix Vitamin. These requisites are passed through four distinctive phases namely.

1. Cleaning 2. Roasting 3. Floor 4. Grinding 5. Packing

The process of ingredients can be mixed with the following ratio to 100 gram energy food

Table 3

Ratio of Ingredients Mix For Manufacturing of Energy Food

S. No.	Basic Ingredients	Ratio of Mix
1.	Wheat	42%
2.	Ragi	5%
3.	Maize	10%
4.	Jaggery	30%
5.	Bengal -grame dal	12%
6.	Vitamin Pre-mix	1%

CAPACITY UTILIZATION AND MANUFACTURE OF ENERGY FOOD

The society manufactured the energy food at the maximum of 10 M.T. (approximately) per day and in turn it leads to total manufacture of energy food is not less than 157 M. T. per month This would workout to a monthly turnover of Rs. 18 Lakhs.

Table 4

Position Of Manufacture Of Energy Food

(Rs. In Lakhs)

S. No.	Year	Amount
1	1997 —1998	38.42
2.	1998 —1999	55.00
3.	1999— 2000	49.97
4.	2000— 2001	N. A.
5.	2001— 2002	N. A.

(N.A= Not available)

The position of manufacture of Energy Food has marked the level of fuller capacity utilization of the machines. As on 31st March 2000, the society manufactured the Energy Food for the value of Rs. 49.97 Lakhs.

COST OF MANUFACTURING OF ENERGY FOOD

It is noteworthy that, the expenditure, which has been incurred upon manufacture of energy food, would count and determine the profit on the part of the cooperative society. Thus, the manufacturing cost includes the purchase of raw materials, taxes and duties on materials purchased, material scrap; wages to workers, chargeable expenses, and factory as well as administrative overheads. This would cost about Rs. 0.15 lakhs per metric tone of energy food.

Table 5

Cost of Manufacture of Energy food

(Rs. In lakhs)

S. No.	Year	Amount
1.	1997 —1998	3.50
2.	1998 —1999	5.29

3.	1999— 2000	6.15
4.	2000— 2001	N. A.
5.	2001— 2002	N. A.

(N.A. Not Available)

The above table shows the details of cost of manufacturing of energy food by the society during the study period. It is clearly understood that the cost of manufacturing of energy food is admissible when the manufacturing activities are carried out by the society.

SALE AND MARKETING OF MANUFACTURE ENERGY FOOD

The manufactured energy food is totally sold to the concerned Programme Officers of Integrated Child Development Scheme (ICD). This has been done on the basis of the quantity ordered by the Programme Officers of respective areas. The following table clearly provides the position of sale of energy food.

Table 6

Position Of Sale and Marketing Of Energy Food

(Rs. In Lakhs)

S. No.	Year	Sale	
1	1997 —1998	44.32	(-)
2.	1998 —1999	53.00	(19.59)
3.	1999— 2000	59.81	(12.85)
4.	2000— 2001	73.82	(33.42)
5.	2001— 2002	94.80	(28.42)

(Figure in Parenthesis indicator Annual Growth Rates)

The above table presents the position of sale of energy food of the society during the study period. It is noted that an increasing trend is attributed with the sale of energy food of the society. Moreover, as on 31st March 2002, the position of sale of energy food was very high i.e.,. Rs. 94.30 lakhs. It is, therefore, cleared that the society is fully involved in satisfying the orders fixed by the ICDs officers and maximizing the productivity in general.

TRADING CHARGES FOR SALE OF ENERGY FOOD

Table 7

Position Of The Trading Charges For Sale Of Energy Food

(Rs. In Lakhs)

S. No.	Year	Amount
1	1997 —1998	2.17
2.	1998 —1999	1.95
3.	1999— 2000	2.69
4.	2000— 2001	N. A.
5.	2001— 2002	N. A.

(N. A. Not Available)

The above table shows the trading charges of the during the study period. During 1999-2000, the charges incurred by the society in Trading of trading activity amounts to Rs. 2.69 lakhs. But, during the 2000-2001 and 2001-2002, audit report of the society had not been completed due to administration drawbacks.

DISPOSAL OF NET PROFIT

The net profit of the society as declared by the Registrar of Cooperative Societies every year is apportioned in the fallowing order;

1. A sum calculated at 3 per cent of the net profit set apart towards the contribution to the Cooperative Research and Development Fund.

2. Two per cent of the net profits set apart for contribution to the Co-operative Education Fund.
3. Twenty per cent of the net profits is carried to the credit of the Reserve Fund.
4. Honorarium may be paid to the members of the Board including President and Vice President not exceeding 10% of the net Profits subject to the provisions of the Rule 94 of the Tamil Nadu Co-operative Societies Rule, 1988.
5. Dividend not exceeding 14 per cent per annum on the paid up value of each share may be paid to the members proportionately to the amount of paid up share capital held by each.
6. Such amount from out of the net profits not exceeding 50% of the net profit as may be decided by the General Body may be paid as Bonus to the members.
7. Such sum as may be decided upon by the General Body not exceeding ten per cent of the net profits in each case may be carried to any or all of the following funds.

   (a) *Building Fund* : The amount to the credit of this fund shall be drawn with the sanction of the Registrar and shall be utilized for the purchases of a site or to construct a building of the society.

   (b) *Price Equalization Fund* : The amount to the credit of this fund shall be utilized to subsequent years for meeting losses, if any, incurred by the society in selling the finished goods at reduced prices.

   (c) *Members Welfare Fund* : The amount to the credit of this fund shall be utilized or the purpose to be specified by the Board of Directors and approved by the Director.

8. Such sum may be decided upon by General Body Calculated at not exceeding 10 per cent of net profits may be carried to a Common Good Fund (CGF) for being utilized on any of the objects specified in Section 2 of the Charitable Endowments Act 1890 (Central Act (vi) of 1890) such as medical relief, co-operative propaganda, maintenance of library, education and relief to the poor.
9. The balance, if any of the net profits shall be added to the Reserve Fund.

PROFITABILITY OF THE SOCIETY

Each and every business entity should relie on expecting certain profit on business against its heavy investments. The society is also a manufacturing unit, it aims to produce and maintain a certain level of profitability on its part. The following table presents the position of the profitability of the society during the study period.

Table 8

Profitability Position Of The Society

(Rs. In Lakhs)

S. No.	Year	Profit Loss
1	1997 —1998	2.29 (Profit)
2.	1998 —1999	4.96 (Loss)
3.	1999— 2000	1.12 (Profit)
4.	2000— 2001	2.19 (Profit)
5.	2001— 2002	9.31 (Profit)

(31st, December, 2002)

The profit ability position of the society shows the continuous profit over the study period from 1997–1998 to 31st, March, 2002, except in the year 1998-1999 (Loss of

Rs.4.96 lakhs.) It is, therefore, understood that the society has achieved its success through earning profit some what extent and this will help to improve its business as well and the betterment of its members.

AUDIT CLASSIFICATION OF THE SOCIETY

An audit includes examining, on a test basis, evidence supporting the amount and disclosures in the financial statement. An audit also includes asserting accounting principles usual and significant estimates made by management as well as evaluating the overall financing statement presentation in accordance with the principles of cooperation.

The audit of the society has been conducted every year in order to elicit opinion and expression about the functioning of the society in terms of cooperative auditing standards generally accepted. The society was brought under 'C' class in all the years under study. However, there is a need for the society to take measures to improve its manufacturing operations and overall functioning of the society.

BOOKS AND REGISTERS MAINTAINED BY THE SOCIETY

The society have been maintaining important books and registers in order to make entries of transactions. They are:

1. Day book 2. General Ledger 3. Member Wages Register 4. Staff Salary Register 5. Production Register 6. Stock Register 7. Finished Goods Register 8. Delivery Challan Register 9. Sales /Invoice Book 10. Postage Register 11. Members Attendance Register 12. Member Admission Book. 13. Bye law Book.

MAJOR FINDINGS

i) The Chinna Salem Energy Food Manufacturing Women's Development Cooperative Society was registered on 20th December, 1988 and commenced its business on 31st January, 1989 which is a short period, it has a galvanized the weaker section of the society.

ii) The area of operation of the society have been confined to the entire panchayat union of Chinna Salem.

iii) The liability of the members for the debts of the society on its liquidation is limited to the share capital subscribed by them.

iv) It was started mainly to detect the vitamin defect and deficiency of Children and Pregnant Women members of the society.

v) The society collect shares from the Women members, TAICO Bank and Villupuram CC Bank.

vi) The society direct to implementation of the Government Schemes and programmes in the area of operation.

vii) The society received collect funds from the World bank

viii) The activities of the society is also being controlled by the Department of Social Welfare.

ix) The society was also registered by the Registrar and Director for Social Welfare Department.

x) The audit classification of the society was put under the category of "C" class.

xi) The society is encouraging thift and saving among women members.

xii) The society do not borrow funda from any higher level financial organizations or institutions

xiii) The society is managed and administered by the special officer (SO)

xiv) The society purchase the major raw materials is wheat form Tamil Nadu Civil Supplies Corporation and Consumers Cooperative Stores.

xv) The society manufacture energy food to a maximum of 10 M. T. per day with monthly turnover of Rs.18 lakhs.

xvi) The study reveals that the cost of manufacturing energy food is about Rs. 0.15 lakhs per metric tone of Energy food.

xvii) The society sale and market the energy food products to concerned persons/officers dealing with the Integrated Child Development Schemes located in various areas in the region.

xviii) The society earned profit in all the years except during 1998-1999.

PROBLEMS AND CHALLENGES OF THE SOCIETY

The society has faced numerous problems such as;

1. Heavy and high cost of wheat which is the basic raw material for the manufacture of energy food.
2. Lack of prompt payment of energy food products supplied in time to the govt. organization/institutions
3. In sufficient storage facilities.
4. Untimely repayment of dues to the suppliers particularly when the society purchased raw material other than wheat.
5. Lack of funds for installation of modern machineries and construction of new building for the society.
6. Untimely and lack of prompt audit
7. Absence of prompt order from Department of Social Welfare and from the Programme officers of the concerned areas.

SUGGESTION

The following are some of the basic steps that are needed

to remove various problems experienced by the energy food cooperative society.

1. The society would require to reduce the cost of formulation of energy foods in order to optimize the price of wheat which is the basic raw material for manufacturing of energy food.
2. The State govt. should participate and provide regular payment of prices of Energy food to the society.
3. The society should strengthen its financial soundness, sufficient and suitable methods for repayment of dues to the suppliers through enhancing marketing and sale of energy food. This would lead the society to get sufficient margin.
4. The State govt. should evolve Schemes for the installation of machineries and construction of new buildings so as to increase the requisite energy food to the needy Children
5. The Social Welfare Department should advice enforce the Programme officers to issue prescribed order to the society on a regular basis and in an uninterrupted manner.

CONCLUSION

The Chinna Salem Energy Food Manufacturing Women's Development Co-operative Society has been providing various services to its women members. It has directly empowered women fold. This society has undertake manufacturing of energy food and sale of energy food at the Cuddalore, villupuram Perambalore, and Ariyalore district limit. This society is also earning more and more profits year by year. However, the society needs its own building, modern machineries also the value addition methods techniques manufacturing and modern processing activities, which may help to provide regular employment opportunities to the widow, divorces and poor women members of the society.

SELECTED REFERENCES

— Agarwal A. K. (1975) "Initiative, enterprise and economic choice in India-A study of pattern of entrepreneurship in India", Munshiram Manoharlal, New Delhi.

— Burrows. D. (1983) "The Development of Small Business in the Pacific; problems and solutions" INA speech series No. 22.

— Capati. A. P. (1985) "cross-cultural characteristics of the Entrepreneur" Entrepreneurial Development and small Industry stimulation in Developing countries

— Drucke peter F. (1985)- "Innovation and Entrepreneurship" Harper & Row. El-Namaki. M.S.S. (1988) "Encouraging Entrepreneurs in Developing countries" Long range planning, XXIV No.4

— Flahvin. A. (1985) "Why Small Business fail" Australian Accountant-LV-9. Government of India (2000)1999-2000 Ministry of Finance, Economic Division, New Delhi.

— Government of India (2000), "WTO and its implication for industry" Office of the economic adviser, Ministry of commerce and Industry.

— Hailey J. M. (1986) "Small Indigenous Business in the Pacific" International Small Business Journal V-I.

— J.S. Canol (1986) "Entrepreneurship and Indigenous business in the Republic of the Marshall Islands", Honolulu East-West centre.

— Kannar H. E. and Herbig P. A. (1994) "Cultural Differences in doing business, Germany and the South Pacific" Review of Business.

— Kilby. P. (1971) "Entrepreneurship and Economic Development", Free press, New Yark.

— Mathur, Sathish B. (1999) "Sickness in Small Scale sector-causes and cure with special reference to the role of commercial banks" concept publishing company, New Delhi.

— Mukherjee Neela (2000) "World Trade Organisation and India's Trade policy in services", Vikas Publishing House, New Delhi.

— Plotkin H.M., (1990) "Portrait of successful small business owners" small business reports XV-1.

— Richard Lynn (1973) " The Entrepreneur case studies", George Allen & Unwin Ltd, London.

— Venkateswar T. Rao and Uday Pareekh (1978) "Developing Entreprenurship–a handbood learning system" New Delhi

— Vasanth Desai (1990) "Entrepreneurial Development and Management", Himalaya Publishing House, New Delhi.

— Samwel Kakuko Lopoyetum, etal "Essential management strategies for cooperative Entrepreneurs and Organization in the era of open market Economy" The Cooperator, Vol. 41 No. 3 pp 88-91.

— Samwel Kakuko Lopoyetum (Nov. 2003) "Cooperative Entrepreneurship A perspective "Kurukshetra, Vol. 52 No.1 PP 20-23

STATUS OF WEAVERS COOPERATIVE SOCIETIES IN TAMILNADU — EMPLOYEES PERCEPTION

Dr. K. Ravichandran*
M. Revathibala**

Cooperatives have now emerged as a vital segment of Indian economy and enjoy the support of about 200 million members covering 100 percent villages and 65 percent of the households in the country. The introduction of Cooperatives in industrial activity first began with Handloom Weavers Cooperatives during 1930s. India account for 58 percent of the global share of looms, consisting of 3.5 million handlooms and 1.8 million power looms with a majority of the handlooms being in the cooperative sector. Handloom Industry in India serves as an age-old source of livelihood for 10 million people in the country with a total decentralized sector is about 5.5 percent. The handlooms meet one-third of the total cloth requirement of the rural masses.

As far as Tamilnadu is concerned, the first Weavers Cooperative Union was established at Kancheepuram in 1905. The liquidation and severe loss of this Union necessitated the Government to establish Madras Handloom Weavers Provincial Cooperative Society in 1935, which gave impetus to the development of the Weavers Cooperative Societies. At present, there are 1414 Primary Weavers Cooperative Societies (WCS) covering nearly 2.92 lakh handlooms with the working capital of Rs. 373.57 crores as on 31, March 2001, functioning across the state.

---

* Senior Lecturer and

** Ph. D. Scholar, Department of Cooperation, GRI, Gandhigram -624302

STATUS OF WEAVERS COOPERATIVES

The reported evidences show that the new economic policies has created both favourable and challenging environment for the WCS.

FAVOURABLE CLIMATE

Some of the WCS like Woraiyur Devanga Cotton-cum-Silk Handloom Cooperative Production and Sales Society in Trichy, who have been pioneers in the popular 'Ernakulam Saris' for decades together, continuously run with profit. Like this more than 12000 looms in 200 WCS in the State are now engaged in export-oriented production through deemed export. During the years 1999-2000 and 2000-2001 handloom goods worth Rs. 25 crores and Rs. 92 crores were exported respectively. For the year 2001-02, the target was fixed at Rs. 125 crores. This has become possible because of new economic policies.

CHALLENGING SCENARIO

The cooperative titans of the recent past viz., Chentex, Erotex, and some of the silk cooperatives in kancheepuram could not withhold their market share in the vicissitudes of the market economy. Many other WCS have become bird watchers and their members have been shifting their occupations. The long years of service in weaving have brought poverty, famine and unemployment.

A study conducted on occupational shift among 200 handloom-weavbing families in Chinnalapatti traditionally 'the handloom corridor' of Tamilnadu found that as much as 55 percent of the weaving families find shelter in other occupations and majority of the younger generation 'the children of viswakarmas' had developed aversion towards their own traditional industry. This resulted in wide spread dormancy in WCS. The political parties in Tamilnadu have gone to the extent of organizing gruel centres to feed at least one meal per day to the dying weavers as incidence of suicides were reported among weavers.

OTHER CONSTRAINTS

WCS in Tamilnadu are affected by several maladies that hamper their efficient functioning and growth. They are viz.,

- Accumulation of stock due to non-linking of Production to market moods and trends
- Mismanagement of Societies
- Increase/fluctuation in hank yarn prices leading to higher production cost and its adverse impact on marketability
- Yarn purchased from Cooptex is of higher price and the quality of yarn was not up to the mark.
- Most of the dyes (Napthal dye) procured by societies are from the National Handloom Development Corporation. Napthal dye packages involved blocking of funds to the tune of Rs.3000 needed for wax packing. Many of the WCS could hardly afford to go in for Napthal packages owing to their liquidity crunch and hence, they seem to knock at private traders who offered to a supply dyes even on credit basis.
- The influence of master weavers on the members whose loyalty to the WCS did not sustain for several reasons like malpractices in selection of members under the welfare schemes of government.
- Dormancy of looms, locking up of working capital loans and accumulated losses.
- Delay in release of rebate on sales by the Government, delay in settlement of dues by of which have contributed to the liquidity crunch at the WCS level hindering their production programmes.
- Delay in settling interest subsidy claims by the Government to WCS.

- ➢ Large numbers of WCS are functioning under C class in Audit Classification– indicative of the unsatisfactory working of a very large number of WCS and their financial ill health and operational inefficiency.
- ➢ Lack of modernization– most of the looms were of the "raised pit-loom" type since the weaver households prefer to weave on raised platforms instead of working on frame looms or jacquard looms in which they can weave more yardage and earn more wages. The average production on a pit-loom was only 4-5 meters per day as against 8-9 meters per day in frame looms.
- ➢ Practices like unaccounted sales have also affected the viability of WCS.

Though some of these constrains are not new, the new economic policies have aggravated these problems.

EFFORTS MADE BY THE STATE GOVERNMENT

- ✓ On the other hand the State Government has been providing the following assistance to the WCS and has some welfare measures for the members of WCS
- ✓ WCS are being provided with working capital finance at normal rate of interest and the government is directly paying interest subsidy of 3% to the WCS. Government of Tamilnadu has sanctioned Rs. 13.58 crores for the year 2000-2001.
- ✓ The State Government permitted the WCS and Cooptex to allow rebate at the rate of 20% for the sale of handloom cloth throughout the year for the retail and wholesale. The rebate claims aggregated Rs. 23.43 crores for the year 2000-2001.
- ✓ Since cotton is the main raw material for the textile industry and as there is a huge gap between the production and consumption in Tamilnadu,

Government of Tamilnadu has set up State Cotton Council to workout a strategy for increase of cotton production and its productivity.

✓ Welfare measures initiated by State Government for Weavers are:

- Hand loom Weavers Savings and Security Scheme
- Group Insurance Scheme for Handloom Weavers
- Central Thrift Fund Scheme
- Cooperative Handloom Weavers Old Age Pension Scheme
- Health Package Scheme for Handloom Weavers

FOCUS GROUP DISCUSSION

Based on this background, a Focus Group Discussion was conducted among employees of WCS of Thanjavur District to understand their perception on the functioning of the WCS in Tamilnadu. Employees were chosen mainly because they act as backbone for the WCS. As there is no democratic management, members lost their identity with their own WCS and they look WCS as only a Government mechanism to dispose of Government schemes for weavers. On the other hand, the new economic policies alienated the government from Cooperatives. Hence employees only act as stakeholders of WCs. Their perceptional management, customers, members, employees and general aspects were identifies and analysed.

PERCEPTION OF EMPLOYEES ON MANAGEMENT

Every cooperative society is autonomous and independent. The democratically elected board of management should manage the affairs of the society. To maintain democracy in the management every one is given equal right through one-man one vote policy irrespective of their shareholding in the society. But as far as Tamilnadu is concerned regular elections to the boards of cooperatives have been negated since 1970s.

1. Decision–Making Process

Since there is no democratic management, the special officers are managing the WCS. Government has appointed one special officer for managing more than one WCS. Also they have been transferred very often. This results in postponement of decision making even for crucial issues. In number of cases, special officers visit was at the end of month to pass the salary bill. Hardly they find time to go deep into the issues, which are faced by the WCS.

2. Political interferences

Unnecessary increase of membership and unwanted appointments because of political interferences questioned the exchequer of the WCS. The financial viability of WCS has been eroded due to non-release of subsidies from Government and unwanted interference of political parties.

3. Professional Management

The Employees perceive that they need a team of professionals to manage the affairs of WCS. Employees find it very difficult to face the onslaught of competition by using the available resources, as there is no guiding force behind them.

PERCEPTION OF EMPLOYEES ON CUSTOMERS

WCS products still have a niche in the handloom market. However, the charging scenario brings a lot of new changes that brings new challenges to WCS.

1. Consumer Behaviour

Handloom consumer's taste and preferences are changing very often because of more choices in the market. Employees felt necessary to have training to produce goods according to the market demand. Further, it is felt that many of the rare varieties in handloom are out of production and the continuance of sickness in the handloom industry would question the employment opportunities of millions of people.

2. Expectations of the Consumers

Consumers look WCS only during festival seasons due to cash rebate. Even during non-festival seasons while consumers visit WCS they demand rebate for their purchase. It seems that if rebate is not provided many of the customers may not turn back.

3. Facilities Needed for the Consumers

The present day consumers expect more facilities during their shopping namely dressing rooms, air-conditioned show room, more varieties, more space for display and selection of cloths etc., but this needs heavy investment. Majority of WCS are not capable of providing these facilities to the customers, as they are financially not viable.

PERCEPTION OF EMPLOYEES ON MEMBERS

Dedicated membership is the base for cooperative effort. But nowadays the number of active members in the WCS has been coming down. This results in wide gap between the members and cooperatives. Employees perception on the relationship between members and WCS is presented below:-

1. Lack of Responsibility

Members have been merely shareholders and not stakeholders, but expect more wages and benefits from the WCS. Members are not interested to maintain relationship with employees and management for development of the society. Majority of them demand simple work from WCS but expect more wages. They have been dolls in the hands of politicians. This affects the routine functioning of WCS.

2. The Problem of overdue

In the WCS every member is provided with adequate raw materials to produce particular variety of cloth in particular design. Many of the times, after producing the cloth, the members sell them in the open market or to the master weavers, hence overdue to the society. The WCS find it very difficult to collect the raw materials/finished products from such members.

3. Production of new designs

Majority of the members are not capable of producing cloth with new designs and the standards necessary for export. The training given for them on producing cloth with new designs have not provided better results. Since majority of the members have crossed their middle age.

PERCEPTION OF EMPLOYEES ON THEIR WORKING CONDITIONS

Employees felt that they are the only stakeholders in the development of WCS at present. If the following issues are settled, they may re engineer themselves for the development of WCS.

1. Unattractive Salary

Salary of employees is fixed on the basis of working capital of each WCS. Because of this, the majority of WCS employees get low salary, which has been a decade old problem. Further, in majority of the WCS the employees could not assure of getting salary during every month.

2. Lack of promotion

Employees work continuously in the same post for years together without any promotion or transfer. Since there is no democratic management, the Government officers are not taking any interest in this aspect. Hence poor salary and lack of fringe benefits has been killing the morale of the employees.

3. Lack of training

Employees demand regular training to update their knowledge and skill on handloom industry, consumer behaviour, management of WCS and public relations. All the employees are not provided a chance to go for training regularly.

Apart from the above, the employees felt that they are facing the following problems in their WCS:

1. Lack of autonomy and independence in the management of WCS
2. Lack of democratic management
3. Competition from private sector
4. Lack of relationship between management and employees
5. Lack of effective management information system
6. The restrictive provisions of the Tamilnadu Cooperative Societies Act 1983 and Rules 1988
7. Lack of organic link between WCS and Cooptex.

PROBLEM PRIORITIZATION

After finding the problems, the employees were asked to prioritize them. As per their opinion, the problems of WCS at present are listed down.

1. Sickness in handloom industry.
2. The interference of Government in all activities.
3. Delay in taking decisions
4. Low salary
5. Lack of democratic management
6. Increasing number of inactive weavers
7. Consumers demand

CONCLUSION

Cooperatives have been given due priority in the programmes of the government during the past nine decades. But one cannot deny the fact that during recent past cooperatives in general and WCS in particular were denied due recognition. The government has turned its face towards market economy. This policy of the government has created both favorable climate and challenging environment for the WCS. However, cooperatives have proved their efficiency even in the a market-oriented economics. In Tamilnadu, too there is enough evidence that the WCS are waking up to face the challenges of new economic policies. But their number is too small. Majority of the WCS have become dormant and the members have been forced to loose their identity. Active members' participation, enlightened leadership, self-reliance in resource mobilization, professional management, autonomy and independence, depoliticisation and debureaucratisation alone would reengineer the WCS. If the cooperators are not sensitizing this, as J. C. Kumarappa once reported 'skilled weavers found breaking stones for road-making for a meager livelihood', would repeat. Yes it has repeated in the case of weavers of Tamilnadu.

Table No.1

Status Of Weavers Cooperative Societies

S.No.	Description	1995-96		1996-997		1997-98		1998-1999		1999-2k	
		TN	All India	TN	All India	TN	All India	TN	All India	TN	All India
1.	No of WCS	1439	18396	1439	18846	1386	19187	1382	19980	1-414	20023
2.	No. of looms	0.04	-	0.04	-	0.04	0.23	0.3	0.24	0.24	0.24
3.	Production	435.76	-	405.29	-	398.2	7713.45	401.97	13207	387.72	13198
4.	Sales	455.6	-	422.56	-	431.66	9514.94	510.62	13132	461.57	15266
5.	Working Capital	221.93	-	268.29	-	270.19	7606.19	304.13	8412.3	373.57	8513

Source : Compiled from (i) NABARD (2002) State level Credit Seminar—State Focus Paper

(ii) NCUI (2001) A Profile of Cooperative Movement in India

INCOME AND EMPLOYMENT LINKAGES IN INDIA AN EXPLORATORY ANALYSIS

Dr. T. R. Jeyaraaj*,
Dr. N. Malathi**

In India the largest growth in output in the industrial sector has generally been associated with low growth in employment. Development of industrial sector has probably taken place not so much on lines of labour intensive small scale and agro-based industries as on the lines of the organized sector. But in developing countries like India with surplus labour and scarce capital, labour centered strategy is essential for employment maximization. Hence it is being increasingly recognized that the village and cottage industries have an important role to play in generating employment and in making up the crucial shortage in the sector of consumer goods and thus keeping inflationary forces in check.

Tamilnadu State occupies third place in the number of nonagricultural enterprises in India and fifth place in the contribution of manufacturing to State domestic product. But the State Comes to ninth place as regards central government investment and unemployment is much higher than the national average. The structural changes since 1970-71 indicate that the commodity production sectors have been and are stagnant or declining in relation to service sector. The growth rates of primary, secondary and service sector are 1.8%, 3.9%, and 6.4% respectively and their contributions to he SDP has changed from 40% to 23% for primary sector, from 26% to 28% for secondary sector and from 34% to 49% for service

* Reader in Development Studies, Department of Economics. Annamalai University,

** Professor of Economics

sector respectively. The secondary sector and in particular the manufacturing sector has registered a higher growth rate than that for the country as a whole. These facts highlight the role of industrial sector in development through economic reforms.

EMPLOYMENT -OUTPUT TRADE OFF

Aggregate employment in the State depends on the structure of production and its labour intensity. But employment objective must not be incompatible with economic efficiency and it need not conflict with maximizing the growth rate of output. The methods of generating employment ought to minimize the cost of creating a job and be sufficiently productive to contribute adequately to the national product. Stable employment of a region requires availability of raw material and existence of demand for the product. It is better that the industrial units create both forward and backward linkages, employment and income multiplier and spread effect. In this context Agro-based industries which have tonic effect on the rural economy through their linkage and spread effects needs to be encouraged to avoid adverse impact of economic reforms. As agricultural sector has reached a stage of stagnation, the growth of employment is only 0.95% in rural areas whereas it is 3.97% in urban areas. The manufacturing sector has high linkage with the rest of the economy (Hirschman) and it can help alleviate the problem of unemployment in rural and urban areas by increasing the number of jobs.

Decentralised concentration of industries is suggested to achieve a shift of future industrial growth from a metropolitan area to secondary urban centres by regional industries and to rural communities by rural industries. These linkages are expected to result in multiplier mechanism of Keynes and spread effect. Synthesis of Gadgil – Sen and Rao approaches is needed to achieve growth with social justice in rural areas. Gadgil-Sen approach links the villages with mandi town to achieve economic growth. But Rao indicates the leakages out of the multiplier in such vertical link up and urges for horizontal link of villages to villages or cluster to cluster. The synthesis of two approaches requires proper combinations of vertical and horizontal links.

The simple employment project arising out of Keynes' theory is that productivity gains of labour will exercise negative effect on labour absorption Lr=Yr— Lpr. The post Kenesian output-employment macro models focus on the relationship between industrial output and employment generation. Models for a dualistic economy with surplus labour by Lewis (1954) and Fei-Ranis consider capital accumulation as the crucial factor for absorption of labour in the modern industrial sector. The 'Big Push' of Rodan through rapid industrialization hence becomes the code word for development.

In this context, it is worth while to note that modern industries using capital intensive technique not only create a few opportunities for employment but also destroy employment in the traditional household sector in the rural areas (backwash effect of Myrdal). Due to the result that labour is not absorbed in sufficient quantities relative to the general population growth and especially the growth of urban areas; problems arise in the absorption of the growing labour in the developing economics. The alleviation of mass unemployment is doubted by Baer & Herve (1966) as capital Intensive technique supposedly lead to increased production potential in the economy without the generation of effective demand.

Raphael-Barel opines that income maximization requires rural industrialization process is based mainly on big plants centralized at local areas whereas employment maximization can be achieved through smaller plants dispersed in rural areas. Even in labour centered strategy some combination is essential between capital intensive and labour intensive industries in order to achieve maximum employment as well as income.

Staley and Morse highlight the fact that small plants have high labour use and labour cost coefficients. Realisation of their employment potential depends on the pace of growth of demand for these products. According to Choget small scale enterprises economise capital, provide more employment per unit of capital and therefore are viable and vital for a labour abundant economy. But due to idle investment and idle capacity the small scale sector which is a strategy for reducing large scale unemployment is not providing as much employment as it would absorb economically.

The development of complementary industries is essential indeed to achieve maximum income and employment multiplier. There is vast scope for the establishment of related cottage industries in rural areas so that a given volume of investment would make a far greater dynamic impact on output, income and employment in view of the chain multiplier effects involved and ensures the speedy improvement in the living standards of the people.

DEVELOPMENTAL FOCUS

It is pertinent to note that labour absorption substantially lags behind output due to an increase in labour efficiency and adoption of more capital intensive technique of production. Price–Incentive Micro Models suggest that the prevalence of factor price distortion in favour of capital has resulted in the labour saving bias of technology which has offset the employment expansion effect of output growth. The growth rate of employment thus depends upon the growth rate of labour intensity and on the rate of investment multiplied by output-capital ratio. Thus comparing to all expectations and predictions high rate of capital promotion has failed to generate adequate employment opportunity.

In order to forge dynamic links between rural and urban areas industrialisation of rural areas will capture rural surplus of its development and sustained growth. A proper combination of an industrial complex leads to efficient linkages and centrifugal spread of prosperity. Leibenstein has pointed out the use of capital intensive technique to generate productive employment on a sustained basis for a labour surplus economy. It is argued that the growth process by capital centered approach would take care of the issues of employment through tickle down process.

But a thorough analysis is also necessary to ascertain the kind of industrial growth in rural and urban settlements as employment elasticity of industrial output or income equivalent of employment in industries is influenced by the size of an enterprise and choice of production technique. According to Barel, optimum combination of labour centered and capital centered strategy of rural industries is needed to achieve employment as well as income. This may be achieved by preferring a mid way between village industries and manufacturing industries according to the suitability of rural conditions of industrial and product diversification through intersectoral and spatial linkages.

In developmental context empirical evidence for the growth of employment is necessary to supplement the theoretical contention employment -output trade off as the largest growth in the output of industrial sector in India has been associated with low growth of employment [Agro-based 0.93, Metal-53, Small=0.64, Large = 0.54]. Hence the , income equivalent of employment growth rates are around two for capital goods and around one for consumer goods industries.

If modern industries require a substantial service sector in order to function, such a requirement would eventually provide a major source for coping with the employment problem of LDCs. Galenson is fairly optimistic along these lines and found from the empirical study of both developed and developing countries that one percent increase in manufacturing employment leads to an increase of 0.6% of employment in tertiary activities. There is stronger service employment impact by capital intensive technique in addition to greater potential for further investment expansion and multiplier effect.

LABOUR INTENSITY, PRODUCTIVITY AND PROFITABILITY

Cottage industrial units or tiny units are yielding quick output through capital light, import light and skill light technology of production. Local market based industries help the producers in reducing selling expenses and transport cost. Development of local resource based industries provides additional employment to people in that region. Employment potential and contribution of labour were analysed through the use of primary data collected from a stratified random sample of 100 cottage industrial units encompassing brick and cement wroks, mat-weaving, cigar, beverages and food product units. The cost of machinery occupies one third of fixed capital while fixed capital constitutes less than 30% of total productive capital. In all these industries cost of raw material and labour charges occupies 50% to 95% of total production cost.

Employment of labour per unit is 8.3, 5.5, 5.0, 3.1 and 4.1 respectively in these units and is smaller for units with relatively higher fixed capital investment. Nearly half of labour employed are female and they are in sizeable number in cigar, brick and mat-weaving units. Family labour constitutes 50 percent of total labour employment. Excepting brick units which do not operate during rainy season other units have casual labour employment for 290 days and family labour employment for 300 days.

In view of social desirability criterion, labour intensity of cottage units is expressed in terms of employment of labour per unit of capital. It is found that as size of productive capital increases labour intensity deceases and as size of employment increases it also increase. If the basic objective is to raise employment and income of the rural people it would be imperative to argument capital in these industries which only appear to be capable of increasing output and income per worker.

Profitability or economic viability of the cottage units is assessed in terms of surplus per unit of capital investment. Little has proved that more labour intensive firms are found to be more profitable. In the sample units the most labour intensive brick and cement works get the maximum rate of return of 31.5%. Thus in spite of less labour productivity relatively more labour intensive units are able to generate more income since the increase in capital per unit of output is more than compensated by the decline in the labour cost per unit of output.

The cottage units generate wage employment in addition to self-employment. But the sample units are depending only on their own source of finance and the owners do not have industrial training. Since these industries are suitable to provide employment opportunities to under-employed and unemployed people appropriate measures are needed as the prosperity of these industries is hindered due to facilities of capital and marketing. For the promotion of cottage units in the long run appropriate asset endowment schemes by the government are essential rather than mere concessions.

CONCLUSION

The low proportions of fixed capital investment affect the gross profit and consequently the capital formation and investment of cottage industries which shows their unstable and unpredictable nature. Extension of bank finance to cottage units and the sanction of working capital finance leading to more capital investment will certainly result in large employment of labour. If efforts are made to acquire new skills and adopt modern technology for better utilization of the capacities as well as resources the nineties may well mark the beginning of a rapid development of cottage industries which in turn will galvanise the economy and bring a new measure of prosperity through economic reforms.

REFERENCES

1. Bar-El,R(1982), Industiralisation and Development, Hebrew : London.
2. T. Choget [1989]; "Efficiency of small scale Industries in India', The Asian Economic Review, Vol. XXXI, p.1743.
3. Fei John, C.H. and G. Ranis (1964), Development of the Labour Surplus Economy: Theory and Policy, Homewood.
4. Gadgil, P. G. (1985), Industrial Economy of India, S. Chand: New Delhi.
5. Keynes, J. M. (1936), The General Theory of Employment, Interest and Money, Macmillan : London.
6. Leibenstein, H. (1957), Economic Backwardness and Economic Growth, Wiley : New York.
7. Little I. M. D, Dipak Majumadar and John M. Page Jr. (1987), Small Manufacturing Enterprises, Oxford University Press: New York.
8. Sen, A. K. (1975), Employment, Technology and Development, Oxford : London.
9. Staley, E., and R. Morse (1987), Modern Small Industries for Developing Countries, McGraw Hill: New York.

RURAL—URBAN LABOUR MIGRATION AND THE GROWTH OF INFORMAL SECTOR IN INDIA

*Dr. Soukath Ali,
** V. Saravanan

INTRODUCTION

Migration of the rural population to urban centres in search of better livelihood prospects is a noteworthy feature of India's economy. Employment opportunities in the urban formal sector, which offers protected employment for certain labour, is what attracts the villagers. But, the limited prospects of the sector pushes majority of them into the hard core of informal sector characterised by unorganised small-scale business ventures operated with skills acquired outside the formal school system. Urban conglomerations in most cases have their own Limitations in affording the migrant villagers. The flow towards urbanisation, couples with the restrictive absorption power of formal sector; is in no way matches with the mass migration of skilled and unskilled labour from the rural areas. Development of villages is hindered by this exodus of productive labour that could have been utilized for integrated development of the rural region. The sad paradox is that neither the urban ventures are able to provide substantial livelihood to majority of rural migrants nor the villages are benefited with the under employed to majority of rural migrants not the villages are benefited with the underemployed urban settlers. Efforts have to be taken at the migration sources to remedy the intricate problem.

---

* Reader, Department of Economics, M.S.S.Wakf Board College, Madurai.

** Ph. D. Research Scholar, Department of Economics, Centre for Research, Arul Anandar College, Karumathur, Madurai District-625 514

URBANIZATION

India is predominantly a rural economy. The gradual transfer from its predominant rural make-up to an industrial nation has much to do with the global development scenario. A four four-decadal analysis of the sectoral composition of the country's gross domestic product (CGDP) shows that the dominance of agricultural sector is declining.

On the other side, the industrial as well as service sector contributes increasing proportion to the GDP (Table 1). During 1960-61, the share of agriculture in GDP was 54.54 per cent which declined to 27.50 percent in 1999-2000, at the same time, share of industry increased from 16.55 percent to 24.63 percent. Industrial growth was supplemented with the development of service sector, which grew from 28.91 percent to 47.87 percent during the four decades. Industrial and service sector growth is viewed as an impetus to urbanisation. The declining trend in the contribution of agricultural sector to GDP could also be attributed to the increasing urbanisation. According to World Bank, urbanisation is a process by which large number of people becomes permanently concentrated in small areas forming cities. It is an index of industrialisation and economic development.

Table –1

Sectoral composition of India's GDP

Sector	1960-1961	1970-71	1980-81	1990-91	1999-2000
Agriculture	1128.48 (54.54)	1425.81 (48.02)	1677.70 (41.82)	2420.12 (34.92)	3167.80 (27.50)
Industry	342.39 (16.55)	589.97 (19.87)	866.05 (21.59)	1697.03 (24.49)	2837.16 (24.63)
Service	598.09 (28.91)	953.53 (32.11)	1467.87 (36.59)	2813.36 (40.59)	5514.95 (47.87)

Source : Government of India (2001)

The change in the proportion of urban population to total population is termed as "degree of urbanisation". The degree of urbanisation increases as the economy develops and it is higher in developed countries as compared to developing countries. In developed countries, roughly around 70 per cent of the population lies in Urban centres, where as, in developing countries the proportion of urban population is mostly around 30 per cent.

A look at the percentage of urban population to total population over the years in India shows that there is an increasing trend in the urbanisation process. As could be seen from Table 2, during 1901, only 10.82 per cent of the total population belonged to urban centres and even that was reduced to 10.27 percent in the next decade. Afterwards, the process of urban population reached a level of 25.70 percent in 1991 and again increased to 27.78 percent in 2001.

Table 2

Percentage Distribution Of Indian Urban Population To Total Population

Census Year	Population (Millions)	% Rate of Growth of Total Population (Annual)	Total Urban Population	% of Urban Population to total Population	Growth of Urban Population (Annual)
1901	238.40	---	25.8	10.82	---
1911	252.09	5.6	25.9	10.27	0.3
1921	252.32	-3.1	28.1	11.18	0.8
1931	278.98	1.05	33.5	12.00	1.8
1941	318.16	1.32	44.2	13.87	2.8
1951	361.09	1.30	62.4	17.28	3.5
1961	439.23	2.00	78.9	17.96	2.4

1971	548.16	2.24	109.1	19.90	3.3
1981	683.33	2.23	159.3	23.31	3.9
1991	846.39	2.16	217.42	25.70	3.16
2001	1027.02	2.13	285.35	27.78	3.12

Source : 1) Raman H. (1994), 2, Government of India 2001

Apart the concentration of urban population, the trend in its growth rate bypasses the overall growth trends, From 1921 to 2001, the growth rate of urban population went over and above the total population growth, During the period, the growth of urban population and total population increased from 0.8 per cent and -3.1 percent in 1921 to 3.12 and 2.13 percent in 2001 respectively. The exceptional growth rate in urban population is the result of natural increase of urban population as well as the net migration from rural areas. The net migration from rural to urban areas is the concomitant of rapid growth and expansion of industrial and service sectors in urban areas.

RURAL-URBAN MIGRATION

There are two principal hypotheses regarding the growth of urban centres and urbanisation (William son, 1988). They are, 1) the rapid growth of population pressing on limited farm acreage, pushing landless labour into cities. The surplus model of Lewis (1954) imprints that, as a consequence of this migration, wage patterns of the modern sector favours the capitalists in augmenting their investments and thereby profits. This two-sector model explains the movement of excess labour in the traditional agricultural sector to the modern industrial sector in search of higher wages. The wages, which is assumed to be constant, is higher in the modern sector compared to the subsistence wage in the traditional sector. The assumption of constant wage in the modern sector is in view of the fact that the marginal product of labour in the traditional sector is zero. This peculiarity helps the capitalists in keeping the wages constant. It will remain so until the entire surplus labour being absorbed from the traditional sector and afterwards induces the marginal product of labour to rise from zero. On the other side, the migration model forwarded by Todaro (1997) is more realistic though it sees migration as purely an economic phenomenon. It explains the paradoxical relationship of accelerated rural-urban migration in the context of rising urban unemployment. The model postulates "migration proceeds in response to urban-rural differences in expected income rather than actual earnings. The fundamental premise is that the migrants consider the various labour market opportunities available to them in the rural and urban sectors and choose one that maximizes their expected gains from migration".

As far as India is concerned, there is little statistics available regarding the number of migrants from rural to urban and also about the percentage of educated unemployed within that category. The aggregate figure for educated unemployed in India is 39.03 million at the end of August, 1997. It increased to 40 million in 1998-1999 and again slightly increased to 40.37 million in the next year. The employment exchange statistics (1999-2000) says that a majority of the job seekers (63.6%) wee in category of workers not classified by any occupation implying that they are inexperienced fresher . The second highest (22.2%) was in the category of production-related workers and transport-related workers. A minor proportion of the job seekers belonged to the category of sales-workers. Those job seekers, who fall within the unspecified occupational category, are employed in some way or other, somewhere amidst their actual expectations of receiving a job in the formal sector. The second largest category of job seekers, who engage in production and transport-related endeavours, also reiterates the possible absorption of labour force by the informal sector. This trend could also be noticed among the women job seekers registered with employment exchange within the country. It is evident that the so-called formal sector could not absorb any significant portion of the skilled or unskilled labour force. Naturally, the labour force would be soaked into the informal sector.

INFORMAL SECTOR

The term 'Informal Sector' was first used in the International Labour Office report on Kenya, 1972 and since then it has sparked a great deal of controversy in development literature over the meaning and usefulness of such a concept. This sector is distinguished with the features contrary to the organised or formal sector. The major features of informal sector are, a) ease of entry, b) reliance on indigenous sources, c) family ownership of enterprise, d) small scale of operation, e) labour-intensive and adapted technology, f) skills acquired outside the formal school system and g) unregulated and competitive labour markets. The features of formal sector activities are obverse to these and includes, a) difficulty of entry, b) frequent reliance on overseas resources, c) corporate ownership, d) large scale of operation, e) capital intensive and often imported technology, f) formally acquired skills and g) protected markets (through tariffs, quotas and trade licences).

The ventures prominent in the urban informal sector could be given priority in the regional rural plans incorporating the potential of skilled and unskilled labourers. The rural urban disparities could be reduced with such a balanced approach of development. The linkages between urban informal sector and the secluded rural production centres could be explored. The development programmes enunciated at the grass-roots level could be maneuvered in such a way as to include the rural migrants.

Informal sector tops in creates in employment opportunities. Informal sector in India is widely disbursed over its numerous city centres and the size distribution or the quantum of employment in the sector was prominent, even by the middle of the twentieth century. One has to rely on several regional studies to have an idea of the sector. Most of these studies show that the proportion f labour force engaged in informal sector is much higher than that employed in the formal sector. Table No. 5 reveals that the data compiled by Mazumdar from various sources shows that 55 percent of the urban labour force in Mumbai city is engaged in informal sector activities. Studies from some major city entries in certain selected developing countries (Jakarta-Indonesia, Belo Horizonte-Brazil, Lima-Peru) also reveal that more than 50 per cent of the urban labour force is employed in the informal sector.

Table 3

Size Of The Informal Sector

Area	Date	Criterion of Employment	Total Employed	%in Informal Sector
Mumbai	1961	Employment reported, Directorate of Employment and Training	1,687,000	55
Jakarta	1971	Registered Employment	Just Over 1 million	Just over 50
Belo Horizonte (Brazil)	1972	Social Security payment	?	69
Lima (Peru)	1970	Size of Establishment	619,000	53
8 cities (Peru)	1970	Size of Establishment	N. A.	62

Source : Mazumdar (1976)

CASE STUDIES FOR GROWTH OF INFORMAL SECTOR

Anand compiled various studies conducted in different city centres of India and came up with a detailed picture of the distribution of informal sector firms, its ownership pattern, employment opportunities and the magnitude of informal schooling. A study from Allahabad found that 80 percent of the total informal sector activity concentrated on the job of trading of goods and services (wholesaling and retailing activities) and only 20 percent concentrated in small-scale manufacturing. An equal degree of concentration was seen in the ownership pattern of informal sector ventures, around 90 percent of the units were singly owned. Majority of the owners (82 per cent) operate their business on the basis of informal and self-taught skills, even though they possess a lower degree of formal schooling. More studies from Kolkata and Ahmedabad, along with Allahabad, showed that the informal sector creates substantial wage and self-employment opportunities. The involvement of women in this sector is meagre, as most the studies have found a negligible percentage of women in the total labour force. Mazumdar's study has located only a small minority of female workers in the Mumbai labour market.

IMPLICATIONS

Overcrowding in cities leads to several social and environmental problems. Homelessness and the subsequent sanitation, health, ecological hardships are a few of such consequences. The latest census has identified 35 city centres with a population above one million. Three metro cities, such as Greater Mumbai, Kolkata and Delhi have an average population of 14 million. The ecological hazards, no doubt, would be directly proportionate to this overcrowding. Supplementary to this, the growth trends of India's economy towards and urbanised path with increasing importance of industrial and service sector in the GDP have contributed much in the upcoming of informal sector. Urbanisation, which is viewed as an index of industrialisation and economic development, is certainly attracting more people towards better employment opportunities. The magnitude of migration is also evident from the rapid growth of urban population. But, contrary to the migrant's expectations, a significant proportion of the labour force found a way outside the formal organised sector.

CONCLUSION

The ventures prominent in the urban informal sector could be given priority in the regional rural plans incorporating the potential of skilled and unskilled labourers. The rural-urban disparities could be reduced with such a balanced approach of development planning coupled with infrastructure development. The linkages between urban informal sector and the secluded rural production centres could be explored. The development programmes enunciated at the grass-roots level could be maneuvered in such a way as to include the rural migrants. Thus, the occasional migrates could be targeted on the basis of their degree of marginalization. In fact, the rural development initiatives are geographically constrained to village inhabitants, keeping away a large gamut of vulnerable segment, the migrants. Geographic and administrative constraints could be relaxed to include development action based on sustainable production potential. Ultimately, the rural-urban equivalence will certainly dilute the hazardous consequences of migration and over-crowding of cities.

REFERENCES

1. Anand V (1994), Informal Sector in Developing Countries; Certain Crucial Hypothesis, The Indian Economic Journal. Vol. No.42, No.2
2. Dewell K. K., J. D. Verma and M. L. Sharma (1995) Indian Economy; A Development Oriented Study, SC&C, New Delhi.
3. Government of India (2001). Employment Exchange Statistics. Directorate General of Employment and Training, Ministry of Labour.

4. Government of India (2001). Economic Survey 2000-2001, Ministry of Finance.
5. Government of India (2002), Census 2001, Office of the Registrar General, India.
6. House William J (1985), Nairobi's Informal Sector; Dynamic Entrepreneurs or Surplus Labour? Economic Development and Cultural Change.
7. Lewis Arthur W (1954), Economic Development with Unlimited Supplies of Labour, The Manchester School, May.
8. Mazumdar (1976), The Urban Informal Sector, World Development. Vol. 4, No.8, pp 659.
9. Meir G. M. (1995), Leading issues in economic development Oxford University Press, London.

EMERGING TRENDS IN SERVICE SECTOR : SOME OBSERVATIONS

N. Mukundan*

INTRODUCTION

As proof of India's economic development since independence the share of agriculture in the Gross Domestic Product (GDP) gradually declined from 57.41% in 1950-51 to 22.16 percent in 2002-2003. Further, it reflected on the share of the primary sector and rise in that of secondary and territory activities. In this context, the "U" turn New Economic Policy gives a new dimension of the Indian economy in the nineties and has been shifted towards service sector. While a little over decade ago the main sectors of economic activity like agriculture, Industry and Services had roughly equaled shares in the GDP. The Service sector has now left the other two sector far behind.

METHODOLOGY

The focus of this paper is 1) To study growth of service sector contribution to GDP during pre and post reform periods. 2) To Study correlation between the growth of sectoral contribution of GDP and its employment. The analysis based on time series data of growth trends in 1983 and 1999-2000.

EMERGING TRENDS IN SERVICE SECTOR :

The service sector in the Indian economy accounted for 28 percent of GDP in 1950-51. This share increased to 37.6 percent in 1999-2000. The component of service sectors like transport, Communication and Trade improved from 12 percent in 1950-51 to 21.9 percent in 1999-2000. The

* Lecturer in Economics, P. G. and Research Dept of Economics, A.V.C. College (Autonomous) Mannampandal-5 Mayuram.

component of service sectors like Transport, Communication and Trade improved from 12 percent in 1950-51 to 21.9 percent in 1999-2000. The agriculture sector contribution to GDP was 38.23 percent in 1983 which had fallen by 16 percent in 1999-2000. It elicits that the agriculture sector being a major contribution in the pre reform period which was a step down in its contribution during the post reform period (as shown in Table-1) As a result of the introduction of New Economic Policy the Industrial sector contribution to GDP which was 24.99 percent in 1983 stepped up to 31.7 percent in 1999-2000. At the same time gradual increase in the service sector contribution to GDP witnessed from Table-1 shows clear evidence that there is also a rise in the growth and dominance over all the three major sectors of the economy during post reform period

Table-1

Gross Product at Industry Origin at Factor Cost

(Rs. Billion at 1995/1996 prices)

Years / Sectors	1983@	1993-94	1999-2000
Agriculture	51190 (38.23)	2217.5 (27.7)	3180.6 (22.3)
Industry	33471 (24.99)	2005.3 (25.0)	4529.8 (31.7)
Service	49254 (33.6)	3008.3 (35.6)	4997.6 (37.6)

Source : Economic S. Rvey 1999-2000. and NCAER, Infrastructure report-2001@ Base 1980-81 prices Figures in parenthesis are percentage

Table 2

Compound Annual Growth of GDP by Economic Activity

(% per annum at 1993 prices)

Years / Sectors	1980-81 to 1990-91	1990-91 to 2000-2001
Agriculture	3.4	2.6
Industry	7.6	5.9
Service	6.7	7.5

Source : Ruddar Datt, K. P. M. Sundaram, Indian Economy 2003

Table 2 explains the sectoral compound annual growth rate of GDP by sectors of the economy. The growth of agriculture showed a decline from 3.4 percent 1980-81 and 1990-91 to 2.6 percent between 1990-91 and 1999-2000. Similarly, the rate of growth of secondary sector came down from 7.6 percent in 1990-1991 to 5.9 percent in 1999-2000. In this context, the growth rate of service sector has picked up from 6.7 percent in 1990-91 to 7.5 percent in 1999-2000.

EMPLOYMENT SCENARIO IN THE SECTORS OF THE ECONOMY

One of the great failures of Indian planning system over the decades is that it has not contributed adequately to the solution of unemployment problems and the existence of poverty and slow rate of increase in human development. The underrating of human resources should be a channelised productive one that is crucial building the nations economy. In this connection, service sector provide more employment opportunities during post reform period. Table-3 reveals that two periods in employment generation may be noticed in the perform period nearly 51 percent of additional employment came from the primary sector 19 percent from the secondary sector and 30 percent from the service sector. Between 1993-1994 and 1999-2000. Nearly 50 percent of the additional employment was generated in the secondary sector and 73 percent in the service sector However in the agriculture sector there was a fall in employment by nearly 24 percent.

Table 3

Growth of Employment (million) by Different Sectors

Pre-reform Period	1983	1993-94	Increased during 1983-93	Share in Increase (%)
Agriculture	208.99	245.16	36.17	50.5
Industry	41.66	55.53	13.87	19.3
Service	52.11	73.76	21.65	30.2
Post-reform Period	**1993-94**	**1999-2000**	**Increased during 1994-2000**	**Share in Increase (%)**
Agriculture	245.16	239.83	-5.33	-23.6
Industry	55.53	66.91	11.38	50.4
Service	73.76	90.26	16.50	73.2

Source : Ruddar Datt, K. P. M. Sundaram, Indian Economy 2003

Table – 4

Correlation Between Sectoral GDP and its Employment

Employment	GDP from sectors		
	Agriculture	Industrial	Service
Agriculture	0.1568 (0.375)		
Industrial		0.8582 (0.1756)	
Service			0.5389 (0.1774)

'P.E.' values are in parentheses.

STUDY FINDINGS:

The relationship between sectoral contribution to GDP and its employment is determined using Karl Person Sample Correlation and to test the significance of this relationship the test probable error value computed. It is noticed that the correlation co-efficient for agriculture sector is 0.15 percent which is statistically insignificant. That is GDP from agricultural sector is not systematically associated with employment generated in that agriculture sector. On the other hand correlation co efficient of Industrial sector (0.85) and service sector (0.53) are statistically significant. It is categorically indicated that in these sectors employment is closely associated with the respective sectoral contribution to GDP.

CONCLUSION

The theory of economic growth also supports the structural change in the composition of national products. Which is proved by advanced countries. In the reciting past decade, Indian economy also experienced a fast improvement in the structural change in the composition of National Income. It is very clear from the data in India, that the service sector contribution to the GDP is increasing year by year steadily and at present it is nearing 40 percent (2002-2003). Similarly its contribution towards employment is also around 50 percent (2002-2003) which confirms the service sectors dominance over the economy. Further, the changing structure of national income needs to be strengthened by stepping up the programme of industrialization and modernization of agriculture and agro based industries. So it can be concluded that the service sector plays a major role in shaping the Indian economy.

REFERENCES

1. Benjamin Higgins., : Economic Development-Problems, Principles and Policy, UBS Publi. New Delhi (1990).

2. Gupta, S. P. ,: Practical Statistics, S. Chand Publi, New Delhi, (2000).
3. Jegadish Gandhi, P., Ganesan, P., : "*Servicisation*" of the Economic Growth In India : it is Real, A Decade of Trade Liberalization in India (Eds) Padmanabhan, k., I. I. P. A. New Delhi (2001).
4. Ruddar Datt, and Sundharam, K. P. M., : Indian Economy, S. Chand Publi, New Delhi, (2003).
5. The Indian Infrastructure Report —Policy Imperatives for Growth and Welfare, Published by NCAER, New Delhi (2002).
6. Economic Survey— Govt. of India, Ministry of Finance, Economic Division, 1999-2000.

RURAL CHILD LABOUR IN TOURIST PLACES OF TAMIL NADU

Dr. G. Karunanithi
Prof. & Head
Department of Sociology
Manonmaniam Sundaranar
University, Tirunelveli—627 012.

Dr. A. Selva Kumar
Reader in Commerce
Pope's College Sawyerpuram
Tuticorin –628 251

INTRODUCTION

Child labour is undoubtedly a universal phenomenon. Especially, India has the largest section of child labour. This social problem is rooted in the socio-economic conditions prevailing in India. Employment of children at an early age would hamper their mental, physical and psychological growth. This, in turn, would affect the socio-economic development of the country to a great extent. Thus, child labour and poverty in India are mutually reinforcing and complementary to each other.

On the one hand, it is an economic pursuit because the poor parents compel their children to work in order to earn money. Consequently, the children become an integral part of the household economy. On the other hand, it is a social problem, because, it tends to interfere with education, play and recreation of the children. Moreover, they are subject to several health problems, which in turn interfere with their physical and mental development.

STATEMENT OF THE PROBLEM

The present study aims at analyzing the plight of child labour in tourist places especially, in Courtallam in Tirunelveli District, Thiruchendur in Tuticorin District and Kanyakumari in Kanyakumari District And which are popular pilgrimage-cum- in tourist centres in the southern most part of Tamil Nadu. The child labour in this study are those who are 14 and below 14 years of age. More or less, they are full time workers engaged in petty trades of their family or other employers, for a pittance.

In the sample area of Coutrallam, Which is located at *Podihai* hills of western Ghats in Tirunelveli District, six different natural waterfalls have been central attraction drawing thousands of people daily from all over India every year especially, during June-October. A famous siva temple close to the main falls is an added attraction to the pilgrims. Children in the age group of 8-14 years are employed in various small trades, for instance, selling fruits, flowers, eatables, artifacts and the like.

In a similar way, Tiruchendur is one of the aboards of God *Subramanaya,* where there is a big temple on the eastern sea-shore. Since thousands of pilgrims visit the temple every day, there are rows of shops in and around the temple drawing their attention. In those shops, an appreciable proportion of children are employed as sales boys, for little wage.

Kanyakumari is situated at the southern end of India, where three seas get conglomerated. It is, therefore considered as an important pilgrimage centre for the Hindus across the country. Everyday thousands of people throng to the place to see the conglomeration of the three seas and have a worship of Goddess Parvathi, who is believed to protect the place from the encroachment of the seas. Several small and big trades are flourishing because people from different ethnic and lingual groups including foreigners are attracted towards the roadside shops close to the sea-shore, selling beautiful artifacts made up of shells, chunks, beads and the like obtained from the seas. In addition to this, some other shops sell eatables and artifacts made up of palmyra leaves. It is obvious to see several children employed in those shops, are engaged in selling those artifact. Some of them are hawkers who take them to crowded places in order to sell them by persuading the tourists.

SAMPLING

In the three sample areas, there are hundreds of shops owned by private businessmen, mostly they are of small type and unorganized. It has been worked out that there are about 700 shops employing about 1500 children, both boys and girls.

While conducting a pilot study, ten children employed in unorganized trade (shops) from these tourist places, were selected randomly and interviewed with the help of interview-guide to collect necessary information.

MAJOR FINDINGS

In Courtallam children are employed in hotels, fruit stalls, flower shops and other shops dealing with eatables, artifacts, oil and the like. Nevertheless, their employment is primarily based on seasons (June to October). They are busy in season times and earn a sizeable income of Rs. 20–25 per day. They are mostly drawn from the sub-urbs and small villages surrounding Courtallam and they are from poor and large size families. Especially, the dalit (Scheduled Caste) children out number the children from other castes in terms of employment in the labour market. Normally, they start their work at 7 a.m. and continue to work till 8 p.m. But, those children employed in hotels do work upto mid-night. Most of them stay in the hotels because they have to start the work at 5 a.m.

It is observed that, half the child labour in Courtallam are hawkers, mostly selling eatables, fruits, flowers, oil, etc., in crowded places. They earn a very low wage (about Rs. 15 per day) when compared to children employed in hotels other shops. They are in the age group of 8-14 years and work for 10-12 hours a day. They are punished orally as well as physically by the shop and hotel owners if they are inattentive and careless in their work. In addition to the assigned work, they have to attend to the personal work of the owners especially, bringing tea or coffee, food and other required items to the owners and also to attend to their domestic work at times.

It is important to note that the children employed in hotels have certain unhealthy practices. For instant, they smoke beedis or cigarettes, drink liquor, use intoxicating drugs, and read pronographic literature. Moreover, they are involved in masturbation, homosexual activities and also indulge in sexual intercourse with sex workers. These practices are handed down to the them by the adult co-workers. This is easily possible because all of them share a single common room to take rest and sleep. They together while away the time by gossiping, playing cards and sex related games. Since they have no privacy, the activities of adult co-workers are very much open to every child worker.

The children employed in various shops, hotels and restaurants in and around the temple are in Tiruchendur are mostly drawn from the town and its neighbouring villages. Most of them are employed in shops dealing with articles meant for *archanai* and *abishekam* at sanctum and sanctoram and also selling eatables especially, the black, brown and white jaggery prepared out of palmyra juice, which is a popular sweet available is most of the shops. Besides some other shops sell items like toys, photos of Gods and goddesses. It is found out that a handful of children are hawkers who sell eatables at the sea-shore. More or less the same proportion of children work in hotels close to the temple and situated in other places of the town . They also have similar unhealthy practices as observed among children working in various hotels at Courtallam.

Generally, the child workers, start the work at 8.00 a.m. and continue to work till 8.00 p.m. for a meagre wage of about Rs. 20-25 per day. Most of them belong to Nadar community (Backward Class) because the surrounding villages of Tiruchendur are mostly populated by Nadars. They are poor mostly depending on agricultural work and selling palmyra products, they do not want to educate their children after primary level and want them to assist in their work. This is perhaps an important reason that the children prefer to work in shops and hotels in Tiruchendur area.

The child hawkers are more in Tiruchendur area as compared to their counterparts in Courtallam. Most of the time they get exposed to hot sun and are always in walk within the temple area even without foot-wear. The children are often subject to oral and physical punishment because, they come late in the morning and to sleep during the business hours. Those coming from neighbouring villages return to their homes after 9 p.m. by walk. Especially, during the festival times, they need to stay back in the shops because of the peak time of their business. They normally take food twice a day.

Kanyakumari is one of the famous tourist places in India. All over the year, tourists from different places of India and abroad do visit Kanyakumari. Therefore, this place is always crowded and highly commercialised mainly to attract the tourists. The children are employed in various shops selling varieties of artifacts mostly collected from the sea, and different types of bags made up of palmyra leaf and other raw materials available in the that area. Some of them work in hotels and other shops selling eatables, juice and soft drinks. The proportion of child hawkers in this area is appreciably higher than their counterparts in the other two places of the under the study. The child workers mostly come from surrounding villages and neighbouring districts and they are from some forward communities also. As in Tiruchendur, they come to the shop at 8 a.m. and work till 8 p.m. IN most of the shops, the girls out number the boys because the owners prefer the girls as sales persons. But, the child hawkers and those employed in hotels and restaurants are invariably boys. They work for 10-12 hours a day and earn (about Rs. 30 per day) more than the earnings of their counterparts in other two tourist places.

The unhealthy practices among them are rampant in this place.

It is concluded that the child workers from these three places belong to the age group 8-14 years, work for 8-12 hours a day, earn an average income of Rs. 20-25 a day, contribute to their family income to a certain extent and undergo physical exhaustion. They turn to child labour mainly because of poverty and negligence on the part of their parents to educate them. However, they have a feeling that they have lost childhood in terms of playing with other children, getting education and enjoying several things as other children from do so. Most of the children are willing to study if they are provided with adequate facilities.

It is noted that, there is delinquent sub-culture emerging among the working children especially, among those employed in hotels and restaurants. They commit to one or two criminal activities uniformly. Probably the new entrance from rural areas, at the age of eight or nine years, may not be aware of these criminal activities in the beginning. But, after one or two years, they slowly pick-up such activities as their seniors do. It is, therefore, concluded that the child workers at the age of 14 years have ample of chances to become delinquents as they are exposed to several criminal activities during their stay in the place of work.

At present Government of India adopts a new Economic Policy consisting of privatisation, liberalisation and globalisation. Under privatisation, business concerns and public undertakings are under the process of privatisation. This trend would results in accumulation of wealth by entrepreneurs. Consequently, they would prefer cheap labour. Thus, there is a possibility to observe a large section of children into labour market.

Under liberalisation, business people are encouraged to start any business free from restriction without hindering the general welfare of the public. This will pave way for proliferation of entrepreneurs across India. They will also look for cheap labour and more profit. As a result of this, more children will get employed all over the country.

Under globalisation, multinationals invest huge sum of money in establishing industries and trade. Though, they are against child labour, their ancillary units to be given to Indian entrepreneurs will employ more children because of cheap labour.

While giving way to New Economic Policy, The Government of India needs to go with the following packages to eradicate child labour.

i) Compulsory education upto secondary level.

ii) Stringent enforcement of laws relating to the elimination of child labour.

iii) Creating awareness not only among the parents of working children but also among public by campaigns organised by the NGOs in collaboration with the State and Central Government.

iv) A monitoring committee shall be formed to eradicate child labour at all levels.

EMPLOYMENT GENERATION THROUGH SELF-HELP GROUPS IN RURAL AREA

Dr. S. Padmavthy*
M. Malarvizhi**

Rural Development is a continuous and comprehensive socio-economic process attempting to improve all aspects of rural life. It aims at improving the economic and social condition of people living in villages. The development programmes are concerned with the principal object of improving the primary, secondary and tertiary sectors of the village absorbing excess labour force in gainful rural employment. In the primary sector, modernization of agriculture and improvement of animal husbandry, fisheries, and forest will be attempted. In the secondary sector, programmes will aim at developing village and cottage industries and enlarging the industrial base of rural life by creating skilled formations. In the tertiary sector, the programmes will aim at creating the necessary infrastructure for processing, marketing, transporting and other allied activities in rural areas. The supply of drinking water, linking of village by rural roads, educational programmes, vocational training and functional literacy, are the other important components of the process. Above all improving the social and economic conditions of scheduled castes and tribes, improving the lot of land less agricultural Labourers and extending help to small and marginal farmers form the vital aspects of the process of rural development.

* Reader in Economics, K. N. Government Arts College for Women, Thanjavur.

** Lecturer in Economics, K. N. Government Arts College for Women, Thanjavur.

There are many models of rural development. Some models aim at development with the existing socio-economic structure. Other models aim at development by altogether changing the existing socio-economic structure.

Since models of rural development aim at comprehensive change and improvement in all aspects of rural life, the approach to rural development should be made with the development of agriculture and modernization, change in socio-economic-cum-political set up, co-operative orientation and honest and dedicated rural leadership.

RURAL EMPLOYMENT SCHEMES

In recent years, the government has started some special schemes of rural development with particular emphasis on reducing rural unemployment.

1. The Small Farmers Development Agency (SFDA)
2. The Marginal Farmers and Agricultural Labourers Agency (MFALA)
3. Crash Scheme for Rural Employment (SRE-1971-1972)
4. Employment Guarantee Scheme (EGS)
5. The Drought-Prone Areas Programme (DPAP-1970-71)
6. Minimum Needs Programme (MNP)
7. Food For Work Programme (FWP-1977)
8. Training of Rural Youth for Self Employment (TRYSEM)
9. National rural Employment Programme (NREP-1984)
10. Integrated Rural Development programme 1978-79
11. The Rural Landless Employment Guarantee Programme (RLEGP 1984)

12. Indra Awas Yojana (1985-86)
13. Million Wells Scheme (1988-89)
14. Employment Assurance Scheme (1993)
15. National Social Assistance Programme (NSAP)-1995)
16. Jawahar Gram Samrithi Yojana (JGSY-1999)
17. Swarnajayanti Gram Swarozgar Yojana (-1999)

LINKAGE PROGRAMME OF NABARD

The National Bank for Agriculture and Rural Development is the apex body which provides credit to the grass root agencies so as to improve the socio-economic condition of the rural poor. The bank has been propagating the idea of SHGs and Bank Linkage Programme since 1992 in order to implement the package of ISB (Industry Service, Business) to the rural poor.

Integrated Rural Development Programme (IRDP), Training of Rural Youth for Self employment (TRYSEM), Development of Women and Children in Rural Areas (DWCRA), Ganga Kalyan Yojana (GKY), which are no longer in operation. The Yojana takes into account all the strengths and weaknesses of the earlier self-employment programmes.

It aims at establishing a large number of micro-enterprises in the rural areas. Persons assisted under this Programme will be known as swarozgaris and not beneficiaries. A significant aspect of SGSY is that every family assisted under this programme will be brought above the poverty-line in three years and as such the programme aims at creating substantial additional incomes for the rural poor. It is proposed to cover 30 per cent of the rural poor in each block in the next five years. '

The programme has been designed to provide proper support and encouragement to tap the inherent talents and capabilities of the rural poor. It will target at least 50 per cent

SC/STs, 40 per cent women and 3 per cent disabled.

It is a holistic programme of micro-enterprises covering all aspects of self–employment, that is organisation of the rural poor into self-help groups and their capacity building planning of activity clusters infrastructure build up technology, credit and marketing. SGSY focuses on group approach. This would involved organisation of the poor into self-help groups (SHGs) and their capacity building. Efforts would be made to preference and progressively majority of the funding will be for self help groups.

Self-Help Group is a forum or association of like minded people who are coming together for economic business. The group is democratically controlled by the members and the profit (or) surplus shall be equally distributed among them. This is the beginning of a co-operative from of organisation.

According to the International Seminar on "Development of Rural poor through the Self Help Group" organized jointly by NABARD and APRACH at Bangalore in May -1995 SHG Group may be defined as "Man by nature is very individualistic in his approach and more particularly in matters relating to finance. So the ultimate objective should be to graduate him, enable him to take loan from banks, instead of perpetuating him in the culture of SHGs".

The main objective of the formation of SHG is to strengthen co-operative move by utilizing the resources available in the area. The members of the SHGs should be from the same locality and of the same income group who have combined together to live with dignity.

Accelerating economic growth and creating an environment for ensuring 'spread effect of growth' have been emphasized, especially during 1990s for poverty alleviation. This macro strategy contributes to the emergence of production indivisibalities in groups only. Moreover, the participation of the poor in the planning and implementation of anti poverty programs is required to reduce the chain of intermediaries between the governmental and the actual beneficiaries and to improve their bargaining power.

Further, the institution -joint family system patron-client relationship and traditional occupation based institutions that provide social security to the poor are breaking down at the grass roots level. Thus, there is an institutional vacuum at the grass roots level to safeguard the interest of the poor. There is substantial evidence that organizing women around thrift and credit services is one of the most effective methods, not only for alleviating poverty but also for empowering women. Thus, the macro and micro concerns are giving rise to the demand for women based collectives centered around thrift and credit services.

Socio-economic empowerment of women through their self-help groups has been initiated in Tamil Nadu as early as in 1989, with its success, Mahalir Thittam was launched from 1997-98. The year 2000-2001 has been the fourth year of the implementation. The schemes had made great strides during this period. A successor of the IFAD assisted Tamil Nadu Women Development Project, Mahalir Thittam has so far facilitated formation of over 45,000 SHGS in partnership with various agencies like Rural Development Department, banks and NGOs. The schemes have made substantial impact on the status of women.

In 1999 Swarna Jayanti Gram Swarozgar yojana (SGSY) with concurrent objectives of economic empowerment and poverty reduction with convergent approach, was launched by the Government of India with major emphasis on the self-help group strategy. The existence of Mahalir Thittam was found to be the foundation on which Tamil Nadu could start operationalising SGSY even in the first year of its launch an advantage compared to most others states, which did not have such as SHG's base. The Rural Development Department and Tamilnadu Corporation for Development of Women have built up a sound Collaboration which has made implementation of both programmes easy.

TNWDP has effected significant changes in living conditions of poor rural women. NGOs have played a key role right from formation of women? Self-Help-Groups to attainment of women empowerment, by providing necessary training and other inputs. The average repayment level of IFAD loans is above 85 percentage consistently and is one of the key indicators of success of IFAD project.

The recent success stories of SHCs show that even the poor can exercise financial discipline. The case of obtaining the loan compensates for higher costs. Although the loan amount is small, it helps in meeting the requirement of the poor. The provision of even little credit helps the poor to improve their income levels. Small amounts of loan, coupled with financial discipline, enforce that loans are given more frequently and hence credit needs for a variety of purposes and shorter time intervals can be met. This is a better mechanism to reduce poverty gradually, as against giving a one time loan for a productive asset, which may to lead to sustained increase in income. Till now, benefits for the poor in terms of social empowerment and economic progress through SHG have far outpaced benefits from other rural development projects.

The impact of SHGs has relatively been more pronounced on social aspects than on the economic aspects, One of the major contributions of micro-finance is towards women empowerment. As women's groups exclusively dominate the SGHs their empowerment both on the economic and social fronts is one of the greatest opportunities for earning through deposits and higher off farm activities to improve their disposable income. Consequently family incomes substantially increased. There are tremendous social changes too. The Women

Command more respect get their due affection and rightful place in the family. Their involvement in family decisions has been substantially enhanced. In addition to meeting financial requirement, the SHG has become a platform for exchange of experiences and ideas beyond social participation by members, especially women. The SHGs are making the process of rural development participatory and democratic and are displaying their sustainability even in the absence of any susbsidy.

The impact assessment covered two aspects, that is poverty alleviation and women empowerment. Regarding women empowerment three dimensions are considered. They are 'Power to' 'Power with', and 'Power within'. The Power to dimension of empowerment indicates the power of women to control their lives. This includes power to survive control over their labour and access to family labour, access to and control over resources, freedom to move and interact, access to leadership positions, control over reproduction and control over body. The Power with indicates the collective power of women members to negotiate their gender, caste, class and other interest vis-vis institutions of market, the community. This includes collective interventions in the institutions of family community, market organisation the state including statutory long bodies. The third dimension 'Power within' indicates the strategic gender awareness.

Women are more efficient than men, sometimes, they contribute a lot to the economic development. In particular, Self-help groups are the central activity which would result in social and economic development. SGHs also facilitated to achieve independence in their lives. Further, SHGs helped to improve their ability through proper education.

PROMOTION OF SELF -HELP GROUPS:

Now -a -days, the formation of Self-Help Groups (SHGs) has empowered the women through their excellent activities with the help of promotional agencies like voluntary agencies and the Government Departments. The Self Help Groups inculcate the habit of savings among the group members and give small amount of loan to them for their urgent need and business purpose with low interest. The members of the group, at least, can meet twice in a month themselves and discuss their problem and elect their leader for managing the group activities.

STATUS OF WOMEN

The Nobel Scholar and Indian economist Mr. Amartyasen expressed in his words, "Unless women are empowered, issues like literacy, health, population explosion will remain unresolved problems of the developing counties". In India the majority of the women still continue to perform their traditional roles in the household and agriculture. The women are the wife of men-the present scenario forces them to depend on men, representation of women has never gone beyond eight percent in parliament, 10 per cent in the State Assemblies, 13 per cent in Council of Ministers, and 5.8 per cent in senior management and administrative posts generation activities. The activities such as starting small industrious brick making, poultry industrious, dairy industrious, providing services like tailoring, greeting cards making, candle making and business activities like vegetable vending, small hotel, huts making for sales. From this point of view, the voluntary agencies implemented their programmes and lifted the rural women to a decent life. Apart from these voluntary agencies provide formal training through which the women entrepreneurs acquire practical skills for managing the small scale enterprises such as garments making, toys making, fruit processing etc. Through the intervention of micro credit, the women entrepreneurs had benefited many things and shifted over their lives from rural areas to semi-urban areas.

RURAL MARKETING

The voluntary agencies provide financial support to start micro enterprises and also suitable place for marketing the products of women entrepreneurs. In order to activate the system of Rural Marketing the Voluntary agencies, Some times, may act as an internal agencies for selling the products produced by women entrepreneurs. The Voluntary agencies insist the SHG members to undergo training for technology upgradation and to give up-to-date market information for creating awareness on the matter pertaining to price trend of commodities in the market through establishing of marketing system in rural areas. The SHG members may easily sell their products in the villages which paves the way for self-sustainability among women entrepreneurs.

The above facts are responsible for the selection of the topic "Employment Generation Through Self-Help Groups in Rural Areas" with special emphasis on the role of SHG.

METHODOLOGY

Area of Study : Two SHGs functioning at Thanjavur are selected for the study.

Period of Study : Data has been collected in the second week of September 2003.

Sample : Among the 35 members in the two groups 16 samples have been selected at random. A special questionnaire is used to collect information from the respondents.

Tools : Tables and percentages are used.

Limitations : There are chances for sampling error. As the answers are given by members of SHG there are possibilities for human error in giving the data. Despite these limitations, this research paper will help in highlighting the role of SHG in employment generation in rural area and some solutions to the same.

Table No. 1

Age Distribution of the Respondents

Age	No. of Respondents	Percentage
20–25	1	6.25
25–30	5	31.25
30–35	3	18.75
35–40	4	25.00
40–45	3	18.75
Total	16	100.00

Source: Computed from Primary Data.

The above table shows the age distribution of the respondents. Among the respondents 31.25 percent belong to the age group of 25.30 and 25 percent of them belong to the age group of 40-45 years. Another personal attribute considered is the caste of the respondents as caste still determines the social status of an individual in India.

Table No.2

Caste-Wise Distribution of the Respondents

Caste	No. of Person	Percentage
Backward Class	8	50.00
Most Backward Class	3	18.75
Schedule Caste	5	31.25
Total	16	100.00

Source : Computed from Primary Data.

The data given in table No.2 reveals the distribution of the respondents on the basis of caste. It shows that 50 per cent belongs to back ward class and 31.25 percent belongs to scheduled caste. In Indian society among the three, scheduled caste people are in the lowest strata and next comes most backward and back ward class people.

The data on the religion of the people revealed the 15 of them belong to Hindu religion and one respondent belong to Christian relation . Martial status indicates that 14 are married and 2 are unmarried.

Whatever be the caste or religion, an individual's status improves through education. Education gives them the self - confidence and courage to face problems experienced in any activity. So education of the respondents is taken up here.

Table No.3

Educational Status of the Respondents

Educational Status	No. Of Persons	Percentage
8-10	3	18.75
10-12	11	68.75
Graduate	2	12.5
Total	16	100

Source : Computed from Primary Data.

The data presented in the above table shows the educational status of respondents. Out of 16 respondents, 68.75 per cent have studied up to higher secondary level, 18.75 per cent have studied up to 10th standard and 12.5 have studied up to graduate level. This shows that the members of SHG and not illiterates. In fact they have enough education to get trained in some work.

The questionnaire contains a question on the source of information to the respondents about the SHG. The answers given by them is given in the following table.

Table No.4

Source Of Information About SHG

Source of Information	No. Of Persons	Percentage
T. V.	1	6.25
Radio	–	–
Friends	6	37.5
News Paper	5	31.25
Others	4	25.00
Total	16	100

Source : Computed from Primary Data.

Among various sources available information from friends occupies the top position with friends as the source of information to 37.5 per cent of the respondents. Next comes news paper as 31.25 per cent of the respondents revealed that they got the information from news papers. Bank managers and health visitors gave the information to 25 per cent of the respondents. Only 6.25 per cent come to know about it through Television even though every one watch TV regularly. News papers and banks can be made use of in popularizing the significance of SHG among rural women.

Even though every body know about SHG, not every one joins SHG. There must be some reason for the members to join such groups. The surveyed respondents have their own option to join SHG which is listed below in the form of a table.

Table No.5

Reasons for Joining the SHG

Reasons	No. of Persons	Percentage
To get Entrepreneurship Development Training	5	31.25
To get loan for self-employment.	8	50.00
To get a loan for Consumption	2	12.5
Without any particular reason.	1	6.25
Total	16	100

Source : Computed form Primary Data.

The above table reveals that 31.25 per cent of the respondents joined the SHG to get Entrepreneurial Development Training. This will enable them to start their own business though on a very small scale. This skill is a basic requirement for self-employment. So many people join Self-Help Groups to under go such training without spending money. Another reason for joining SHG is to get a loan for self–employment. This is the prime cause for joining SHG as 50 per cent of the respondents joined SHG to get a loan for self-employment. These loans are used for the purchase of sewing machine, cattle, raw materials etc. Only 2 persons joined SHG to get a loan for consumption another person has joined SHG without any particular reason.

Since majority of the respondents joined SHG for getting trained and to get a loan for self employment, they were asked to mention the type of training given to them. The type of training and the number of persons who have undergone such training is given in the form of a table.

Table No.6

Type of Training Undergone by the Respondents Through SHG

Type of Training	No. of persons	Percentage
Entrepreneurship Development Training	8	50.00
Entrepreneurship Development and Leadership Training	2	12.50
Leadership Training	2	12.50
Nil	4	25.00
Total	16	100.00

Source : Computed from Primary Data.

Out of the 16 respondents surveyed, 8 of them have undergone Entrepreneurship Development Training, two members have been trained in leadership and two in Entrepreneurship Development and leadership training. Four members have not attended any such training programme. Among the two, one person has joined SHG without any motivation. The other being a government servant has no inclination to attend such training courses as she has a secured income.

These training programmes have changed the occupation of some of the respondents and some other respondents who so far remained idle have started their own business. To find out the impact of training occupation if other respondents before and after joining SHGs are considered.

Table No. 7

Occupation Before Joining SHG

Nature of Employment	No. of persons	Percentage
Self -Employed	1	6. 25
Private-Sector	3	18.75
Government Sector	3	18.75
Others	2	12.50
Nil	7	43.75
Total	16	100.00

Source : Computed from Primary Data.

To find out the influence of Self Help group on the employment of the respondent nature of employment of the respondents before joining the SHG is analysed. The data given in table No.7 shows that only one person come under the category of self – employment. Three persons work in Private sector and 3 persons work in government sector. Those who cannot be brought under these categories are included in other category list. It its seen that 7 respondents remained unemployed and they wasted their skill till they join the SHG.

The occupation of the respondents after joining SHG is also analysed to find out the impact of SHG on employment of members. It shows that all those who remained unemployed have taken up a job

Table No. 8

Change In Respondents Occupation After Joining SHG

S.No.	Type of Business	No. of Persons	Percentage
1.	Tailoring	4	25.00
2.	Telephone Booth	1	6.25
3.	Saree sales	1	6.25

4.	Mess	1	6.25
5.	Live stock	1	6.25
6.	Sandal garland	1	6.25
7.	Pappad Making	1	6.25
8.	Toys making	1	6.25
9.	Nil	5	31.25
10.	Total	16	100.00

Source: Computed from Primary Data.

It is gratifying to note that even the persons working in government sector has undergone training through SHG and is doing the work of toy making. This adds to her income. All the 7 members who remained idle at home have taken up works like tailoring, running a mess, sale of sarees pappad making etc. One respondent who already had some livestock increased the number by getting a loan through SHG. This is a very big achievement as far as SHG is concerned. It has enabled many members to identity their talents and made them to utilize the resource available for the betterment of their life.

Income of the family determines the economic status. So to find out the impact of SHG on the economic status of the members their monthly income before and after joining SHG are analysed.

Table No.9

Monthly Income Before Joining SHG (in Rupees)

S.No.	Monthly Income	No. of Persons	Percentage
1.	Less than-500	1	6.25
2.	500-1000	5	31.25
3.	Above 1500	3	18.75
4.	Nil	7	43.75
5.	Total	16	100

Source : Computed from Primary Data

Monthly income of the members given in the above table shows that income of one member was less than Rs. 500 and that of five members is more than Rs. 500 but less than Rs.1000. The income of 3 members was above Rs. 1500. These three members are employed in government organizations and have a fixed salary. The remaining 7 members earned no income before joining the SHG.

To compare the economic condition of the members their income after joining SHG is given below.

Table No. 10
Monthly Income After Joining SHG (In Rupees)

S.No.	Monthly Income	No. of Persons	Percentage
1.	500–1000	6	37.5
2.	1000–1500	4	25.00
3.	1500–and above	3	18.75
4.	Nil	3	18.75
5.	Total	16	100

Source : Computed from Primary Data.

The data on monthly income after joining SHG reveals that the income of 6 members ranges between Rs.500 and Rs. 1000. No one gets less than Rs. 500. The income of 4 members ranges between Rs. 1000 and Rs.1500. The Government employees still get more than Rs.1500 per month. It is to be noted that only 3 members do not get any income after joining SHG. This shows the improvement in the economic status of the members after joining SHG.

Another factor considered in the present study is monthly savings of the members.

Table No. 11
Monthly Savings Before and After Joining SHG
(In Rupees)

S.No.	Before Joining		After Joining	
	Saving	No. of Persons	Saving	No. of Persons
1.	50	3	100	4
2.	100	4	150	5
3.	Nil	9	200	7
4.	Total	16	Total	16

Source : Computed from Primary Data.

Before joining SHG 9 members did not have any saving and 3 members saved Rs.50 per month. Only 4 members saved an amount of Rs.100 every month. But after joining SHG all of them have started saving money and the minimum saving is Rs.100 and maximum is Rs.200. This is a proof for the improved economic status of the members.

FINDINGS

1. Age distribution of the respondents reveal that 31.25 per cent belongs to the age group of 25-30 years in the SHG.
2. An important personal attribute considered is the caste of the respondents. Caste still determines the social status of an individual in India. Scheduled caste women constitute 31.25 per cent in the present study.
3. All members are literates and 68.75 per cent of them have studied up to Higher Secondary level in the group. In fact they have enough education to get trained in some work.

4. Religion of the people revealed that majority of them belong to Hindu religion in the SHG. Martial status indicates that 87.5 per cent are married.
5. Main source of information about SHG is friends followed by newspaper.
6. Most of the of respondents joined SHG to get a loan for self employment. These loans are used for the purchase of the sewing machine, cattle, raw materials etc.
7. Among the samples 62.5 per cent have under gone entrepreneurship development training. These training programmes have changed the occupation of some of the respondents.
8. Before joining SHG 43.75 per cent of respondents were not employed. But after joining SHG all of them are doing some work which yields income
9. Before joining SHG the minimum income of the group was less than Rs.500/-. But after joining SHG this has increased to a minimum of Rs.500 to Rs.1000
10. Before joining SHG nine members never saved any money. But after becoming a member of the SHG all of them save money and the minimum amount is Rs. 100 and Maximum is Rs. 200 per month.

SUGGESTIONS

1. As the members are literates, regular training programme in various arts and crafts can be given to them through NGOs.
2. Entrepreneurship training and leadership training should be made compulsory to the members so that they can develop the skill of starting a business of their own.

3. Marketing is major problem experienced by SHG members. So NGO's can arrange for marketing of the products produced by SHG member.
4. As the members regularly repay the loan, they may be encouraged to borrow more loans and invest in new ventures. The bank can play a better role in this regard.
5. Organisation of members into SHG has increased employment of members. All members engage themselves in one work or other and get additional income to the family. Hence these successful members can be trained to motivate members of other groups also. These suggestions may be considered for implementation as it will help in the generation of employment opportunities in rural areas like Thanjavur.

EMPLOYMENT GENERATION PROGRAMME THROUGH SELF-HELP GROUPS IN THOOTHUKUDI PANCHAYAT UNION

Dr. D. Solomon Raj*

INTRODUCTION

The self-help group is an effective tool for delivering the credit to the rural poor for their economic empowerment and social development. The population growth has declined from 2.5 per cent per annum in 1983-1994 to 1.9 per cent per annum in 1994-2000. But the rate of employment generation has fallen from 2.7 per cent during 1983-1994 to 0.53 per cent during 1994-1999. The decline in the employment generation was mainly due to the decline in the employment in public sector establishments. Unemployment among the rural males in the age group 15-25 has increased from 9.5 per cent to 11.1 per cent and among rural females from 7.6 per cent to 10.6 percent between 1993-1994 and 1999-2000.

The growing problem of unemployment cannot be solved through creating adequate job opportunities in wage-paid and salaried employment due to the sharp declining trend in the employment market both under public sector and private sector. Therefore, in the context of present economic crisis, it cannot be ignored that there is no other alternative way than self-dependent. Owing to the responsibility, the central government and the state government has launched many self-employment schemes to solve the unemployed problem.

* Reader in Economics, Pope's College, Sawyerpuram-51, Thoothukudi District

This paper attempts to analyse the employment potentials and prospects of self-help groups for a period from 1999-2000 to 2002-2003. The results of the recent studies showed that women are better credit risks than men, preference is given to Self-Help Groups formed by women. This study tries to find out the reasons for which men are not actively participating in the group activities and give possible suggestions.

REVIEW OF EARLIER STUDIES

The brief review of a few research articles connected with this paper is discussed below. The Bangala Gramina Bank with an out reach of 2.1 million clients, Bangaladesh Rural Advancement Committee with an out reach of 1.5 million clients and Association For Social Advancement with an out reach of 4 million clients and the pioneer in the field of micro credit to self-help groups. Benjamin Kunjukunju in his article, "Impact of Rural Institutional Credit on Employment" indicates that the pattern of not only the rural poor had a favourable impact on the employment pattern of not only the borrowers, but also his family members and hired workers. Among the sectors, agriculture and allied activities ranked first in self-employment generation (103.6 per cent) followed by rural industries (80.6 per cent). Mathew, ET (1995) in his paper 'Unemployed and Self-employed job preferences and employment perspectives' states that a major factor contributing to the growth of educated unemployment in Kerala is the preference for salaried employment especially in the public sector and aversion to self-employment among educated job seekers. Adhihkam, C.S. (2000) in his project report, 'Enterprise employment for Rural Employment' stated that given the modernization of agriculture and the slow down in organised industry, the rural non-farm sector will have to provide employment to the growing population. The central idea is to provide a catalyst to a qualified professional and to income generating activities in rural areas.

NABARD initiated a pilot project in 1992 that aimed at financing self-help groups across the country through the banking system. The banks financed about 600 self-help groups by March 1993. Ten years from 1992, the informal delivery strategy developed for the banking system by NABARD in collaboration with non-formal development agencies through the vehicle of self-help groups has grown into the largest micro-finance programme in the world in terms of its out reach. On the basis of the above studies, the following objectives are framed:

i. To study the potentials and possibilities of self-employment generation through self-help groups in the study area.

ii. To know the reasons for which men are not actively participating in the group activities.

iii. To highlight the problems and to give suggestions for the improvement of the self-help groups.

AREA PROFILE AND METHODS OF STUDY

In the Thoothukudi block, there are 29 revenue villages. The geographical area of the block is 31,488 hectare. The block has the total population of 1,54,385 consists of 77,788 males and 76,397 females. The Thoothukudi block has 25 village panchayats and no town panchayats. It consists of 196 small villages. It has 30 Mahalir Mantrams.

The study was conducted by secondary data. The study is a descriptive one. Data regarding the loan scheme of self-help groups were collected from the Thoothukudi Panchayat Union Office. Simple statistical tools like percentages, averages, etc. are used to analyse the data collected. The responder had visited some of the self-help groups to know their problems in order to give suggestions for their improvement in future. The present study covers the period from 1999-2000 to 2002-2003.

SELF-HELP GROUPS AND ITS DIFFERENT MODELS

A self-help group is a small economically homogeneous and affinity group of rural poor, voluntarily formed to save and mutually agree to contribute to a common fund to be lent to its members as per group decision. It usually consists of a group of twenty people from a homogeneous class, who come together for addressing common problems. They are encouraged to make voluntary thrift on regular basis. They use this pooled resource to make small interest bearing loans to their members.

The social intermediation for forming and nurturing self-help groups is handled by a large number of NGOs and several community based organisations like farmers clubs, local bodies, field level workers of governmental agencies and bank staff. The existing formal agencies like state government departments, UNICEF, banks and NABARD also co-ordinate to create people based structure for generating resources.

THERE ARE THREE DIFFERENT MODELS OF SELF - HELP GROUPS :

i. Self-help groups formed and financed by banks. Under this model, banks themselves act as self-help promoting institutions i.e., forming and nurturing the groups, opening their savings account and providing them bank loans. As at much 2001, 13 per cent of total number of self-help groups financed were from this category.

ii. Self-help groups formed by NGOs and formal agencies, but directly financed by banks. Under this model, NGOs and formal agencies act as facilitators. They propagate the message, organize groups, trains them in thrift and credit management and nurture than over a period. Banks, in due course, link these groups by directly providing loans to them. Major scheme of self-help groups linked as at March 2001 (76 per cent) is under this model as compared to 70 per cent as at March 2000.

ii. Self-help groups financed by banks using NGOs a financial intermediaries. In this model, NGOs take on the dual role of facilitators and financial intermediaries. They help in formation of self-help groups, nurturing them, training them in thrift and credit management. Eventually, the NGOs approach banks for bulk loan assistance for lending those self-help groups. The share of cumulative number of self-help groups linked under this model is relatively small i.e., 11 per cent. This could eventually develop into an effective method to control transaction costs through economic scale.

BENEFICIARIES OF SELF-EMPLOYMENT THROUGH LOAN SCHEMES

On the basis of the policies and programmes of Tenth Plan Period, it is expected to generate employment for 19.3 million persons per year, out of which 20 million from rural employment generation programme.

The Table 1 shows that for the year 1999-2000, there were 19 beneficiaries of the loan scheme received Rs.13.58 lakhs as against Rs.13.29 lakhs as subsidy. The total number of beneficiaries have increased to 218 per the year 200-2001, increased Rs. 16.22 lakhs as against Rs.15.53 lakhs as subsidy.

The number of beneficiaries have decreased to 63 for the year 2001-2002, received Rs.5.23 lakhs loan amount as against Rs.4.80 lakhs as susbsidy. The number of beneficiaries have still decreased to 37 for the year 2002-2003, received Rs. 277 lakhs loan amount as against Rs.2.27 lakhs as subsidy.

Table –1
Beneficiaries Of Self-Employment Through Loan Scheme From 1999-2000 to 2002-2003

(Rs. in lakhs)

Sl. No.	Year	No. of Beneficiaries	Estimated Amount	Loan Amount	Subsidy
1.	1999–2000	191	26.87	13.58	13.29
2.	2000–2001	218	31.75	16.22	15.53
3.	2001–2002	63	10.03	5.23	4.80
4.	2002–2003	37	5.04	2.77	2.27
	Total	509	73.69	37.80	35.89

Source : Records of the Office of the Thoothukudi Panchayat Union.

It is clearly understood from the above table that the employment generation programme in rural areas through self-help groups is directly reflecting the upliftment of rural people below poverty line. The success of this scheme depends on the subsidy and NGOs involvement in implementing the programmes by the government through the banks.

BENEFICIARIES OF SELF-EMPLOYMENT THROUGH LOAN SCHEME

The dependence of the rural poor on the money lenders continues, particularly in the resource poor areas. The NGOs have actively promoted the informal groups of the rural poor to encourage thrift and also weaning the poor away from the money lenders, The concept of non-formal agency for credit supply to the poor in the forms of 'Self-help group' of the poor is emerging as a promising partner of the formal agencies.

The members of the self-help groups benefited through revolving fund scheme for 1999-2000 were 183, received Rs.1.95 lakhs credit as against Rs. 1.30 lakhs as subsidy. The number has increased to 309 for 2000-2001, received Rs. 2.70 lakhs loan amount as against Rs.1.80 lakhs as subsidy. The number has sharply decreased to 142 for 2001-2002, received Rs. 150 lakhs loan amount as against Rs.150 lakhs loan amount as against Rs.100 lakhs as subsidy. Again the number has increased to 203 for 2002–2003 received Rs.1.95 lakhs loan amount as against Rs. 1.30 lakhs as subsidy.

Table – 2

Beneficiaries Of Self-Employment Through Revolving Fund Scheme From 1999-2000 to 2002-2003

(Rs. in lakhs)

Sl. No.	Year	No. of Beneficiaries	Estimated Amount	Loan Amount	Subsidy
1.	1999–2000	183	3.25	1.95	1.30
2.	2000–2001	309	4.50	2.70	1.80
3.	2001–2002	142	2.50	1.50	1.00
4.	2002–2003	203	3.25	1.95	1.30
	Total	837	13.50	8.10	5.40

Source : Records of the Office of the Thoothukudi Panchayat Union.

The beneficiaries of self-employment through revolving fund scheme are now confident enough to sustain in their efforts to find jobs by themselves. They get credit at a low rate of interest. They have to have easy access to bank through self-help groups.

CATEGORIES OF SELF-EMPLOYMENT GENERATION AND THE SEX-WISE BENEFICIARIES OF LOAN SCHEME

The Table 3 states that the beneficiaries utilized the available funds for starting up of different categories of self-employment schemes like palm leave box making, goat and cow rearing, pickle, masala, dress and soda making, etc. Beneficiaries form men category were found in cow rearing scheme alone. For 2000-2001, out of 33, 24 were men and 9 were women. For 2001-2002, there were 14 men and 48 women. Again for 2001-2002, there were 15 men and 8 women beneficiaries of the Scheme. More number of women beneficiaries is engaged in palm leave box making self-employment scheme.

At the national leave, it is very important to note that employment position of men has been reducing continuously. It is surprising to see that involvement of men in self-help groups is discouraged even at the implementation level of the programme. Though, we are of the opinion that men are more credit risks than women, they are courage enough to take up any venture than women.

Table 3

Categories of Self-Employment Generation and the Sex-wise Beneficiaries of Loan Scheme From 1999-2000 to 2002-2003

Sl. No.	Categories of Self-Employment	Scheme Period							
		1999-2000		2000–2001		2001-2002		2002-2003	
		Men	Women	Men	Women	Men	Women	Men	Women
1.	Palm Leave box making	-	56	-	68	-	13	-	-
2.	Goats rearing	-	60	-	11	-	-	-	-
3.	Cow rearing	24	9	14	48	15	8	-	-
4.	Pickle making	-	26	-	-	-	-	-	-
5.	Masals powder making	-	16	-	43	-	15	-	-
6.	Dress making	-	-	-	34	-	12	-	17
7.	Soda Making	-	-	-	-	-	-	-	20
Sex-wise Total		24	167	14	204	15	48	-	37
Total		191		218		63		37	

Source : Records of the Office of the Thoothukudi Panchayat Union.

SUGGESTIONS FOR IMPROVEMENT OF SELF-HELP GROUPS

The field level observation helps the researcher to give the following suggestions:

1. The formation of self-help groups among unemployed men can be encouraged and each male member of the group should have a guarantor who may be his mother in the case of bachelor and wife in the case of married one.
2. The students of schools and colleges should be aware of the self-employment generation programmes of the government. They can be encouraged to form self-help groups to practice the habit of saving. Educational loans to students under below poverty line category can be rooted through only self-help groups.
3. It is also observed that disparity is being shown taking into account the community in which the members of a particular self-help group belong. Therefore, efforts should be taken by the government through NGOs, community organizations and clubs working social upliftment to bring communal harmony and religious tolerance.

CONCLUSION

It is concluded that the formation of more and more self-help groups can able to generate sufficient employment opportunities in the wake of severe unemployment position in India.

REFERENCES

1. Adhihkan, C. S, (2000) Enterprise Development for Rural Employment-Project Report, Economics and Political Weekly, Vol. XXXV, Nos. 20 and 21, pp. 1858-1864.

2. Prasanakumari, K (2003) 'Tenth Five Year Plan and Employment Generation', Workshop conducted by the Economists of Tamilnadu and Adhithanar College of Arts and Sciences, Tiruchendur.

3. Monograph on Micro Credit (2003): NABARD-Past, Present and Future, M.O.P. Vaishnav College for Women, Chennai, pp.3-21.

4. Rajalakshmi, N., (1999), 'Tamilnadu Economy', Business Publications Inc. Mumbai.

5. Perumalsamy, S., (1996) 'Economic Development of Tamilnadu', S. Chand and Company Ltd., New Delhi.

6. Ajit Ghose, 'Current issues of Employment Policy in India', Economic and Political Weekly, Sep. 4., 1999, pp.592-2609.

7. Solomon Raj, D., (2003) 'Role of Banks in Micro Credit to Services Sector in Tamilnadu with special reference to self-employment', Paper presented in a National Seminar on 'Micro Credit' by M.O.P. Vaishnav College for Women, Madras.

8. Tamilnadu - An Economic Appraisal, 1997-1998.

9. India 2001, Publications, Division; Ministry of Information and Broadcasting, Government of India.

INDEX

T